THE FAMILY PROJECT:

DISCOVERING THE ROAD BEYOND SHAME

DR. DAVID F. ALLEN MD, MPH

MEDIA ENTERPRISES LTD
2025

Other books by Dr. David F. Allen

Ethical Issues in Mental Retardation

The Cocaine Crisis

Crack: The Broken Promise

In Search of the Heart

Shattering the Gods Within

Contemplation: Intimacy in a Distant World

Pudgy: A Bahamian Parable

Daily Discovery: A Devotional

Shame: The Human Nemesis

Publisher's Cataloguing-in-Publication data
Allen, David F.
The Family Project: Discovering the Road Beyond Shame
Description: Nassau, BS: Media Enterprises Ltd., 2025
p. cm

ISBN 13: 978-0-9971609-6-3

Cover design by Ross Miller
Design and layout by Media Enterprises Ltd
31 Shirley Park Avenue, P.O. Box N-9240, Nassau, Bahamas
Tel: 242-325-8210
E-mail: bahamasmedia@gmail.com

Contents

THE FAMILY REMEMBERS Those who have gone before… Hebrews 12:1		v
Testimonials		vi
Introduction	Professor Alexis Abernethy	x
Acknowledgments		xii
Prologue:	The Parable Of Pudgy	xiii
Poem:	There is a coldness in the world by David Allen Jr.	xvi
CHAPTER 1	The Family: People Helping People Project	1
CHAPTER 2	Shame: The Human Condition	14
CHAPTER 3	The Contemplative Discovery Pathway Theory	34
CHAPTER 4	The Evil Violence Tunnel	56
CHAPTER 5:	The False Self: The Internal Saboteur	71
CHAPTER 6	The Still Point: The Healing Of Silence	77
	Forgiveness by Richard U. Rosenfield	87
CHAPTER 7	Discovery: The Freedom To Be Fully You	90
Epilogue	The War for Peace Within Ourselves	101
Appendix		113

Epidemic Free-Base Cocaine Abuse: Case Study from the Bahamas. The Lancet Ltd, 1986;1:459-462.
Nine Years of the Freebase Cocaine Epidemic in the Bahamas. American Journal on Addictions, 1994, 3:14-24.
Cultivating Gratitude: Contemplative discovery pathway theory applied to group therapy in the Bahamas. Journal of Trauma. Treatment 3(3) 2014
Cocaine Addiction: The Nemesis of Modern Culture by David F. Allen, MD
Presented at the Jack W Provonsha Lectureship for the Alumni Postgraduate Convention on March 3, 1997
Adapting Group Therapy to Address Real World Problems: Insights from groups offered in the Bahamas. International Journal of Group Psychotherapy 68 (1), 17-34 2017
A Resocialization Intervention Model in the Prison - The Family: People Helping People Project, Sociology International Journal, October 16, 2017
Spirituality and transformation in a community-based group in the Bahamas Mental Health, Religion & Culture 2019
A social intervention for court-ordered adolescents—The family people helping people project. Examining social identities and diversity issues in group therapy Routledge 2020
Community-based treatment of suicide through the family: people helping people project Japan Journal of Medical Science 2025

Cartoon by Stan Burnside, published in The Tribune, 9.9.91

THE FAMILY REMEMBERS

Those who have gone before...
Hebrews 12:1

Angela Ward

Rita Thompson

Danise Christie

Burt Carey

Mark Beckford

André Chappelle

Testimonials

Michaela Bethell-Stuart

The Family means Hope for me. It embodies a group of people from all classes of society seeking a common cause. I felt welcomed and loved in my first meeting. I made a commitment to myself to follow through with my therapy. Depression is not a good space for anyone and seeing that I was not alone made a world of difference to me. Everyone's story is different, yet everyone's pain seems familiar to my pain. Dr. Allen has a way of making everyone feel welcomed and that they matter. We learn how to talk through our trauma, we laugh and cry without judgment. I call it my functional dysfunctional family where we have a safe space to talk about our trauma and are allowed to work through our grief. We are sharing our burden and people are actually listening with an empathetic ear. The sessions are not just designed to be about sadness. They are designed to form a unit, to be our brother's keeper and it reminds me of the prayer of St. Francis of Assisi, "Lord, make me a channel of your peace".

Col. Gill Brown

A good friend introduced me to Dr. David Allen in the Washington D.C. family group several years ago. Since then, I have been able to leverage Dr. Allen's wisdom through frequent interactions about my life and the lives of other people in the group. I have been particularly impressed with his teaching on shame as the gap between what we expect and who we are. This has challenged me to do my own personal work that led to the publication of my own book describing my journey in the U.S. Army. Dr. Allen is a special treasure to many of us in the D.C. area, and we always enjoy being with him, either in the Bahamas or in D .C.
- Colonel Gill Brown, retired U.S. soldier.

Andrea Johnson-Thompson

In July, 2023, I received a call from a member of the hierarchy of the Royal Bahamas Police Force asking me to meet with Dr. David Allen to help bring awareness about deadly Fentanyl in The Bahamas. My beloved twenty-eight year old son, Dre, was killed on August 28, 2022, from one pill containing Fentanyl. I agreed to meet with Dr. Allen the following day because I was feverishly seeking justice for my son's death. I was being consumed by grief and anger. This decision would change my life forever. As I sought to bring awareness about my son's death, educate the people about the deadly impact of illicit Fentanyl, and compel the police investigators to help me to get justice for Dre, I walked into a new chapter of my life called "The Family."

Days after meeting with Dr. Allen I found myself the guest of honor at a "Family" group grief therapy session led by Dr. Allen. It was my first time attending this group, and I had never heard about it prior to meeting with Dr. Allen. It was one of the most difficult things I've ever had to do in my life. I had never experienced talk therapy in any group setting. I felt like a fish out of water. My breathing felt labored. It felt like a heavy stone was sitting on my chest. The pangs of my heart were very real. I was covered in shame, as a Godly mother whose son was killed by illicit drugs. As I shared just some of Dre's story I felt as if I would have a heart attack. I sobbed the entire time. The pain I was feeling and the shock, pain, anger and occasional groans from the people in the room were almost palpable. Many of them cried with me and they were very gracious as they listened.

That day was the beginning of a new season and chapter in my life. From that fateful day on, I was a consistent attendee at all of The Family group meetings. I am now a facilitator for the overall group, trained by Dr. Allen himself. To date I have remained constant in attendance, and for the first eighteen months I don't think I missed any meeting of any group. I realized that God had ordained that I connect with Dr. Allen so that I would learn from his wisdom. I have begun to walk in my healing and also help others to do the same. My consistent attendance at group meetings allowed me to be poured into, and I am also able to pour into others.

I've learned that healing is not linear and no healing journey is identical to anyone else's. I've learned that there are two poles in grief–the sadness pole and the anger pole. Dr. Allen taught me that it's best that I remain at the sadness pole, because hope will return when we understand that Jesus is close to the brokenhearted.

The Family sessions have taught me that healing can be very difficult, but it's possible. It takes work; we must work our healing and our healing will work for us. My healing journey with The Family has helped me go back and rescue my child self. Along this journey I am falling in love with little Andrea. I have asked her forgiveness and made peace with her for leaving her behind, and for putting her through so much in my adolescent and adult life. I've introduced her to our sons and granddaughter, and I've promised her that I will never leave her behind again. I'm beginning to feel wholeness, since I've reconnected with my little princess Andrea.

From the wells of my life-long painful experiences, I have learned that I was grieving since I was five years old, when I was molested. I've had to open the vials of deep, deep trauma, sit with every loss, and accept that I lost myself along the way. Working with The Family has helped me to face myself in the mirror, to accept that I have a responsibility to own my mistakes and poor decisions and HEAL! I've discovered the beauty of being honest with myself and my feelings. I've learned to stand up for myself, setting boundaries concerning people's access to me and speaking out against abuse and mistreatment. This is self-care.

The Family has also helped me to walk in forgiveness towards those who have hurt me so deeply. Because of the work I've done on myself through The Family, I have accepted that losing so much of myself while trying to win other people's love and acceptance is my own doing. I've found that forgiving myself is oftentimes more difficult than forgiving others, but my overall healing requires that I do. I no longer wear the cloak of shame. The rejection, humiliation and abandonment I suffered are not my portion. The Family has helped me to rise up and be who God has called me to be. I am no longer hiding and I am no longer afraid to come off the wall and face my oppressors.

I am so thankful that God threw me a lifeline at the lowest time of my life...,that lifeline is Dr. David Allen and The Family Group.

Curt Ashburn

It goes without saying that Dr. David Allen is a gifted psychiatrist, but it is his God-given gift to discern the hidden gifts in others that changed my life. After knowing David only casually for 15 years, he asked me to teach his work on recovery to the homeless men at Washington, DC's Gospel Rescue Mission.

That unexpected opportunity in 2009 began a deep transformation in my life. As I immersed myself in his writings and shared them with the men, I found myself on a journey to my own heart.

In small group settings, I took note how David found ways to lead people to share their stories of past and current hurts and trauma. No one was exempt from his insightful questioning, including me. It became clear that my hurt trail, beginning with childhood, was the source of my debilitating shame.

David always creates a safe, nonjudgmental environment that brings gradual but profound healing which led me to eventually discover my love story. It was by telling my story that I found a pathway to uncovering shame, recovering from hurt, and discovering a new life based in love and not fear.

David ultimately formalized this healing through story by establishing groups that he calls Families. It was in one of these families that I witnessed the true power of story to heal deeply traumatized people, including myself. From this journey to my heart, I found what David calls the Contemplative Discovery Pathway out of shame and into a life full of meaning, dignity, identity, and value.

Rod Wenner

I was involved with Dr. Allen in 1992 when he formed The Haven (predecessor of The Family) at The Gospel Mission, a non-denominational Christian homeless shelter for men in the inner-city of Washington, D.C. Over a period of more than 20 years, The Haven helped homeless men recover from addiction and return to their families and to their communities.

In the early 1990's, as part of President George H.W. Bush's "Thousand Points of Light" program, U.S. Senators Jack Kemp, Dan Coates, and Sam Brownbeck met with Dr. Allen and others from The Mission to recognize The Haven's success in helping those in need..

Priscilla Sands

Having experienced the value of individual and group therapy for 40 years, I quickly joined The Family Group three years ago following the death of my second husband.

The grief journey began again. Not only did I re-learn how to grieve the loss of my husband, but this time I discovered that I was experiencing other losses – unknown to my conscious mind and which could be traced back to childhood.

The Family, by giving me a confidential and loving space, helped me to identify those losses, which in turn stimulated me to work them out at home. I discovered a deep shame (Self Hatred Aimed at ME) in the bottom of my soul. As I shared weekly with The Family and other members shared their stories – I began to see that I was not the only one experiencing such shame.

By God's grace, The Family and Dr. David Allen's loving patience & encouragement, I was able to surrender that shame. What freedom of my soul! It didn't happen overnight: it was a 3-year journey, traveling to the mission field of my own heart. It took courage and stickability.... The Family is indeed a grieving chamber, providing a safe, supportive and confidential space to mourn. We also have fun in The Family as our stories are filled with humor and universal applications.

May I invite you to join a Family? It's a FREE opportunity for support and to work on yourself.

Pastor Joshua L. Sands Jr

In an age where sociocultural and religious theories abound, David Allen has managed to organize and orchestrate a magnificent display of introspection and involvement through his weekly gatherings to form a new alliance of what family life can be.

Participants coming from various societal groupings gather faithfully from week to week to confront personal and collective habits of behavior ingrained from years of spiritual and psychological mismanagement.

Having shared in the group meetings as a supportive coach and encourager, I have become convinced that David Allen has crafted a magnificent approach to helping people face their fears and anger issues. We observed participants work through the shameful acceptance of painful abuse and find new ways of not only coping but enabling others to bring about a renaissance of life. Through the family therapy groups we saw persons confront social demons through contemplation and discovery to formulate new behaviors and develop new thought processes that will ultimately reflect the grace of God and produce new behaviors.

Kudos to David Allen and his team of dedicated counselors in breaking new ground. Truly heaven has a cause to smile once again in seeing family life in the Bahamas rise to a new level of excellence.

Introduction
by Professor Alexis D. Abernethy

I REMEMBER WHEN MY COLLEAGUE, Dr. Jim Steinwedell, mentioned that he wanted me to meet a psychiatrist who was doing important group work in the Bahamas. I am forever thankful for that introduction.

Dr. Allen has led and trained others to lead innovative community-based process-oriented groups that have transformed lives and he has conducted research on these groups to assess changes in members over time. Dr. Allen is a skilled and creative clinician, a teacher who is committed to mentoring future group leaders, and a researcher whose work has been funded by the Templeton World Charity Foundation.

In our article, Adapting Group Therapy to Address Real World Problems: Insights from Groups Offered in the Bahamas published in the International Journal of Group Psychotherapy by Alexis Abernethy, David Allen & Marie Allen Carroll, we describe

> ""The Family" as a supportive process-oriented community-based group intervention. The approach is an integration of interpersonally oriented, role-playing, and supportive techniques based on the Contemplative Discovery Pathway Theory (CDPT; Allen et al., 2014)."

Seven of my students have had the opportunity to experience his leadership of these groups in the Bahamas. I appreciate his generosity and hospitality toward me and my students. At least eight dissertations and three master's projects have been completed by students in the School of Psychology & Marriage and Family Therapy at Fuller Theological Seminary based on Dr. Allen's work with The Family.

Observing his groups has deepened my appreciation for the power of group as a vehicle not only for individual, but communal change. When I am teaching group therapy, my students appreciate the classical approaches to group therapy, but they will ask me how do we make group offerings more available to the community, particularly those who have limited health care access. Also they question whether our models of group therapy need to be culturally tailored for certain communities. Dr. Allen's work has provided me with a vibrant, creative example of this tailoring and increased accessibility.

Again, we note in the group psychotherapy article "This adaptation can serve as a model for community contexts where there are few mental health professionals, where there is a need to serve a large number of people, and where there are significant challenges related to community violence and societal fragmentation."

He is an example of someone who has been well trained, but never forgotten the community where he grew up. He has literally risked his life to help to transform the Bahamas.

We have published another article, Spirituality and Transformation in a community-based group in the Bahamas (Abernethy, Grannum, & Allen, 2019), published in Mental Health, Religion, and Culture. The qualitative study aims were to clarify the interrelationships among transformation, spirituality, and forgiveness in this community-based group. Sixteen group participants from the Bahamas were selected and interviewed. Themes related to prayer, group connection, and compassion were prominent. Participants noted that modelling by the group provided support for them to forgive and change.

Dr. Allen was invited by the American Group Psychotherapy Association to give the 2018 Mitchell Hochberg Memorial Lecture at the Annual Meeting in New York City. He gave a phenomenal talk on "Group Process as an Intervention for Resocialization in the Bahamas." His presentation resulted in subsequent collaborations and invitations to publish several book chapters.

Dr. David Allen was trained in medicine at Saint Andrew's University in Scotland and in Psychiatry and Public Health at Harvard University in Boston. He is certified by the American Board of Psychiatry and Neurology, with added qualification in addiction. Dr. Allen has taught at Harvard, Yale and held a clinical professorship in Psychiatry at Georgetown Medical School in Washington, DC. Dr. Allen is a Distinguished Life Fellow of the American Psychiatric Association for his innovative scientific research. He is the author of numerous books, most recently Shame: The Human Nemesis. Additionally, he has published numerous scientific papers. Dr. Allen is the Director of the Discovery Clinic, the Renascence Institute, in Nassau, Bahamas.

Alexis D. Abernethy, Ph.D., Clinical Psychologist and Professor of Psychology in the School of Psychology & Marriage and Family Therapy of Fuller Theological Seminary in Pasadena, California.

Acknowledgments

I WOULD LIKE TO THANK THE Templeton World Charity Foundation for their gracious support which helped the Family to expand exponentially. The Templeton grant provided funds for qualified therapists to expand the work of the Family to the prison and many marginalized areas in Nassau. I'm especially indebted to Professor Andrew Briggs whose counsel and advice allowed me to think through many challenging issues in the Family. Professor Briggs attended a number of sessions and helped me to conceptualize my psychological theory, the Contemplative Discovery Pathway Theory on which the Family was developed. Professor Briggs has been a constant advisor and support.

I would also like to thank Professor Andrew Serazin. Director of the Foundation, who was supportive in many ways.

I also thank Mr. Dawid Potgieter whose strategic advice helped me prepare and develop the grant application. Mrs. Betty Roberts of the Templeton Foundation who provided much encouragement. Mr. Ron Attkinson graciously provided his time and accounting expertise to supervise the funds of the grant. Miss Keva Bethell worked tirelessly compiling the praxis reports and the research project of the Family. Without her expertise, the research component would not have been possible.

Special friends Mr. Frank Crothers of Lyford Cay and Mr. Rod Wenner of Washington, D.C. provided helpful counsel.

Finally I'd like to thank my dear wife, Dr. Victoria Allen, for her hard work in preparing manuscripts and providing insights about the work.

The motivating force in all my community work is the Lord Jesus Christ who has stood with me to develop The Family Program in Nassau and Washington, DC. To Him goes all the glory.

Prologue: The Parable Of Pudgy

PUDGY WAS A LITTLE FISH THAT lived on the western end of Nassau in The Bahamas. His parents warned him that he shouldn't swim too close to the shore because the large waves, especially around the month of October, would wash him up onto the beach and he would die.

But Pudgy knew best. As far as he was concerned he could swim better than his parents or siblings; after all he had gone to a better swimming school than all of them. So, against the advice of his elders, one October morning Pudgy went swimming close to the beaches on the western end of Nassau. A large wave tossed him up on the beach and, as he watched the water ebb away, he realized that he was beached. He flipped his tail. He twisted his body. He tried to jump off the sand, but try as he might; he was unable to get back into the beautiful aquamarine sea. Afraid and trapped, he now remembered all his parents had told him; after all, hindsight is twenty-twenty.

As the Bahamian sun grew hotter, water evaporated from Pudgy and he became weaker. As the morning wore on, Pudgy went into early shock. He tried and tried to get back into the water, but the waves lapped just short of him, leaving him stranded. His heart beat faster and his fear now turned to terror.

Along the beach came a very sophisticated lady. Fascinated by the spectacle of the little fish on the beach, she stooped down to tell him how excited she was to meet him. But even before she could open her mouth, Pudgy blurted out his plea for help, crying, "Please help me, I'm beached. Put me back into the water—a fish out of water will die."

"Oh," said the lady, "I understand, but you see I belong to the Bahamas Independent Society and we believe that if people are just given the chance to help themselves, they can handle their problems much more effectively. In fact, I am on my way to the Independent Society meeting at our church down the street. So, little fish, you just keep on trying and I'm sure you will be able to do it all by yourself."

"Please, help me," cried Pudgy, growing ever weaker.

"Please put me back into the sea, you can even kick me back into the sea. A fish...out...... of water...........will... DIE."

"Don't be preposterous," replied the lady. "I would never kick one of God's little creatures, in fact I volunteer at the animal society weekly; God knows I would never harm one of his vulnerable little animals, so don't think like that, just keep on trying. You know the saying, 'Try and try again, boys, and you will succeed at last' Anyway, I must be off to my meeting now—but

I'll stop by on my way back and we can discuss your position further. Cheerio, and have a good day."

Pudgy tried again and again but became progressively weaker until he could hardly move. He was almost dead. Then a little girl came walking along the beach. Seeing Pudgy, she stopped and quickly scooped him back into the water. "Now that's better!" she said smiling as Pudgy slowly regained his strength and started his journey home.

A little later our lady returned to the beach to check on Pudgy. When she arrived at the spot where Pudgy had been, she exclaimed in a loud, joyous voice, "I knew he could do it, I will never forget that little fish. He is now swimming with all the other fishes in the Bahamian sea. He had a problem, and, just like we said in our meeting this morning, he faced it. Now he is swimming happily ever after with all the other little fishes in the sea." The little girl, who was playing in the sand nearby, spoke up. "No, that's not what happened. He was dying so I rescued him; I put him back into the sea. If I hadn't, he would have died."

What was lacking between the woman and the fish? They spent time together; she stopped long enough to hear him explain his inner longing, his need for survival. She talked with him, she encouraged him, she advised him, she even sought to nurture and motivate him, and she tried to build up his strength and self-esteem. She then took the time to come back and check up on him; in our modern scientific lingo, she did a follow-up study. But she didn't meet Pudgy's need. This lady was not malevolent. In fact she rejoiced at the thought of the fish conquering his problems and swimming happily in the sea again. But she didn't meet Pudgy's need. Her formidable intellect and education did not help her to connect. Does this parable remind us of the lack of intimacy that exists in the modern world?

Overwhelmed by the powerful information revolution and our exciting new technologies, we grope toward a global village—but deep in our hearts we feel a paralyzing distance from each other. We can be involved with each other, spend time with each other, but still so easily miss each other. Pudgy is that friend who calls out to us for help. Pudgy is our husband who is trying to tell us that things are not well and are falling apart.

Pudgy is our wife who screams in silence, warning us that her heart is breaking. Most sadly, Pudgy is our child. Seeing our children daily, we continue to ignore the cry of their hearts and the pain of their existences. And one day the cry stops. No, the pain did not go away, it was buried and over time that part of the heart died. Pudgy is also our own heart, which calls us by day and night, asking us to stop, to slow down, to take some time to smell the roses, to give up destructive habits, or just to become authentic.

But one day the heart is silent. No, its needs did not go away, but that part of the heart died. A person dies many times before they die. The tragedy of life is not death itself, but that we allow so much of ourselves to die before we die, some of us living 40 to 60 percent below our potential. The challenge is to keep our childhood simplicity without being childish.

In this story the woman's idea about independent self-determination is very good and reasonable, but it is not applicable to helping the fish in its desperate situation. In spite of the perceived closeness, there was an empathic block between the heart of the woman and the heart of the fish, making it difficult for the woman to hear the fish's cry for help. She was caught up in the prison of the familiar, addicted to her internal idea of independence, which she projected onto the fish instead of listening to its cry. Seeing only her internal representation, the ideas in her head, she was able to ignore the external reality around her.

Sadly this is not uncommon in the way we live. Made in the image of God, we are born into intimacy with God but have to discover or come to an awareness of that reality. We cannot be without the presence of God, but it is possible to live without the awareness of his presence. Through contemplation we can discover intimacy with God—he calls us to a total transformation of consciousness so that our lives are based on his love. This is manifest by a new ability to see the world as God sees it, to care for each other, and by an empathic concern for the environment.

There is a coldness in the world

David Allen Jr.

There is a coldness in the world
That was not here before;
One sees it in the sky,
One feels it in the air,
The trees, though root the same,
Are somewhere far away

There is a coldness in the world
That was not here before;
Is something in the wizened night,
The stars, though shining,
Are not bright,

The moon, though fresh positioned,
Is not new.

There is a coldness in the world
That was not here before;
The climes of season tell,
Spring flowers, though open,
Do not bloom,
And summer's timely fruit,
Fail to ripe,
And winter's virgin snow,
Is not white.

There is a coldness in the world
That was not here before;
One sees it in the people's eyes,
As foreigners passing by,
The mothers, through birth,
Do not give,
The children, though sparrows,
Do not sing,
The church bell, though tolling,
Does not tell.

From where comes this coldness in the world
That was not here before?
From where the dying,
From where the old,
From where the sunless day,
From where the boring night?
Where goes the heart from love,
And beauty from its sight?
Who closed this stable door,
For all the rich and all the poor,
Though blanketed,
Still shivering.

CHAPTER 1

The Family: People Helping People Project

"God places the lonely in families" (Psalm 68:6).

MANY COUNTRIES IN THE AMERICAS AND the Caribbean suffered tremendously from the crack cocaine epidemic of the 1980's. The Bahamas, a small archipelagic nation, experienced the first country-wide epidemic of crack cocaine (outside of South America).[1] This epidemic and its continuing sequelae, along with international economic downturn, has created a serious social fragmentation process. Having organized and written the Bahamas Task Force Report on Drugs, it is painful to see the havoc and destruction that the drug problem has created in what is one of the most beautiful places in the world. Having described crack cocaine academically, with its havoc of personal destruction, I was not aware of how it could cause such widespread family and community disintegration in my country. The Bahamas, consisting of about 350,000 – 400,000 people, is known as a quiet, simple-living, family bonded society, where people have a strong commitment to the Judeo-Christian faith or tradition. Sadly, the crack cocaine epidemic broke through everything that we as a country hold sacred, that is, our personal lives, our intimate connections, our family and society. But most tragic of all, it shattered our socio-cultural value system where life became cheap, property was not respected, the work ethic diminished and the family was desecrated. This social fragmentation is manifested by continued drug trafficking, along with its evil executions and the crippling of the once serene and safe neighborhoods. Crack cocaine was the first drug that feminized drug addiction. In the Bahamas, like many other parts of the world, the women held the family together. With the onset of crack addiction, mothers became addicted and were ejected from the homes, many of which were already fatherless, leaving the children to fend for themselves. With the onset of high youth unemployment, this dynamic led to the formation of violent youth gangs, which terrorize the community.

In 2004, I returned to my country after spending 10 years working in the Washington, D.C. area. I was involved in starting a number of programs dealing with homelessness, drug addiction, prostitution and other societal ills. Having done a number of papers following the publication of the Lancet paper in 1986 in reference to the follow-up of the crack cocaine crisis, it was clear to me that violence was on the increase and that the quality of life in many areas had changed. When I returned, I went to review the community prevalence of drugs and to write a follow-up paper on the outcome of the initial paper describing the crack cocaine epidemic. What I found was so devastating that I felt it was no point publishing another paper, portraying the continued horror, chaos and destruction of the sequelae of the original crack cocaine epidemic of the 1980's. What was needed was an effective intervention in the appalling social fragmentation, prevalent in so many areas of the country. I was contacted by a mother who had lost her son to murder who told me that there were a number of other mothers who had suffered like her and they wished to meet with me. We met together and they told me that because of the leniency of the bail system, they would see the alleged murderers of their children walking in their neighborhoods. As a result, they were paralyzed by fear and felt that their life was in danger because they could be seen as possible witnesses or persons to give evidence concerning a trial in court. These mothers (about six total) taught me about the deep, painful loss produced by the murder of a child. As a psychiatrist who had worked in the field of addiction, I felt I had explored the depths of grief. But in working with these mothers, I was appalled by the multiple layers of grief in a mother's heart when a child is killed. In the sessions, they would groan from the deep part of the abdomen, what I call a womb-groan, which somehow ricocheted in my mind as a powerful clap of thunder, heralding an oncoming destructive storm. They presented feelings of helplessness, rejection, abandonment, humiliation. They felt judged by the society, implying that if their son was killed, they must be involved in some type of illegal or nefarious activity. In our discussions at times, the atmosphere would actually darken, as the gloom of helplessness and despair and the powerful desire for revenge presented itself. I had known a little bit about the academic and intellectual aspects of revenge, but the revenge which I experienced from their heart was like a saw that sawed through me and exploded, creating a sense of nothingness. In other words, it became evident that the desire for revenge was a desire for self-destruction and everything else. As our time went on and we talked together, one of the ladies talked about the shame. When asked to describe what she meant by this, she said you feel disrespected, unwanted and used up. When I went into the community to talk to the young men, they did not use the word shame. Instead, they said they felt 'dissed'. They described that the feeling of being dissed is so deep, you have to block yourself from it. What I found was that the country was suffering from a serious social fragmentation, which seemed to have its base in the shame process. For the sake of the work, I define social fragmentation as a process by which persons are victimized by the negativity of shame, giving them a diminished view of themselves, others and the world. Shame, or being dissed as the young men would say, is a powerful master emotion, resulting from the shattering of cherished wishes, expectations and dreams. Usually hidden, it manifests itself as the faces of shame such as anger, violence, revenge, addiction, intimacy dysfunction, loneliness, dehumanization etc. As a result, the individual is overwhelmed by intense negativity, producing a devaluing of the self, but most sadly, the inability to develop positive, interpersonal bonds in forming meaningful or constructive community.

Resocialization, on the other hand, involves liberation from the negativity of shame, by sharing our painful life stories in a contemplative atmosphere of love, mindfulness, support and non-judgmental listening. As a result, a powerful healing bond develops, leading to the experience of positive emotions, such as love, forgiveness, gratitude and healing community.

I was challenged by the rising murder rate in the country and asked, "What can be done in marginalized communities to reduce social fragmentation and develop constructive community?' As I interviewed people, I saw strong individual negativity, manifested by anger, violence, revenge and intimacy dysfunction. It became obvious that hurting people were not particularly interested in what I could do for them, but were very willing to share their pain and hurt in an environment of trust, love, and non-judgmental listening. The stories of their lives embedded the deep pain they had experienced. As they shared their stories in a group process, a powerful, healing bond developed which allowed people the freedom to release their pain and shame. This bond we call 'Family', hence the name of the project: 'The Family: People Helping People'. Within the dynamics of shame (Allen, *Shame: The Human Nemesis*, 2010), when young people said 'I felt dissed', they were saying they felt shamed and shut-out from the surrounding society, either because of drug addiction, poverty, violence or a prison sentence. So in our work, social fragmentation could be defined as persons who are victims of the anger and negativity of shame, leading to a diminished view of the self, others and the world. Resocialization is the liberation of a person from being the victim of the negativity of anger (shame) to discover the positive emotions of love, forgiveness, gratitude and healing community. Thus, we became involved in developing a model psychotherapy called the Contemplative Discovery Pathway Theory (C.D.P.T.) to help persons release their shame and move towards the discovery of love, gratitude and meaningful community. C.D.P.T. is a psycho-dynamic theory, with elements of various therapies like cognitive behavioral theory, psychoanalytic dynamic therapy, and contemplative psychology.[2]

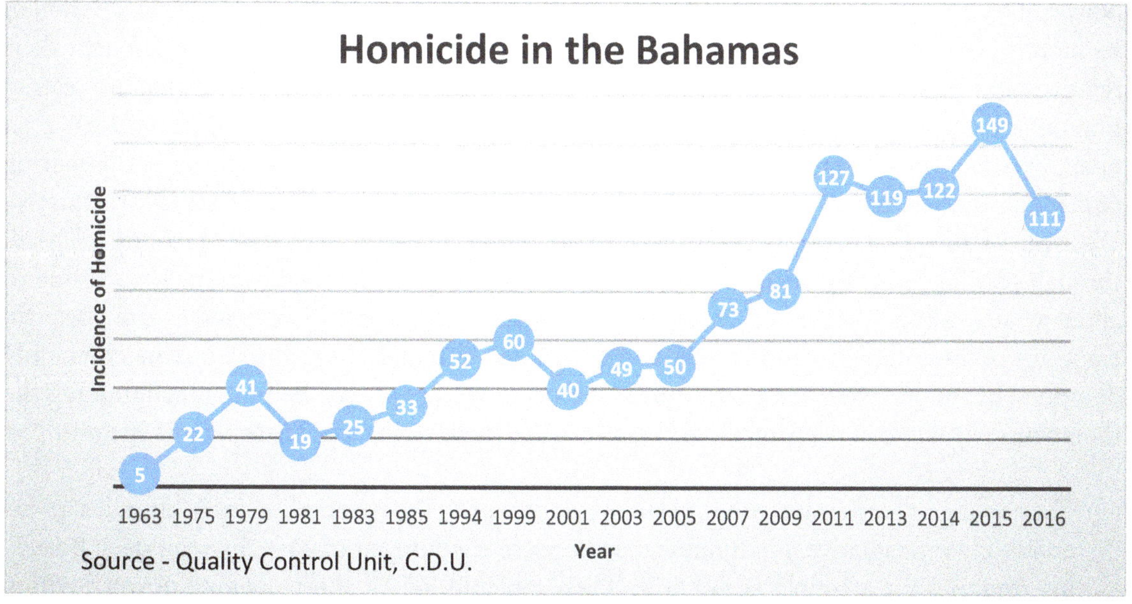

Figure 1 – Incidence of Homicide in the Bahamas (1963-2016) (Section, 2015).

The Family: People Helping People Project is a group process intervention of social fragmentation based on the Contemplative Discovery Pathway Theory (C.D.P.T.). In theory, the group creates a therapeutic replica of the family, allowing us to confront our issues of hurt and shame in a safe, contemplative environment involving love, mindfulness and non-judgmental listening. The Family provides support and efficacy for its members allowing them to discover themselves and grow as individuals. The types of problems addressed include: delinquent and violent behavior, domestic violence, alcohol and drug abuse, revenge elimination, anger management, conflict resolution, alternative sentencing by the courts and traumatization due to natural disasters or other types of violence. The groups meet each week for two hours. The sessions are open. New participants are welcomed to join at any time. Each group meets in a room where chairs are arranged in a large circle so the members can see each other. The sessions begin in contemplative mindfulness, where people are exposed into an exercise in deep breathing, followed by relaxation and a short prayer. The Family group is then described as a place where we share our stories.

The Formation of the Family: People Helping People Project

After I had a structured, workable definition of social fragmentation, I started a program to enhance resocialization, using an intervention technique of a group process model. Starting with ten persons, who were victims or relatives of persons who were murdered, violently assaulted, suffering from drug addiction or the woes of financial disaster, we met once a week for two hours. I came to realize that what hurt people wanted more than anything else was not necessarily what we can do for them, but our willingness to stand with them in their pain. As they shared their deep, painful stories of shame, involving murder, violent crime, domestic violence, addiction, or job loss in a contemplative environment of love, support and non-judgmental listening, a powerful healing bond developed in the group. This bond I define as 'family'. Within a period of six months, the group had grown to over forty persons, because those in the group brought their relatives and friends. Unlike the classic group therapy model, this group process had no restriction on size and required no contract for payment or attendance. This intervention became an open, dynamic, supportive group process model, involving transformation through the sharing of personal stories (narratives) based on the psychotherapeutic principles of the Contemplative Discovery Pathway Theory (C.D.P.T.)[2] Resocialization began to happen as persons released, through painful catharsis, their anger, hurt, jealousy and grief. In doing so, they were able to enter what I call the process of discovery of their authentic selves by opening to the powerful emotions of love, humility, forgiveness and gratitude. Although the curative factors commonly described by Yalom[3] were evident, a number of other factors proved helpful in maintaining the therapeutic dynamic in the group, particularly as it increased in size. These factors include:

(a) The sharing of stories in a contemplative atmosphere– By opening the meetings with an exercise of contemplative mindfulness, people were encouraged to participate in deep breathing exercises for a couple of minutes. Then someone said a short opening prayer inviting God's love and grace to be present to us as we open our hearts to share our pain. The sharing of painful stories in a contemplative atmosphere of love, mindfulness and non-judgmental listening, develops a powerful healing bond, which we describe as 'Family'. In reference to this, Dr. Curt Thompson, speaking of Dr. Daniel Siegel's work, writes "...an important part of how people change...is through the process of telling their stories to an empathic listener. When a person tells their story and is truly heard and understood, both they and the listener undergo actual changes in their brain circuitry. They feel a greater sense of emotional and relational connection, decreased anxiety, and greater awareness of and compassion for others' suffering"[4]

(b) Confidentiality – this is not easy to achieve, especially in marginalized communities, where people are very sensitive and secretive. However, we have found that over time, as people see the benefits of the group, they tend to trust us more. We share with them that the trust they have for us as the leaders of the group must be the trust they have for themselves and each other. The idea is that if after the group they spend time talking about another person's issues, this is no benefit to them. It's pure gossip. But at the same time, if they use the group to work on how the group affected and benefited them, they will grow. In our experience, this has been a very powerful dynamic which has helped persons to realize that the group really is about them and the development of their life.

That which is most personal, is universal and each person's story is related to our own story. We explain to participants that as the healing bond develops in the group, they will tend to see themselves in each other and share each other's wounds. Obviously, confidentiality takes time to develop and so we stress it throughout the process, encouraging the group to examine how the discussion applies to that person. Our other finding is that as the persons mature in the group, they come to realize that if they can own their problems and commit themselves to work on them outside the group, they have a better chance of working toward their solution. On the other hand, if they deny their personal issues and focus on gossiping about persons in the group, there's little chance that they can move to the resolution of their problems. Thus, as the group becomes more cohesive, the group tends to recognize the importance of confidentiality, and the process becomes more effective. The other thing we find helpful is to directly ask the group how are we doing with confidentiality. When someone shares a breach of confidentiality, we make that a topic of discussion. Thus by involving them, we get them to be involved in structuring the confidentiality process. When we started the work in the community, this was one of our major issues. But we are gratified to report that confidentiality develops with cohesiveness. Thus the goal of the group must be to work toward inter-group bonding, where persons take ownership of the group. For example, in prison, after the group became cohesive, the inmates claimed it was their group and even gave it their own name, 'The Free Your Mind Group'. They themselves warned people coming to the group for the first time of the importance of the confidentiality clause. So we find that when the group itself takes up the issue of confidentiality and reminds other group members of its importance, that is a sign that the group is on its way to maturity.

(c) Silence – silence is a powerful absorber of deep negativity, pain and shame, allowing us to heal in an atmosphere of mindfulness and love. In our experience, the sharing of deep pain – e.g. the murder of a relative, the death or abuse of a child – is so painful that it can only be received at the silent level, where words are inadequate to express what the group is feeling. When this occurs, words act as a distraction, moving us toward the circumference, rather than the center of the deep hurt. Again, this was not an easy dynamic to teach and for the group to learn, because in marginalized communities, noise is the order of the day. In fact, many persons, upon entering the group, become frigid and uncomfortable during the silence. But again, it's a teaching point. We actually try to help the members to realize that no matter how much we talk or feel about the deep pain of the death of a child, for example, we are limited in understanding. But if we can allow ourselves to be silent, we invoke the spirit of God to join us and as a result, help us with dealing with the tragedy. We must stress that the Bahamas has a cultural, inherent spirituality. When the silence is called for, group members are reminded that God is present. "Be still (silent) and know that I am God" (Psalm 46:10). In other words, silence means being still, reverent and open to the healing presence of God. Opening our heart to silence releases the unconscious hurt, shame and wounds of a lifetime and as described in this book, in silence, chronological time (chronos) intercepts with eternity or the fullness of time (kairos), producing what T.S. Eliot calls the 'Still Point'. At the Still Point, we experience the united field of consciousness and the interconnectedness of all things in the now or present. The now is not only what is happening at the present, but it is the field of consciousness in which the mystery of our life unfurls. At the Still Point, we experience healing and open to the eternal mystery.

(d) Empathy – empathy is essential for psychological healing. It must be stressed that before empathy develops, we all experience a powerful sense of vulnerability. This vulnerability means that someone may say something to hurt us and so we start to go in protective mode. On the other hand, only when we feel safe and have some type of bonding connection to others, we in turn, allow our vulnerability to move toward the development of empathy. It is important to stress that a new group takes almost six months before the dynamic of vulnerability becoming empathy develops. This is where the test of good leadership or facilitation is evoked. It takes time, patience and most of all, understanding the process of the overt and latent themes of what is being presented in the group. Empathy involves a process of projecting ourselves into the psyche or heart of another person, feeling what they feel, yet remaining true to ourselves. The fact is, empathy only occurs when people feel safe. Vulnerability lead ing to empathy is the gateway to compassion, forgiveness and healing community. But like trust, the development of empathy takes time, patience and understanding. We have found that, in waiting for a group to move toward empathy or cohesiveness, our individual praxis or the group process occurring in the mind of the facilitator, was examined for the small signs that burp out of empathic connection. These elusive signs are a sudden tear appearing when another is sharing, the up and down movement of the head when a person is sharing their story, the movement to be close to another who seemingly is having a hard time sharing their story or as is often the case, a person shouts out 'you too?'. When confronted by that expression, the person then explains that they didn't realize that someone else was undergoing what they experienced. When this happens, the powerful bonding is taking place in the group, leading towards cohesiveness.

(e) Role Play – we have found role-play to be a powerful process of psychodrama, of allowing painful experiences to be released in real present-time. This means that the role play releases deep hurt and allows us to move from the here and now to experience the there and then, and vice-versa. Providing new perspectives on old hurts, role-playing challenges the individual to move from being a victim to becoming a survivor. A profound and complex art, role-play requires contemplative listening and compassion to understand the pain of another, allowing us to experience the destructive action of the perpetrator in real time. When this occurs, the group is often stunned and challenged by the pathos of a situation, resulting in a powerful catharsis, releasing deep hurt and pain. For example, a lady who had attended the group for about three years was challenged about her repressed hurt and anger, particularly regarding her husband. Obviously challenged by this, she retorted, "I am not angry". At this time, I arranged for one of our members who had become proficient in role-playing, to act as her husband. They were both placed in the center of the group and the client was told to talk to her husband. The role-player asked her why she was so difficult with him at home. To the group's surprise, she screamed at him, telling him he was lazy and left her to carry all the responsibility. The role-player said 'you seem to like carrying the responsibility'. At this point, the lady rose up and attempted to hit the role-player, who ran out of the room as she ran after him. When she came back, I asked her how she felt. She said 'I did not know I was so angry'. From then on, her demeanor in the group changed and she started to work on the hurt from her family of origin, where she was the beast of burden and somehow assumed the same role in her marriage. After the group, she personally said to me 'that was a shock. I didn't realize I was so angry. I really felt like killing him'. At that point of the role-play, she actually saw her husband saying the same things to her, and a surge of anger moved up to her heart, rendering her uncontrollable.

(f) Centering – in the process of centering, we invite the person sharing their pain to come to the center of the group, where they are joined by the therapist, other facilitators and participants in the group who identify with their situation. As a result, the group becomes two concentric groups: the inner being the pain sharers and the outer being the pain bearers. As the painful story is released, a powerful catharsis results, not only releasing the pain of the victim, but enabling others to express their pain as well. The catharsis is followed by a deep sense of reverential silence, reflection and understanding. At this point, the group is extremely cohesive and persons have difficulty leaving. For example, a lady shared that the hurricane had blown the roof off her house. As she huddled together with her four children, this was a deeply painful experience for all of them. To make matters worse, the following day, the older son, who was 16 years old, was murdered in an empty building next door. As she was centered in the group and shared her pain, the surrounding group, the pain bearers, were powerfully moved by the pathos and pain of the situation. Some were in shock, others were meditating, others were praying and some were crying. The silence was deafening as the pain shattered our feeling of composure and peace. Eventually, we all were so moved that most of us were crying and feeling a sense of helplessness. After waiting in silence for a while, I announced the group was over, but people just sat as an amazing calm came over the group. A lady in the group sang a well-known hymn sung at funerals 'It's All Right Now'.

(g) Social Activities – in classical group theory, participants are not involved in social action. But in the Family, we have found that social activities, for example a birthday celebration, a hospital visitation, picnic or holiday party, are extremely important and have a powerful healing effect on the group. We are convinced that often a very challenged person is encouraged and blessed by visiting or celebrating with another hurt person. A number of persons have shared how social activity helps them to feel a part of the group, release their pain and give them courage to face the future. For example, a lady called me at 10:00 pm, saying that she felt in danger of killing her husband. I called two Family members and they were able to go to her house immediately. When the police arrived, they were shocked to find the two Family members present. The officer was so impressed with the way they dealt with the lady that when I called back to talk with my Family members, the officer said they felt the lady was in good hands and they didn't have to stay. At the next group, the lady shared how blessed she was to have two Family members come to help her at a very trying time. Even more so, I noticed that the two Family members had a deep sense of well-being and excitement over being able to provide the assistance needed.

(h) Singing – singing has become a unifying force in the group, calming the intense emotional experiences of anger, violence, grief and revenge. The Negro Spirituals have proven particularly helpful. For example, 'Sometimes I feel like a motherless child, a long, long way from home...sometimes I feel like a fatherless child, a long, long way from home'.

At the Kemp Road Family, where participants have suffered tremendously from violent crime and the ravages of poverty through the lack of unemployment, they receive much solace at the end of the group by singing 'Bind Us Together'. The resonance of the words of these songs have a powerful effect on the group as they are reminded of their faith and a positive future where one day they will be at peace. Sometimes, as the spiritual or other songs are sung, tears stream down the faces of many participants as they release their deep hurt and shame. At the end of the song, the silence absorbs the pain and longing so prevalent in the group. Another example of the power of song was when a Family member shared the painful story of being at her sister's death bed and how her faith enabled her to sing a song to her sister which made her smile and gave her hope to face death. When this was shared in the group, at the point of sadness, one of the facilitators sang 'His Eye is one the Sparrow'. The group then experienced a powerful sense of oneness and healing.

In summary, music and song have a wonderful way of providing a sense of connection and a continuation of the healing effect on members of the group, even after the session is terminated.

(i) Humor – The heart with deep pain responds to humor. However, to be effective, the humor must be intimately connected to the process while expressing the opposite. For example, the Bahamas has a Christian cultural orientation. It is not uncommon for people in the group to assure each other by saying 'God will be there for you'. At that point, the facilitator may tell a story about the mother who told Johnny to get the broom from outside while it was dark. Johnny replied, "Mummy, I'm afraid of the dark". Mother said "Johnny, don't be afraid of the dark. God is everywhere". Taking her literally, Johnny opens the door and shouts into the darkness "God, since you're everywhere, can you please pass me the broom?" Despite the sadness, the group breaks into laughter, releasing hurt and shame. Humor allows people to see themselves in perspective and not take themselves too seriously while releasing them, if only temporarily, from their hurt and pain.

(j) Insights from neuroscience: Neuroscience offers novel ways to think about the benefits of the Family. In his book Brainstorm (2013), Daniel Siegel claims that we interact with the world in two views of reality: the physical world of objects and mindsight. Sadly, modern life has become more dependent on physical sight than recognizing the importance of our mind connection. This is challenging because without the mind connection, people can treat others without respect or compassion. The Family project is based on mindsight where we help individuals to develop their internal world to relate more effectively to themselves and others. According to Siegel, focusing our mind on multiple interactions - for example, telling our stories, listening, singing, meditation, social action, etc. – helps us build new circuits in our brain enabling us to adapt creatively to new experiences while increasing our health and developing harmonious relationships. Mindsight includes three fundamental skills: insight, empathy and integration. Insight is our ability to appreciate our inner mental life, helping us to understand the present, past and future. When we reflect on things going on inside of us, we develop mindsight mapping of the brain, activating our pre-frontal circuits where the inner and interpersonal experiences are coordinated and balanced. Empathy is the ability to sense the inner life of another person, enabling us to see them from our perspective and imagine what it is like to walk in their shoes. The gateway to compassion and kindness, empathy is the key to social intelligence, allowing us to understand the intention and needs of others. In this light, relationships can be defined as the sharing of energy and information between persons. Insight and empathy cultivates integration empowering us to coordinate our relationships with each other. Sadly, when integration is blocked, chaos results in our internal and external relationships, developing a powerful rigidity which destroys individual and community development. These neuroscientific insights validate the effect of The Family where people share their stories of pain and shame in a contemplative environment, creating mindsight (insight, empathy and integration) in the participants leading to coordination, balance and self-regulation.

(k) Spiritual teaching - At the end of the group when people are overwhelmed by the pathos and suffering of others, a spiritual teaching gives a sense of calm, encouragement and hope. Examples of spiritual teachings that have been used effectively include: loving when the dream of love has shattered (the story of Ruth and Naomi), facing the painful giants in our life (the story of David and Goliath) and forgiveness (parable of the prodigal son by Jesus particularly as portrayed in Rembrandt's painting).

Case Vignettes

Abuse: When Shirley (not her real name) came to the Family, she was broken and deeply hurt. Incested and abused by her father for many years, she was threatened if she ever revealed the family secret. Seeking to escape her abusive family, she married a man who at first seemed loving but eventually became verbally and physically abusive, threatening her life many times. Distraught and depressed, Shirley became suicidal and was referred to the Family. When she was ready to share her story, Shirley was invited to come to the center of the group, supported by therapists and persons who identified with her pain. After a while, Shirley was able to release her pain, exploding into powerful catharsis screaming at the top of her voice for three minutes or more, releasing the pain and shame of a lifetime. This was followed by a powerful silence in the group where persons prayed and others meditated or cried. After the catharsis, persons in the group comforted and encouraged Shirley. Having been in the Family group for five years, Shirley is a changed person. She is a healer who has helped many persons face and work through their painful experiences of abuse. Recently receiving a promotion at work, she has become one of the first graduates of the therapist facilitator training program.

The terror of poverty and social deprivation: Rejected by his family, John left home at 13 years old to fend for himself on the streets. Living on the beach and in abandoned buildings, John hustled daily to make ends meet. He was severely abused - physically and sexually. Later on John was shot in his face and side and admitted to hospital. On the third day of his hospitalization, the person who shot John was also shot, admitted to the same hospital and placed two beds away from John. Angry and filled with revenge, John wanted him dead. The next day John's gang came to the hospital seeking to kill the person who shot John. They begged John to point out the shooter to them. But John refused to identify his shooter. Instead, he surrendered his feelings of revenge and prayed for a better life. After release from hospital, John's life became worse. He lived in a tomb in one of the graveyards and was eventually referred to the Family project. Facing a loss of confidence in himself, John was shy, ashamed and unable to speak. The group was very receptive and showered him with love, giving him odd jobs, clothes, food and money. After a number of sessions, John began to speak freely and socialize with the participants in the group. A few months later, he shared that when he first came to the Family, he felt his life was hopeless. He said he is now determined to live again because of the love he found in our sessions. John is still in the Family, has a job and volunteers in the Family basketball outreach program to marginalized youth.

Revenge and its destructive effects: Many persons in the Family have experienced the murder, violent attack or abuse of a loved one. As a result, revenge is a major issue in the Family which may involve wanting the perpetrator killed or his family injured. Feeling of revenge are very powerful and extremely destructive. A young lady walked into the Family screaming, "They killed my brother this morning, I want to kill, I want revenge". Continuing to scream, she said, "My brother supported my family and paid for my schooling. Now we'll drop back into poverty and I may even have to quit school." Sitting quietly, the group listened attentively as she poured out her heart. After a while, an elderly lady with bowed head and tears in her eyes walked slowly toward the young lady. Looking intently at her, she said, "They killed my son a year ago. It was terrible! I know how you feel. I wanted revenge but realized that the destructive feelings could destroy me. I came to the Family to work through my pain and release my feelings for revenge. I can't tell you what to do, but I encourage you to release the feelings of revenge. If you don't, you will have two murders on your hands: the murder of your brother who is dead and the psychological murder of yourself from the poison of revenge." The young lady and the group were tearful as they listened to the elderly lady. The group ended and persons left quietly and respectfully. Three weeks later I received a letter from the young lady thanking me for The Family. She said the love of the older lady and the support of the group encouraged her to let go of the revenge for her brother's murder. She said it still hurts deeply and she misses her brother. But she realized she had to release the feelings of revenge in order to continue with her life. She ended the letter 'thank you for preventing me from committing murder'.

Violent behavior: The Family deals with many persons involved with violence. Taking a non-judgmental approach, we encourage them to make the perceptual shift from shame and violence to love and gratitude. A young man who came to the Family was very active with gang leaders and highly respected on the street. On weekends he drank alcohol heavily, smoked Marijuana and bidi and acted out violently. He said that after taking his mixture of alcohol and drugs, he had a feeling of invincibility. One Friday night, under the influence, he returned home to find the doors locked with his wife and son inside. Banging on the door, he shouted at his wife to let him in. She was afraid because she knew he was intoxicated and violent. Because she refused to open the door, he became exceedingly angry. He threw bricks through the window and eventually broke down the door. Terrified, his wife grabbed the child and locked themselves in the bathroom. Threatening to hurt them, he tried to break into the room, but was unsuccessful. Eventually the police were called and stabilized the situation. He was referred to the Family where he has spent time working on himself and his marriage. He has made excellent progress and has been able to reconcile with his family. In the Family for five years, he continues to work on his addictions and has been able to be productive on his job. Graduating from the therapist facilitator program, he has helped many persons struggling with gang activity and violence. He has been particularly helpful in the Family's trauma rescue program, making calls to persons threatening or suffering from violence throughout the day. Acting as a personal assistant to the leader of the Family, he has accompanied him to other islands to facilitate very difficult situations involving violence and murder.

Terminal issues and death: A pleasant young lady was referred to us suffering from a serious type of Leukemia. On her first day in the Family, she shared that the money she had saved up for her consultation in Miami was stolen. They also stole her computer which she hoped to use to Skype her nine year old daughter while away. She said these losses were painful, but the most difficult experience was to hear her daughter ask if the robbers would return. The group was overwhelmed with her pain and the pathos of her situation. At the next meeting, she was much brighter and more positive. When asked how she was doing, she replied that she was encouraged because some members of the Family visited her, replaced the stolen money and bought her a new computer. As a result, she was now able to continue planning the trip to Miami for the consultation. During the next year, she was hospitalized a number of times. When she was able to attend the Family, we were all blessed by her beautiful smile. She was particularly upset when persons talked about suicide. She would say to them, "You don't know how valuable life is. You only realize how valuable your health is when you're faced with a terminal illness, and there's nothing you can do." Even as she became weaker, she continued to attend the Family and encouraged us. Eventually she died and Family members attended the funeral. We remember her fondly because she helped us to realize that death may destroy a life but not a relationship.

Addiction: From recovery to discovery: In the Family, we have a number of persons who suffer from addictions to alcohol, drugs and other issues. A young man was a drug addict who lived on the street for many years. He went in and out of treatment programs, experiencing recovery repeatedly, only to find that after the removal of the drugs in his life, he would still feel meaningless and irritable. This feeling of emptiness haunted him, and before long, he was back on the streets. Terrified, he wanted to give up because he was depressed and hopeless. In fact he said he felt so bad about himself that he would only steal from people he knew could kill him. In other words, he was so depressed and suicidal that he took the risk of the theft being successful to get what he wanted, but if it was not, he did not mind being killed. In the Family, he shared his hurt and the powerful shame that governed his life. As he shared his painful story, he said the loving environment of the Family impacted him deeply. Sharing his pain in the presence of people who truly accepted him, allowed him to experience a depth of love that he had never encountered before. In the Family, he was valued, and as a result, his life had meaning and purpose, allowing him to reach out and help others. Having experienced discovery, that is the vision of love in his life pushing him toward meaning and hope, the young man trained to become a therapist facilitator. Despite his issues, he is now an active outreach worker of the Family, working with marginalized young men.

Conclusion

The Family's mantra is summed up in this quote: "Each person's life is a challenging journey from being a victim of their shame false self-based in fear and anger to the discovery of the glorious freedom of their authentic true self based in love, compassion, humility, forgiveness and gratitude". The Family is a place where we tell our authentic stories to empty our heart so that we can absorb the love coming from the contemplative environment of the group. All love comes from God, 'the Love which will never let us go and the Face which will never turn away'. When that love enters our life, we change our mind, change our life and change the world. As T.S. Eliot said, "We shall not cease from exploration, and the end of all our exploring will be to arrive where we started and know the place for the first time".[5]

REFERENCES

1 Jekel JF, Allen DF. Podlewski H, et al:(1986) Epidemic freebase cocaine abuse: a case study from the Bahamas. *Lancet* 1986; 1:459-462
2 Allen DF, Mayo M, Carroll M, et al: (2014) Cultivating gratitude: Contemplative discovery pathway theory applied to group therapy in the Bahamas. *Journal of Trauma Treatment*, 3(3)
3 Yalom, I *The Theory and Practice of Group Psychotherapy*. (New York, Basic Books. 2007)
4 Thompson, C. *Anatomy of the Soul*. (Carol Stream: Tyndale House 2010)
5 Eliot, T, S. "Little Gidding" *Four Quartets* 1942

Chapter 2
Shame: The Human Condition

Liberation is no longer being ashamed in front of oneself.
–Friedrich Nietzsche

THE WORD SHAME IS DERIVED FROM a Germanic root meaning "disgrace" and has been traced back to an Indo-European root meaning "to cover or to hide." The notion of hiding is intrinsic and inseparable from the concept of shame. An ancient concept, shame appears in the Genesis story of Adam and Eve in the Garden of Eden. When Adam and Eve disobeyed God, they were ashamed and instinctively covered their nakedness with fig leaves. In spite of its ancient history, shame has been little discussed in the psychological literature. Why is this so? One hypothesis is that shame was repressed, denied, and ignored because therapists and psychiatrists were not in contact with their own shame.

No longer neglected, shame is now known as the Master Emotion. It combines the powerful effects of anger, hurt, remorse, rejection, abandonment, and humiliation. A powerful bolus of pain, shame strides like a colossus across the length and breadth of our heart, mind, life and society.

Examining the dynamics of shame is imperative because it is the principle impediment in all relationships: parent-child, teacher-student, therapist-client, or husband-wife. Violating inner security and interpersonal trust, shame inflicts wounds not only on the self, but also on the family, groups, entire nations, and the diplomacy of international relationships. Because of shame and our Shame False Self, being judgmental occurs when we feel vulnerable to help us cope with our inner feeling of fear and hurt. Being judgmental strengthens shame's powerful attempt to isolate us, creating distance to make us look down on each other. But sadly, with a judgmental attitude of shame, the distance grows and isolation increases.

In recent developments of neuroscience, the most powerful dynamic of shame is that it interferes with the flow of energy and communication in the mind. According to interpersonal neurobiology (IPNB), the mind is no longer what or how we think, but is the regulation of the flow and balance of energy and information among neurons. The energy involves electrochemical communication among neurons and information involves the perceptions passing through different domains of the mind as well as interpersonal relationships. Sadly, shame blocks this flow and balance, making healing, empathy, insight and integration more difficult. As a result, when we expose shame and release it, we improve healing, empathy and integration in the brain, enhancing intrapsychic and interpersonal connections. In our work, Discovery is opening to our True Self. This occurs when we choose to release the shame and pain of our individual stories and decide to be known authentically. As will be discussed later in the book, when we release our shame and pain, we become more integrated and desire to be involved in our vocational gifts and purpose given to us by God.

Shame produces comparison and competition, translating differences into being better or worse. As a result, shame disintegrates all our endeavors, leaving us as disconnected individuals, isolated from each other. According to Dr. Curt Thompson in his book *The Soul of Shame*, "Shame is ubiquitous, the emotional pigment which colors the images of everything – our bodies, marriages, politics, successes and failures, friends and enemies...It ends wars, only to start them again. It fuels injustice, creating excuses for doing little if anything about them.[1] Shame is a powerful motivator of students, athletes and employees. For example, a successful wrestling coach shared with me that he found shame a powerful motivator of his most victorious wrestling teams. During the matches, he would shout, 'Kill, kill, kill them' and the young men would just push themselves to their ultimate strength and often win the match. As I continued listening to the coach, his tone changed and he looked sad as he remarked, "Even though shame was a good motivator, I believe I was wrong to use that approach to motivate the young men because it had a devastating impact on their personality". He described that the young men were very successful in wrestling but found it difficult to regulate their life in a healthy and loving manner. As a result, a number of them became depressed, frustrated and failed miserably in interpersonal relationships. Even after the matches were over, they were still thinking of dominating people by shaming them. The coach said after experiencing the renewing of his life through opening to the Christian faith, he changed his approach. Instead of motivating the young men through shame, he encouraged them to do their best in loving the opponent and respecting their dignity and value. He began to ask the young men to imagine themselves as serving God's purpose in love during their wrestling. In so doing, the point of the match was not only to be an excellent wrestler but to treat the person with dignity, love and respect. Thus whether they won or lost, he claimed the young men were more relaxed after a match and became balanced human beings in developing meaningful relationships.

Shame is particularly present in the stories of our life. Occurring in our early development before speech, shame lodges in our right brain around the eighth to the fifteenth month. The right brain is intuitive, compassionate, nonverbal and visuospatial. As we learn to share our story, we give words to our shame but find that guilt is also present. Shame develops earlier and is the structure on which guilt rests. Guilt usually develops in the formation of the left brain, occurring in the third and fourth year of life. Therefore, guilt requires a cognitive approach. For example, 'I have made a mistake'. On the other hand, shame is deeper and it is 'I am a mistake'. When we tell our story, often, we are sharing a cognitive experience of what others have told us about ourselves. Guilt is present but shame is not expressed. As we become more familiar with our personal narrative, we begin to share deeply our story and ourselves, not only in the cognitive sense but also in the deep emotional release of shame. When this occurs, we are very cautious and sensitive as to how people around us are perceiving us. After we mature in giving our authentic story, we release our deep shame and pain, liberating ourselves to discover our Authentic or True Self. When discovery occurs, we find that that which is most personal, is universal. As a result, people around us start to connect with shame experiences in their personal life. This creates a ripple, healing effect between the sharer and the listener, benefiting both. It is important to realize that our stories separate us from the rest of creation and relate to our function, purpose and meaning. In a strange way, we all live within the story we believe about ourselves. Sadly, though many of us are not conscious of this, our story is part of the human story that unites us all. The bottom line is that shame permeates every aspect of our story. Therefore, the ability to develop a coherent understanding of our story demands that we release the shame in our life.

Shame is more than a feeling, because there is always an undercurrent of it being a sensed emotion, meaning that we can experience shame with it being transmitted through our brain structures. When we are shamed, our face hangs down, we feel terrified and seek to hide or want to die. For example, we experience 'I am bad', 'I am hopeless', 'I am not enough', 'I am unlovable' or 'I am a failure'. A major part of shame is that we are able to project it onto other persons, making us judge and blame them. Thus, the sad reality is that shamed people usually shame others.

The healing of shame requires exposure. Once exposed, shame decreases. But if it remains hidden or unspoken, it increases. Thus, shame's healing requires the counter-intuitive act of turning toward that which most terrifies us. This is not easy because this vulnerable exposure can be great and it may seem even life-threatening. It is the movement toward another and the connection with someone who is safe that allows us to develop the ability to release our shame and experience the freedom from our in-built shame prisons. Sadly, in this vale of tears, life, it is impossible to eliminate shame totally from our individual and interpersonal relationships. But we can be intentional in learning to change our response to shameful experiences and discover the freedom of our own authenticity.

Shame is an internal, hidden phenomenon that appears in society as the external faces of inferiority, shyness, failure, anger, addiction, shattered dreams, and broken lives. Shame destroys the quality and the meaning of life and creates a gap between what we expect for ourselves and what we are. Facing this gap is very painful and many of us seek to avoid it, deny it or rationalize it. Shame is the underlying dynamic in many psychopathological issues such as depression, anxiety, intimacy dysfunction, and violence. In modern society shame has become a predominant factor for the following reasons.

(a) Shame-based dysfunctions such as addiction, abuse, and eating disorders are our society's dominant diseases. Treatment is often sabotaged or inadequate unless the shame core in these illnesses is worked through.

(b) The burgeoning problems due to the breakdown of the family with increasing numbers of single parents, blended families, dual careers, latch key kids, and post divorce families. All of these expose children to painful experiences that result in evolving layers of shame.

(c) The breakdown of the family has also placed an enormous burden on the school, mandating teachers to act as parents. Teachers cannot replace parents. Children are raised with a deep sense of inferiority, anxiety, and pain which develops into shame. The absence of meaningful, comforting environments in the modern home leads to poor separation and individuation processes and identity formation. This, too, feeds into the development of shame.

(d) The exploding technological revolution in modern society has produced a new transparency and openness. Facebook, emails, YouTube, MySpace, Twitter, and smart phones have revolutionized our way of life. Everything is open and out there for everyone to see. Shame implies hiding and there are few places to hide. Even the deletion of email is an illusion because it circulates in cyberspace.

(e) Finally the development of Self Psychology through the work of Heinz Kohut, Joseph Lichtenberg, and others has created a greater awareness of the development and importance of the self as opposed to the dynamics of intra-psychic conflict. Since shame involves the evaluation of the self, the evolution of the Self Psychology movement has projected shame into public prominence.

What is Shame?

Shame is **S**elf **H**atred **A**imed at **ME**. Revealing a rupture of the self, shame exposes the self to the self and others. Interfering with interpersonal experiences and communication, shame is portrayed by looking down and is associated with a feeling of terror and withdrawal. Shame makes a person feel embarrassed, self-conscious, and worthless. Shame is associated with disappearing, covering or hiding. Sadly, shame often rejects the love it craves and like Adam and Eve after being shamed or found naked, we cover ourselves with our self-made fig leaves, representing different versions of our Shame False Self.

Feeling useless and fundamentally flawed, shame-prone persons have a sense of deep loneliness and haunting self-doubt. Shame seeks a reunion with the person who shamed us, creating an uncomfortable state of hating and desiring to be loved simultaneously. There is an intimate connection between the shamed person and the person doing the shaming, our Nemesis. Nemesis was the goddess of retribution and indignity in Greek mythology. She was a personification of the resentment and indignity aroused in us when we are shamed by others.

A former client was a lovely lady, but deeply hurt. Married and pregnant, she was terrified when her husband left her for another woman. Her shame came from feeling abandoned, rejected, and humiliated. Hate for her husband drove her to constantly contemplate revenge. As she drove past the exit on the highway leading to his house, she would scream out at the top of her voice, "I wish you'd die. I hate you. You destroyed my life. You betrayed me." The thoughts of revenge were so deep she even thought of paying someone to kill him. Crying profusely, she told me, "I know I shouldn't think like this. But it really hurts."

She wanted to die and thought of killing herself or running away. But what would this do to her children? They were not at fault. Why should they suffer? The shame penetrated her emotionally and then started to affect her physically. She developed muscle aches, irritable bowel syndrome, and periodic, severe heart palpitations. Thinking of her husband, she would literally shake and break down crying uncontrollably.

Life was miserable and almost intolerable. She felt like exploding. Even church became ineffective. The songs and the sermons had no effect on her. She tried to pray, but it seemed as if her prayers bounced back off the ceiling. Life lost its luster. She kept on performing but stopped living. She was ashamed!

Andrew Morrison writes in *The Culture of Shame*,

> Much of human misery stems, I believe, from the gap between what we wish to be (or think we should be) and what we believe we are. This gap – influenced by the largeness of our aspirations on one hand, and lowness of our own self-image on the other – is the breeding ground for shame. The nature of this gap, between our ideals and our convictions about ourselves, is both universal and individualized, often leading to feelings of embarrassment, self-loathing and humiliation.[2]

Shame (**S**elf **H**atred **A**imed at **ME**) is a feeling of self-castigation, self-loathing, or hatred arising in us when we feel something about us is wrong, flawed, or weak. Shame is a hateful vision of the self through our own eyes. As a result, it may determine how we expect and believe that others see us.

Accompanied by a sensitive self-consciousness and conviction of failure, we are driven to hide or conceal ourselves. Hence the common expressions when we feel embarrassed, "I could have died" or "I could have sunk into a hole." Mortification is a synonym for shame. Whereas guilt generates confession and hope for forgiveness, shame, on the other hand, seeks concealment and self-deprecation.

Here is how one young professional describes the shame and turmoil of his life:

Warped and Twisted

Harsh words and violent blows
Hidden secrets nobody knows
Eyes are open, hands are fisted
Deep inside I'm warped and twisted
So many tricks and so many lies
Too many whens and too many whys

Nobody's special, nobody's gifted
I'm just me, warped and twisted
Sleeping awake and choking on a dream
Listening loudly to a silent scream
Call my mind, the number's unlisted
Lost in someone so warped and twisted
On my knees, alive but dead
Look at the invisible blood I've bled
I'm not gone, my mind has drifted
Don't expect much, I'm warped and twisted
Burnt out, wasted, empty and hollow
Today's just yesterday's tomorrow
The Sun died out, the ashes sifted
I'm still here, warped and twisted.

Shame has emerged as the "Master Emotion". Beginning in early childhood, shame influences the total human experience and, although rarely recognized, shame may be the cause of much conflict in interpersonal relationships. Shame is a powerful internal phenomenon which penetrates every segment of life producing mortification or making us want to disappear into some deep hole.

Ralph Ellison describes shame in this passage from *Invisible Man*.

> I am an invisible man.... I am a man of substance, of flesh and bone, fiber and liquids – and I might even be said to possess a mind, I am invisible, understand, simply because people refuse to see me.... When they approach me they see only my surroundings, themselves or figments of their imaginations – indeed, everything and anything except me....I am only ashamed of myself for having at one time been ashamed.[3]

Shame is having a diminished vision of our selves. Shame impales us under the magnifying gaze of our own eyes. Like a deer in the headlights, "We are," in the words of Jean-Paul Sartre, "frozen by our own inner gaze." He goes on.

> I was a fake child...I could feel my acts changing into gestures. Play-acting robbed me of the world and of human beings. I have no scene 'of my own'... I was giving the grown-ups their cues... my own reason for being slipped away; I would suddenly discover that I did not really count, and I felt ashamed of my unwanted presence in that well-ordered world. My truth, my character, and my name were in the hands of adults.

> I had learned to see myself through their eyes... when they were not present. They left their gaze behind, and it mingled with the light. I would run and jump across the gaze, which preserved my nature as a model grandson...a transparent certainty spoiled everything: I was an imposter.... The clear sunny semblances that constituted my role were exposed by a lack of being [a real self] which I could neither quite understand, nor cease to feel. I was not substantial or permanent...I was not necessary ... I had no soul.[4]

We have all experienced shame at some time or other. Sometimes it motivates us towards positive action. At a certain point, however, shame becomes toxic and destructive. It overwhelms and blocks our relationships with others and our own selves. Multi-layered, multi-dimensional, and transgenerational, shame beats at its own frequency and self-replenishes, triggered anew by life's events. Shame is ever rising like the phoenix. We cannot eliminate shame from our lives, but we can learn to recognize the difference between constructive, God-given shame and self-destructive shame, the human nemesis.

The Impact of Shame

The principal effects of shame are hiding, paralysis, and transparency. Hiding is an attempt to reduce scrutiny by seeking to cover the self. In paralysis, speech is silenced, movement interrupted, and the self frozen. Feeling the total exposure of our innermost being with our insecurities and flaws produces a painful transparency.

Shame makes us want to be found out when we feel like imposters and failures. For example, an expert witness in a trial said he was so ashamed of doing such a terrible job in court that when the police came to handcuff the defendant, he thought they were coming to handcuff him. Overwhelmed with shame about his poor performance, he felt he deserved to be punished.

Self-validating shame makes us believe that we deserve the pain we feel inside. Blurring the distinction between subject and object, shame is an experience of exposure of the self by the self. The universal look of shame is the head bowed and eyes looking downward and away from the shaming persons. It is accompanied with blushing of the face because of self visibility known as "the loss of face." A head lowered in shame or an inability to look others in the face is associated with low self-image.

Shame has many faces. Embarrassment is shame in front of an audience. Shyness is shame in the presence of strangers. Discouragement is shame about failure and defeat. Inferiority is shame permanently located in the self. Self-consciousness is shame about performance, e.g., public speaking, dancing.

Shame causes many reactions. Fear is the warning anxiety of anticipated shame. Distress is the crying and sadness that covers the underlying shame. Rage is the protection we use for the exposed self.

According to S. S. Tomkins, "If distress is the effect of suffering, shame is the effect of indignity, transgression, and of alienation. Though terror speaks to life and death and distress makes of the world a vale of tears, yet shame strikes deepest into the heart of man."[5]

Father Thomas Keating says, "Shame is felt as inner torment. A sickness of the soul...the humiliated one feels himself naked, defeated, alienated, lacking in dignity and worth.[6]

Components of Shame

Shame, manifested in our hurt trail or shame core, has many components (Diagram 3):

1. **Shame scene and scripts**
2. **Shame thoughts**
3. **Shame voices**
4. **Shame whip**
5. **Shame behavior**

1. Shame Scene and Scripts

Shame is an affective experience stored in memory as scenes which are dynamic, photographic slices of life with scripts, such as being slapped in the face or being teased and laughed at. Storage of a shame scene depends on the intensity, duration, and repetition of the affect. Since negative effects are more easily remembered than positive effects, shame or fear scenes are more easily remembered than those of joy.

Interconnected with and magnified by other affect laden scenes, they combine to form the hurt trail or shame core. Continuously beating at its own frequency, the shame core seeks replenishment and may capture or dominate us. All shame scenes have scripts, that is, voices or language which allow us to predict, interpret, and avoid them.

Shame scenes and scripts are reactivated by the effects of imagery and/or language. Images include people who were present, facial expressions, and actions performed. Language includes words spoken or unspoken and consciously or subconsciously remembered. Some shame reactions occur unconsciously without imagery or language. A gentleman with a successful career recalls a powerful shame scene from his childhood.

The door to my room suddenly burst open. My father rushed in screaming and angrily criticized me for my poor report card. Shouting at the top of his voice, he called me stupid and said I would never amount to anything. Shocked, I became extremely anxious. My face flooded and I was lost for words. In the dreadful silence, looking down and away from my dad, I felt like a total failure. Hopelessly ashamed, I wanted to disappear.

This scene and script is permanently etched in his memory. It is reactivated at home by his wife and at work by his boss. The gentleman became emotionally upset as he described the shame scene in therapy. His father is dead and long gone, but the shame scene and script play on. In his own words he said, "My father is controlling me from the grave!"

2. Shame Thoughts

Shame thoughts come to us as a very critical inner voice that demeans our personhood. Shame thoughts are painful, soul destroying, and destructive. The nature of shame thoughts are, "I am alone," "Nobody cares about me," "I am ugly," "I am a failure," "I cannot make it," "I am stupid," "I should have known better," and "I am weak." These thoughts are incessant and bombard our minds creating depression, anger, and isolation.

3. Shame Voices

Shame voices are the words of others playing over and over again inside our minds. Painful and destructive, shame voices are experienced as hyper critical memories of the words of others. Shame never stops judging us.

Shame voices criticize and demean us with such statements as, "You stupid person, why did you do that?" "Can't you do anything right?" "You are a loser." "You had it all and you blew it!" "You should be ashamed of yourself." "How could you mess up so badly?" "People are laughing at you." "No one likes you." Note how our own shame thoughts echo the shame voices of parents, relatives, teachers, employers, peers or partners.

4. Shame Whip

Besides shame thoughts and voices, the shame-based person develops a masochistic whip that is used to beat, punish, and eventually destroy the true self. A form of chronic penance, the shame-prone person creates his or her own shame cross to penalize or destroy the self. The shame cross has a vertical pole of self-hatred and a horizontal pole of hatred for others. At the point of intersection—the shame violence point—the person is a danger to self (suicide) and to others (homicide).

A man, who had attended a top boarding school in England since he was seven years old, told me this shame memory. He had received years and years of severe corporal punishment from a tough and cruel senior master for poor behavior, inadequate class work, and refusal to do homework.

Now married and successful in business, this man lives a shame-based life with a shame whip and a shame cross. Arriving home after a bad day in the office, he screams at his wife, goes into the bathroom and repeatedly slaps himself in the face for about three minutes. Relieved, he then joins the family for dinner. The shame recording of his youth keeps on playing. Like footprints on fresh cement, shame lasts for a long time!

5. Shame Behavior

Shame thoughts, shame voices, the shame whip and cross lead to shame behavior. Shame behavior validates the unworthiness, failure, and pain of internalized shame. The shame that we fear and despise often leads us to a cycle of more shame.

Causes of Shame

Shame has multiple factors and has many causes and associations. Freud, who wrote, "Shame, which is considered to be a feminine characteristic par excellence," believed shame is caused by genital deficiency.12 Females and males each have specific shame-based areas in their lives. Females tend to feel shame regarding relationships and body appearance. Whereas in males, shame is usually associated with failure in achievement, job, competition, and financial success.

Shame radiates continuous waves of deep hurt and fear as a result of the gap between our expected self (what we and others expect of us) and our actual achievement.

The causes of shame include:

1. Abuse in all its forms, sexual, physical, emotional, mental, and cultural produces repeated cycles of shame.

2. Addictions and eating disorders subtly tend to be shamed based in causation and effect. They cannot be treated effectively until the shame is defined, confronted, and resolved.

3. Natural disasters and illness impact people negatively producing various levels of shame.

4. Oppression and discrimination dehumanize people and create deep shame and low self-image. This type of shame is common in certain populations or minorities.

5. Failure and the shattering of cherished dreams of all types result in unending cycles of pain and shame.

6. Stress overload reduces our margin for compassion and love when it exceeds our limits resulting in a painful saga of shame.

Characteristics of Shame

Shame is a complex, evasive, but ever-present phenomenon occurring throughout our lives. The following is a limited discussion of some of the characteristics of shame I find in my own experience and work with others.

1. Construction of Emotion

Shame-based persons have difficulty integrating feeling with thinking and act out of emotion rather than cognition. But the affect tends to be consumed with one form of anger or the other. Anger pervades all areas of life ranging from constant complaining, fear, paranoia, uncontrollable rage or boredom. The shame-prone person recognizes shame issues and tends to repeat them. It is a sad dance moving between the experiences of being a victim and manifesting victimizing behavior.

For example, a shame-based teenage girl with childhood trauma compensates for the pain by excelling in academic achievement. However, at the height of her achievement she has a child and, to her surprise, becomes extremely and emotionally labile and depressed. Crying profusely, she is terrified of not being a good enough mother to her child. The birth of the child exposed her to the trauma of shame (abandonment, rejection, and humiliation) of her earlier life. If the shame is not worked through, it will be passed to her child and the shame cycle continues.

2. Shame and Addiction

Addiction has genetic, environmental, constitutional, and behavioral factors. It is generally accepted that shame is a causative and an associated factor of addiction. The early childhood trauma of abandonment, rejection, and humiliation creates a deep protest of various hurt feelings such as sadness, anger, frustration, and despair. If the protests are unheeded, the deep hurt, and shame move deeper into our heart with a superficial numbing effect.

As the pain deepens, the first schema begins and the individual seeks to medicate the pain with different types of addictions. The addict seeks gratification in compulsive attachments to the addictive object restricting choices and roles, e.g., drugs, money, sex, people. As the addiction deepens, the addict becomes more attached and the behavior is covered up with lies and multiple deceptions.

Addiction associations include:

- Unawareness of the thought and feeling processes
- Distortion and denial
- Dysfunctional relationships because of manipulation instead of intimacy
- Strong dependency needs
- Excessive guilt and powerlessness
- Living from crisis to crisis (strong self-absorption)
- Dishonesty (reconstructing reality)
- Low self-image and powerlessness over the addiction
- Unresolved loss or aborted grief creating a cycle of multiple addictions

Codependency is a form of addiction, an attachment to pleasing or controlling other people. Codependents medicate their pain by pleasing and controlling others. Caused by dysfunctional family systems, codependency stems from the family of origin and evokes enmeshment and over responsive caretaking. As a result, they become martyrs or victims and chronic caretakers with compulsive behaviors such as overeating and workaholism.

Unable to stand alone, the shame prone codependent craves attention and the support of others. Often extremely talented, codependents are only able to express themselves or state their views in an environment of total acceptance.

3. Interpersonal Relationships

Shame is an impediment to interpersonal relationships when one partner dominates or abuses the other. Having poor boundaries, the shame-based person finds it difficult to pull way. Conversely, some shame-prone persons hurt in the power/control area and have deep humiliation. As a result, they become contra-dependent by developing rigid boundaries and seek control over the codependent partner with weaker boundaries.

4. Negative Vision of Ourselves — Loneliness

Shame is associated with a negative vision of self seen through our own eyes. The negative vision determines how we see others and particularly how we expect others to experience and treat us. Loneliness characterizes shame-based persons. Lonely people have the same amount of social contacts as non-lonely people. The difference is that shame-based persons tend not to reach out and reciprocate hospitality shown to them.

Speaking about loneliness, Frederick Buechner writes,

> To be lonely is to be aware of an emptiness which it takes more than people to fill. It is to sense that something is missing which you cannot name. 'By the waters of Babylon, there we sat down and wept, when we remembered Zion,' sings the psalmist (137:1). Maybe in the end it is Zion that we're lonely for, the place we know best by longing for it, where at last we become who we are, where finally we find home![7]

5. Mortification

Shame makes us feel like hiding or sinking into the ground, wanting to die — mortification. Shame is now! In the 1960s at the age of sixteen, a girl became pregnant. Her parents took her for a medical consultation. She was ashamed and apprehensive about seeing the doctor. Her fears were realized as the doctor berated her saying she should be ashamed of herself for being pregnant. She had destroyed her parents' dreams for her.

When she told the doctor that she only had sex once, the doctor laughed at her and said no girl gets pregnant after having sex once. Even though forty-five years had passed, the woman told me, "I feel the same shame now as I felt then. I wanted to die, fall into a hole in the ground and disappear." There is no time in the heart. Shame is a painful melody playing over and over again.

Shame destroys or dumbs down the possibilities of our lives and creates "dead living people." The tragedy of life is not death, but that shame destroys so much of our life while we are still alive.

6. Self-Absorption

Self-absorption is healthy in infancy and early childhood, but in adulthood it restricts our life to personal concerns giving little or no attention to others. Deprivation of the basic instinctual needs of childhood leads to self-absorption which results in narcissism, vulnerability, defensive self-sufficiency and arrogance. Self-absorption is a characteristic of shame and impediment to relationships.

7. Focus on Limitations and Avoidance of Potential

Shame encourages us to focus on our limitations and ignore our potential producing a triumphant mediocrity. The graveyards and crematoria are filled with so many unwritten books, unfulfilled dreams, unsung songs, and untried solutions to the problems of humanity because our shame made us believe the lie that we are not good enough to make such contributions to the world.

8. Repetition Compulsion

Sucking us into ourselves, shame seduces us to live the repetition compulsions of our pain. It blinds and draws us toward the pain and hurt we know and fear. As a result, we often marry our childhood trauma and repetitively regenerate it through our children. Sadly, the hurt trail goes in circles and keeps returning to the same painful memories of shame. Shame never ceases to create the repetitive compulsion of the pain we fear.

A woman told me that when she was ten, her father became upset on Christmas day. He had been drinking and overturned the table set for Christmas dinner. She remembered the pain she felt scooping the cranberry sauce, the turkey, and stuffing off the floor. She promised herself that she would never marry an alcoholic. Forty years later, telling me this story in my office on Christmas Eve, she said with tears in her eyes, "Dr. Allen, I am married to an alcoholic. How could I do what I said I wouldn't do?"

9. Living in the Gaze of Others

Ignoring the true self, shame encourages us to live and dance in the gaze of those people who are important to us. Even after they leave us or die, we continue to live in the make-believe world of their gaze. We feel insubstantial, irrelevant, and hidden as if we have no soul or life.

A famous film director with world acclaim said that his life was like a film playing on a movie screen. Sadly, in his later years, the projector is off, the lights are out, and his life is now a blank screen because no one is watching.

10. Passivity and Aggression

Bogged down by the burden of hurts and low self-image, shame encourages us to succumb to a bland passivity or an empty aggressiveness. For example, a lady came to my office who had just received a promotion. She said that she would not leave until we talked to her boss to tell him she did not want the promotion. She said the promotion would destroy her life because people under her were difficult and would shame and disobey her. Together we talked to her boss. She refused the promotion and told him she preferred to be what she called an ordinary worker.

11. Loss of Face

Shame creates inner feelings of disgrace encouraging us to hide our faces. Overwhelmed by feelings of fear, distrust, and latent rage we construct walls that block us from ourselves and others. Sadly, when we build walls to hide the garbage, we also block out the beauty around us, the people, the flowers, and the trees.

Challenged by this psychotherapeutic insight, a reticent, young professional woman decided to break down her walls. She determined to travel and open her life to meet people of different backgrounds. To her surprise, within a few months she found the love of her life and married him, had a baby, and is extremely happy. Shame builds walls for protection, but they often become a prison!

12. Chronological Fatalism

Paralyzing us with fear, shame encourages a self-fulfilling prophecy by making us believe that nothing we do makes a difference. We suffer a sense of chronological fatalism. We magnify our problems, we constantly complain and we see the glass half empty rather than half full. As a result, many of us rush into marriage, change jobs, or escape to new geographical horizons only to find that wherever we are or go, our shame goes with us.

As Shakespeare's character Cassius said, "The fault is not in our stars, but in ourselves." Shame can only be counteracted by an intentional, deliberate, and counter-instinctive commitment to face the pain in our hearts. As one song says, "I have been to Nassau, Paris, and New York, but I have never been to ME!" The antidote to chronological fatalism is faith. Faith is the light that brightens the darkness of our shame and despair converting our fear into the freedom of love.

13. Identification with the Oppressor

Oppressed or marginalized people feel cultural shame when they are excluded or disenfranchised by the broader community. Paradoxically, shame-based persons tend to identify with the oppressor because shame seeks union with the person doing the shaming. Sadly, they tend to treat other oppressed or down trodden people even more terribly than the oppressors. This is a well-documented phenomenon in the history of revolution.

14. Learned Helplessness

Shame produces "learned helplessness". It destroys passion, purpose, and perseverance. It creates paralyzing inner psychic structures. Even though we could perform certain tasks, a self-induced form of helplessness makes failure a self-fulfilling prophecy. As a result, we do not show up for our life. In fact, where we are...we are what is missing!

15. Dance of Seduction, Exploitation and Destruction

Shame is associated with a powerful dance of seduction, exploitation, and abandonment. For example, a shame-based young man is seduced to take cocaine. When he is high, he is encouraged to use more cocaine. As a result, he is exploited. He took cocaine and then cocaine took him. Eventually, he is overwhelmed and the cocaine destroys him.

16. Splitting Off and Inferiority

Shame encourages incompetent feelings and acts. There is often clumsiness or feelings of stupidity in the presence of persons perceived to be more distinguished or competent than ourselves. Shame splits off our adequate parts and projects them onto others making us feel inadequate and inferior.

Shame-based persons are vulnerable to being controlled and dominated by persons in power. Cultures and organizations also produce a sense of powerlessness. Fertilizing the soil for dictators to rise and rule without restraint or opposition, shame encourages the splitting off of the adequate parts of their subjects which are projected onto the dictator making him or her even more powerful. Conversely, the shame-based authoritarian leader splits off his inadequate parts and projects them on his subjects thus making them feel inferior and impotent.

17. The Past-Future Prison

Shame encourages us to dwell on the pain and hurt of the past and projects negativity and hopelessness on the future causing us to ignore opportunities in the present. As a result, freedom is compromised and we settle for the prison of the status quo.

18. Suicide/Homicide

The triangle of depression, shame, and anger in intimate relationships is an explosive mixture often resulting in suicide, homicide, or both. As the shame-based person is isolated, the pain is magnified, and the perceived hope of anyone helping is minimized. Alienated and alone, the person walks into the darkness of suicide or homicide.

19. Comparisons

Encouraging comparisons and envy of others, shame leaves us sad, dejected, and discouraged. As a result, we lose our uniqueness and become what the psychoanalysts call "as if" persons. In other words, shame takes away our personhood and it is only "as if" we were persons.

20. Pathological Jealousy

Shame is jealous of the joys and successes of others. It cheers for their failure. This is known as the "crab syndrome" because crabs pull each other down when trying to escape confinement. The crab syndrome is manifested by disloyalty, jealously, anger, opposition, and sabotage.

21. Destructive Gossip

Shame is usually the root cause of gossip which produces betrayal, fragmentation, and destruction. For example, a talented young female left her well-paying job because of the gossip saying, "It's destroying me!"

The Healing of Shame

This book will deepen your understanding of shame. However, this is not a typical Christian "How To" book. Shame is difficult to treat. It is ubiquitous, evasive, deeply internalized, and associated with the wish to conceal. Unlike other emotions which are released with catharsis and weeping, shame is difficult to admit and discharge. Shame has little or no facial expression; you might even say it has no face. The only signs may be turning away or downcast eyes.

Therefore, integrity and medical ethics require me to state that, for some readers, confronting the shame core will require a skilled therapist who has faced and worked through his or her own shame. Hiding behind the masks of anger, contempt, depression, inferiority, denial, and superiority, therapy is often ineffective if the therapist's shame has not been faced and unmasked.

Reading this book is an indication that you are serious about removing your shame masks and dealing with the deeper underlying core of shame, self-loathing, and organized hurt. I encourage you to work at this with others, a friend, spouse, or small group. There is shame-busting power in being accountable to others both in honesty and emotional support. However, if you find yourself struggling, do not let shame itself keep you from going to a good therapist.

Developing a meaningful therapeutic alliance with a shame-based client takes patience, tolerance, compassion, and understanding. Most importantly, be aware that the therapist sometimes becomes the disavowed object of hate, rejection, and disgust as the client releases deep-seated shame. Receiving this transference in a loving manner with a sense of self containment, respect, and a non-judgmental attitude is no easy task.

The Treatment of Shame

The healing of the shame is complex. However, following are eight suggestions that have been helpful in my experience. They are addressed to therapists, but every reader will benefit from them as a foundation for understanding and busting the shame core.

1. Working Through

As the shame-based person works through the hurt trail with the aid of psychotherapy, psychodrama, role playing, and therapeutic letters, ripples of pain, sadness, hurt, and anger are released freeing the patient from the bondage of shame. To paraphrase Albert Einstein, a problem occurring at one level of experience, awareness or consciousness cannot be solved at the same level. Working through the shame core requires the development of a deeper awareness and consciousness of a loving therapeutic alliance.

The therapist treating the shame core must exhibit patience, understanding, and compassion. At the same time, the shame-based person with deficits of trust may seek to sabotage the alliance with a mixture of negative, unstable transference feelings towards the therapist. Challenges to the shame issues of the therapist can create a confusing medley of feelings.

By listening longer and deeper I have learned that I have often responded defensively to the compensation of my own shame issues. The following incident brought this home in a powerful way. One afternoon, a very attractive and highly qualified young lady came for an assessment interview. After hearing her list of distinguished accomplishments, I said, "You have accomplished a lot, congratulations." She became extremely angry and shouted at me asking, "Why does that matter?"

The truth is that she was shame-based and worked hard to compensate for her inadequacy. Drawing attention to the compensation for her shame, she unleashed it on me. The more successful shame-based persons are, the angrier they become in therapy especially when complimented. When a holding environment of stability, consistency, and predictability is provided, the therapeutic alliance, though fragile and labile, will slowly develop.

2. The Release of Affect

Confronting destructive anger is time consuming because of the underlying compounded resistance and defenses. Much understanding and patience is required to work through resentment, bitterness, hardness of heart and grudges. Much care and caution are necessary because when shame-based affect or feeling is released, the therapist becomes the target. Therapists working with shame have to be willing to carry negative introjects and painful affects to allow patients to break through their bondage of shame in opening to the freedom of love.

Janet Gibbs, a distinguished psychoanalyst, claims we have to be careful not to storm the barrier. Using the Trojan horse metaphor, she warns that we have to be wise and infiltrate barriers of resistance subtly and wisely. In her own characteristic way, she warns that shame-based persons can infuse different counter transferences in the therapeutic relationship, dropping us into the pit of despair and as a result make us feel deeply inadequate.

3. Surrender - The Perceptual Shift

Shame circulates around poles of anger and sadness. Facing the anger, we have to choose to open up to the sadness. Conversely, when dealing with sadness, we have to be aware of anger. We need to give up control over our Ego Addictive False Self which is based on fear. This surrender is how we make the perceptual shift to our true self in love.

If the therapist is lacking experience and has not established a therapeutic alliance bond based on mutual positive regard with the patient, the perceptual shift is blocked. The result is that the patient becomes stuck in the destructive cycles of shame and fear leaving the therapist with feelings of gross inadequacy. The patient may even sabotage the therapy.

In my experience, our ability to help patients make contact with their deep shame is the determining factor for the length and effectiveness of the therapy. Only a loving, caring environment melts shame and encourages the perceptual shift. But real love is hard and truthful, not limited, evasive, or superficial.

4. Letting Go

As patients surrender, they have to decide to let go of hurt feelings whether caused by them selves, the perpetrator or others involved in the shame scene. Letting go is to not try to change the person, but to accept what has happened. Letting go is releasing fear and opening to love. Letting go does not mean changing the past but deciding not to let it strangle us. Letting go means not blaming another, but the willingness to face our truth regardless of how painful it is.

Letting go is forgiving the past and choosing to live in the freedom of the present and to grow into the future. Letting go is to not be dogmatic about being right, but to be willing to learn and grow in self-understanding. Letting go is to not be forced into simplistic reductionist solutions. Letting go is to learn to live with the questions so that we can grow into the answers. Finally, to let go is make the perceptual shift from fear to love.

5. Forgiveness

Similar to letting go, forgiveness is the only process in life that can heal a wound from a past that cannot be changed. Forgiveness is the personal experience of leaving the prison of our hurt to work through our feelings so that when the painful memory comes to consciousness, it loses its sting and does not affect us. Forgiveness helps us to realize that we can have a tomorrow different from our yesterday. We come to realize in forgiveness that the enemy is not the other, but the doubt we harbor about ourselves buried deep in our soul.

We can choose to separate ourselves from the hurt experience and know the freedom of our true being. This freedom liberates us to see others, even the perpetrators of our pain, for what they are. They are accountable for their deeds, but they do not define our self- worth or wellbeing. We alone are accountable for our wellbeing. Finally, forgiveness lifts the burden of life's changing circumstances. It lets us let go of the past, enjoy the present and grow into the uniqueness of our own true being.

6. Gratitude

When we make the perceptual shift from fear to love, forgiveness follows. Experiencing the healing of love, our defenses drop, pain is released and automatically we develop an attitude of gratefulness. Receiving a gift is one thing, but when we say thank you, we give of ourselves. Gratitude means that the shame core has been impacted and, like the butterfly leaving the cocoon, we experience a discovery of self.

Speaking of the journey to self, T. S. Elliot wrote, "We shall not cease from exploration and the end of all our exploring will be to arrive where we started... and know the place for the first time." At the end of Henri Nouwen's life, his last words were, "Tell them I am grateful." Gratitude is the crowning splendor of life lived as "the beloved."

7. Laughing at Self

Laughing at self is a powerful antidote to shame. It is self-transcendent and allows a person a sense of mastery. It is a form of surrender in which a person realizes that his essential being (true self) cannot be characterized by shame. Surrender is opening up to the consciousness in which the mystery of our life unfurls.

An elderly man who suffered much of his life from depression with multiple hospitalizations said, "My life is hopeless." After listening attentively, I said, "Hopeless?" He said, "Yes, I feel hopeless." I said, "You are feeling hopeless?" "Yes", he said. I confronted him and asked, "Isn't feeling hopeless different than being hopeless?" As the insight dawned on him, his sad face changed into a smile and then he laughed. If he feels hopeless and is not hopeless, his being is intact and there is hope.

8. Contemplative Prayer

Contemplative prayer is a powerful antidote to shame. The regular practice of Lectio Divina includes Scripture reading (Lectio), reflection (Reflectio), oral prayer (Oratorio), silent prayer (Contemplation), and taking the experience into our daily life (Operatio). This spiritual exercise calms and neutralizes the deep pain in our psyche. In silent prayer, the psyche releases the deep shame feelings of anger, hurt, fear, and despair. Contemplative prayer has blessed many persons including me.

The lady betrayed and shamed by her husband in the opening paragraph of this chapter found great release in prayer from her deep shame and hurt. Experiencing the freedom and peace of surrender, she was able to call her husband and forgive him. Shocked, her husband burst into tears and apologized profusely for having hurt her so deeply and wanted to do anything to make it up to her. He was puzzled how his wife could be so peaceful and forgiving in the wake of such tragedy. Releasing the hurt, she was given the deep freedom of love and experienced the peace that transcends deep shame and hurt.

> Thou wilt keep in perfect peace
> Whose mind is stayed on thee! (Is. 26:3)

Tennyson said, "More things are wrought by prayer than this world dreams of." Jesus tells his disciples in Luke 18:1 that "People ought always to pray and not be overwhelmed by shame" (author's paraphrase).

John's Fight to Surrender

John was a severe alcoholic who became violent when he drank. It sometimes took up to ten policemen to hold him down. He was a public nuisance and disturbance. The police often locked him up. Upon release, he would do more of the same. One day, while drunk, he attacked his mother and was committed to the State Hospital. In the darkness of a corner in his room, he saw the pain and suffering of the people around him. John felt ashamed of his behavior. He sobered up and came to his senses. John said that as he thought about his life, all he could see was shame, darkness, and destruction. Overwhelmed and afraid, John prayed and promised that if he ever got out, he would stop drinking alcohol and would change his life.

Taking his sobriety seriously, John attended individual, group therapy, and AA regularly. For awhile it looked like he had turned his life around. Unfortunately, after being sober for six months, he broke out again around Christmas. But again, he fought against the deep shame with its negative thoughts and voices and persisted in group therapy and AA. Sober once again, John was restless. Life was dull and empty. Although sober, John was miserable. Worst of all, the shame voices were vicious, "Nobody trusts you." "You know you are a failure." "You can't make it."

John berated and beat himself down with the shame whip and on the shame cross for the painful memories of hurting so many people. He was driven back to alcohol (his shame behavior). The situation seemed hopeless, but John began attending regular contemplative prayer sessions each Sunday. John told us that he was fed up because he had made a mess of his life.

Continuing in contemplative prayer and AA, John became sober. Miserable and tormented by his shame, John said, "I finally get it, I have to surrender." Sitting in the silence and healing of contemplative prayer, John let go of his past and his fear of the future and surrendered to God's love. This is no quick fix or cake walk. Surrender, John said, is a decision he has to make hour by hour and day by day. Sober for over five years, John said, "I have seen hell and I do not want to go back."

Surrendering his shame and fear along with attending his AA group, John is an ardent participant in contemplative prayer. He has blessed our group and whenever I am late or missing, John chastises me saying that I should know better. Learning from John, he has taught me that my life too is unmanageable and I need a power greater than myself. "My soul waits in silence for you, O God, and you alone" (Ps. 62:1). John has come home to his beloved.

St. Augustine wrote in his Confessions, Book 10:22:

> How late I am to love you, O beauty so ancient and so fresh, how late I came to love you! You were within me, while I had gone outside to seek you. Unlovely myself, I rushed towards all those lovely things you had made. And always you were with me, and I was not with you... You called, you cried, you shattered my deafness. You sparkled, you blazed, you drove away my blindness. You shed your fragrance, and I drew in my breath, and I pant for you. I tasted and I now hunger and thirst. You touched me, and I now burn with longing for your peace.

REFERENCES

1 Thompson, Curt. *The Soul of Shame.*(Lisle, Illinois: InterVarsity Press, 2015)
2 Morrison, Andrew P. *Culture of Shame*, (Chicago: Ballantine Books, IX, 1996)
3 Ellison, Ralph. *Invisible Man.* (London: Penguin Classics. 2001)
4 Sartre, Jean-Paul
5 Tomkins, S.S, *Affect Imagery Consciousness: Vol II: The Negative Affects* (New York: Springer Publishing Company. 1963), 118
6 Keating, Thomas. *Open Mind, Open Heart: The Contemplative Dimension of the Gospel* (New York: Continuum International Publishing Group, 2006)
7 Buechner, Frederick. *Whistling in the Dark: A Doubter's Dictionary* (Harper/San Francisco, 1993), 83.

CHAPTER 3
The Contemplative Discovery Pathway Theory

"We shall not cease from exploration and the end of our exploring will be to arrive where we started and know the place for the first time."
- T.S. Eliot

IN MY JOURNEY IN PSYCHIATRY DURING the past 50 years, I have explored multiple psychotherapies. These include psychoanalysis, cognitive-behavioral therapy, positive psychology, psychopathology, contemplative theology, addiction rehabilitation, and theories of social justice. But in the 1980's, when I led the fight against the world's first national crack cocaine epidemic in the Bahamas (Jekel, et at. 1986), I was confronted with the developmental trauma of shame, which was resistant to much of my psychoanalytic training. After using multiple approaches, the Contemplative Discovery Pathway Theory (CDPT) emerged as an integration of existing models, including aspects of my Judeo-Christian spirituality and social justice convictions.

A developmental model, CDPT posits the self follows a step-wise path from the Natural Self at birth to the Shame Self, with a defensive Shame False Self in childhood, to a healthier Authentic Gracious Self (True Self) in adulthood (Allen, et al. 2014 leading to the formation of their authentic (true) self, allowing them to grow beyond their limitations to discover their potential. CDPT postulates that the self moves from the Natural Self at birth to the Shame Self and its antithesis, the Shame False Self in early development to the healthier Authentic Gracious Self (True Self) in adulthood. (Allen, et al., 2014) With the practice of the spiritual disciplines, the theory also implies that a person may develop a Contemplative Transcendent Self. Thus each person's life is a challenging journey from being a victim of their Shame and False Self to discovering the glorious freedom of the Authentic True Self. This journey involves moving from fear and anger to love, gratitude and healing community. In the following sections, we describe each of these stages in greater detail.

The Natural Self at Birth

According to the Judeo-Christian tradition, human beings are made in the image of God and stamped with the authority of meaning, dignity, identity and value. We come from love, are born to love and upon death, return to love. Our being, the Imago Dei, is the Immortal Treasure. "In Him we move, live and have our being" (Acts 17:28). Yet "We have this treasure in earthen vessels (our body) that the power is of God and not of us" (2 Corinthians 4:7). At birth, this divine immortal treasure is noticeable but shrouded in mystery. "Before you were born, I knew you" (Jeremiah 1:5). According to Wordsworth,

> "Our birth is but a sleep and a forgetting:
> The Soul that rises with us, our life's Star,
> Hath had elsewhere its setting,
> And cometh from afar:
> Not in entire forgetfulness,
> And not in utter nakedness,
> But trailing clouds of glory do we come
> From God, who is our home:
> Heaven lies about us in our infancy!" (1807)

The child at birth has three basic instinctual needs: survival /security (safety), affection /esteem (connection), and power/control (empowerment) (Keating, 2006) (Figure 1). These basic instinctual needs represent powerful sources of energy that interact as the infant struggles to establish basic trust (Erikson, 1993). According to Margaret Mahler, a child exposed to a meaningful environment of stability, consistency and predictability undergoes a healthy separation-individuation process from the primary caregiver (often the mother) to form their own identity as they learn to trust in themselves (Mahler & Bergman, 1974). The internalization of the primary caregiver (the nurturing object) provides for the development of self-object transferences within the child. In Heinz Kohut's self-psychology theory (Kohut, 1984), the self-object relationships maintain the cohesion, vitality, strength and harmony of the self. In the mirror transference, the child basks in the delightful gaze of its mother, leading to affirmation, self-esteem and self-confidence.

The twin-ship transference, in which the infant becomes aware that the caretaker experiences similar painful and challenging feelings, creates an empathic bond, the basis of human community. The idealized or transcendent transference allows the child to develop respect for that which is bigger and more powerful than themselves. This deep sense of respect gives us the ability to show reverence and honor for authority. This may be considered as the origin of our desire to worship God or a higher power. These relationships are bolstered by the continuing love story that moves from our parents through all stages of our life. Sadly, life is wounded and imperfect. Thus the infant is exposed to the hurt trail which is like a red, hot, pulsating wire, throughout their development. The impacted hurt leads to the formation of the Shame Self (Allen, 2010).

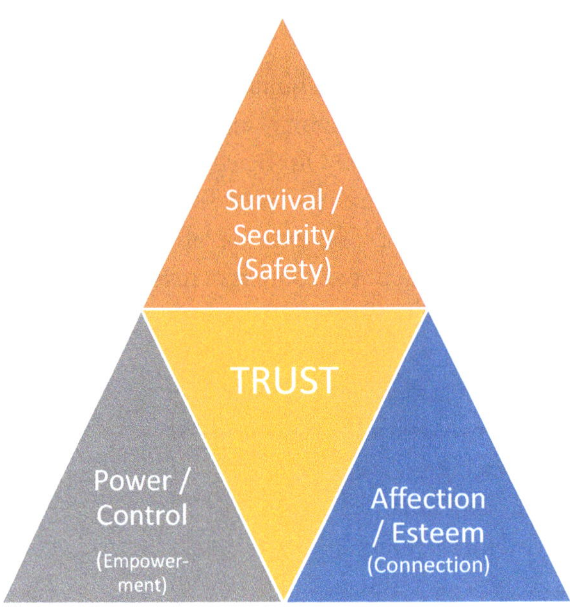

Figure 1 - The Natural Self at Birth

The Shame Self

As an individual develops, they face many challenges involving both success and failure. Sadly, the depreciation of the instinctual needs of safety, connection and empowerment lead to the experience of shame involving abandonment, rejection and humiliation (Figure 2). Shame, as described in Chapter 2, is usually hidden, and manifests itself through anger, violence, addiction, destructive conflict, revenge, abuse etc. Shame is a deep, painful, internal feeling that usually occurs when a cherished dream or expectation shatters. Our basic instinctual needs in the infant or natural self, make up the dreams of our life. When a dream shatters, a lie is born. As our hurt trail develops throughout life, our shattered dreams and impacted shame have a powerful negative effect upon us. When the dream of safety shatters leading to abandonment, we become open to the lie "I am hopeless" or "I am not enough". When the dream of connection shatters leading to rejection, we experience the lies "I am unlovable" and "Nobody wants me". When the dream of empowerment shatters leading to humiliation, we are open to the lies "I am a failure" and "Nothing will ever work out for me". Sadly, when these lies are allowed to linger in our psyche or heart beyond a critical point, they become our truth. Regardless of what a person accomplishes, they are haunted by the lies of "I am hopeless", "I am unlovable" and "I am a failure". Sadly, like Adam and Eve, when human beings believe the lie, they are more vulnerable to hide from love. The result is a deep shame which makes us reject the love that we crave, leading us to become destructive to ourselves and others.

Human beings with continuous, relational trauma and shame experience deep hurt and woundedness such as abuse, violence, revenge, intense loneliness and intimacy dysfunction. Thus, when persistent trauma and pain continue in our lives, all the major instinctual needs are deprived, producing a shame schemata (Table 1).

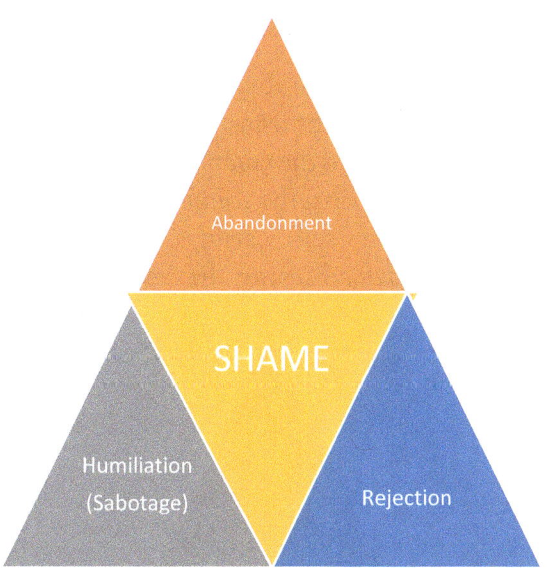

Figure 2 - The Shame Self

	Shame Schemata		
Manifestation	**Abandonment**	**Rejection**	**Humiliation**
Anger	Not aware	Afraid of anger	Vindictive cold anger
Boundaries	Few or impenetrable (may switch)	Fragmented	Rigid
Consumer Needs	Materialistic reductionism	Materialistic comparison	Powerful consumerism
Control	May manipulate by controlling or allowing self to be controlled	Controllable	Controlling
Decision-making	Indecisive	Unstable	Decisive
Dependency	Either co- or contra-dependent	Co-dependency	Contra-dependency
Esteem	Low self-esteem, feeling of inadequacy	Variable self-esteem, make comparison to others	Low/High self-esteem, competitive
Fear	Paralyzed by fear	Copes with fear by pleas-ing others	Defends against fear with bravado
Frustration	Manipulative	Passive aggressive	Aggression
Isolation	Isolated	Connects to prevent isolation	Connects for selfish interests
Motivations	Confused between feelings and thoughts	Controlled by feelings	Controlled by thoughts
Self-absorption	Extreme	Moderate	Extreme

Table 1 - Shame schemata and manifestations

The Shame False Self

The emotional experiences, associated with the Shame Self, are so painful to the heart or psyche, that the mind, through a series of neuromechanisms, develops a defensive Shame False Self . The deprivation of the instinctual needs leads to the compensation and hence the development of the Shame False Self (Figure 3) to defend against the painful feelings of abandonment, rejection and humiliation. The False Self is an illusory self, serving a very important function. Starting in a child from ages 3-4 years, it seeks to defend against the devastating blows of shame.

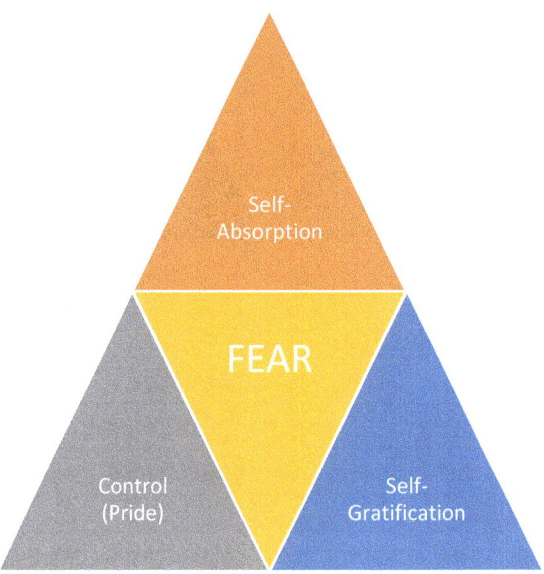

Figure 3 - The Shame False Self

According to Masterson (1988), "The False Self plays its deceptive role, extensively protecting us – but doing so in a way that it's programmed to keep us fearful of being abandoned, or losing support, not being able to cope on our own, not being able to be alone" (p.. 67).1 The False Self is a perverse rescuer, promising relief but often catapulting us into more pain. Controlled by deep fear and anger because of the possibility of being thrown back into the Shame Self, The False Self develops as a multi-layered defense involving:

(a) Self-absorption. In seeking to avoid the pain of shame, the person becomes conceited, arrogant and unable to empathize or connect with others. Enhancing narcissistic entitlement, they have difficulty developing reciprocal relationships, destroying the possibility of teamwork or working together. The focus is on 'what's in it for me?' This ingrained narcissism leads to an inflated view of self that seeks to use rather than work or relate to others. Much of the energy is spent in comparing and competing with others to show superiority. As a result, they are adept at controlling others and seeking to use them to do their own bidding. In the end, they become extremely isolated, lonely and may even self-destruct. This self-absorption leads to an identity formation based on 'what I have', 'what I do', or 'what I possess'. This makes life very precarious, for when we cannot do, feel or think, we are not. This modern form of idolatry is very predominant. As a result, we worship whatever we consider to be ultimate. According to Diarmuid O'Murchu, M.S.C.:

"Anything to which we are deeply committed can become a 'god'. Money, power, possessions, pleasure, scientific certitude and religious dogma are among the leading gods of our age. Insofar as none of these can bring us ultimate happiness or fulfillment, they are false idols. We worship them not out of love, but out of an unconscious need for power" (O'Murchu, 2004).

(b) Self-Gratification, The tendency of the False Self is to bury itself in pleasure and pleasing others to distract from the underlying shame and pain. This leads to a powerful sense of attachment or codependency, seeking to please others, and addictions involving drugs, sex, gambling and various emotional reactions. It also creates a powerful consumerism where we have a strong attachment to things to give us a sense of empowerment or ascendance over others. This determination for self-gratification propels us to seek identification with special groups by corroborating our prejudices and biases and our false belief that we are better than others. Sadly, this dynamic can only go so far and we find ourselves feeling empty, hurt and experiencing more shame.

(c) Obsessive Control. This deep form of hubris gives us the illusion of power and creates a desire to reconstruct reality. As a result of this, we become involved in scapegoating. Control is usually manifested by various types of scapegoating. The scapegoat tradition originates from the ancient Israelis, who at the end of the year, would choose a goat on which the priest would put the sins of the people and release the goat into the wilderness. The idea was that the goat carries the sins of the people, releasing them from their shame and pain. This happens more subtly but is very common in our modern society. For example, a mother disciplined a young girl. But the young girl realized she was too small to fight back her mother. So she grabs her doll and beats her profusely, saying 'bad doll, bad doll'. In this example, the young girl is hurt by her mother but she deals with her hurt by projecting it on to the doll as her scapegoat.

This is demonstrated in the diagram where persons A and B both have an adequate self and an inadequate self. In sadistic scapegoating, A splits off their inadequate self and projects it on to B and then sees B as totally inadequate or inferior, while at the same time, B is carrying their inadequacy or pain. This defense of sadistic scapegoating is used widely in society and is manifested by racial discrimination, oppression, abuse, human trafficking and the discrimination against certain persons. On the other hand, masochistic scapegoating occurs when A projects their adequate part on to B, leaving themselves feeling inadequate, unworthy and lacking in confidence. This is often common where people self-sabotage themselves as the defense against shame, but move themselves further into self-destruction and annihilation. These two forms of scapegoating are very prevalent in social fragmentation, where the oppressed becomes the oppressor and people not only take out their anger on others but also themselves. The False Self is a major part of these dynamics because it blocks us from our true essence, potential and human community. The False Self is the destroyer of human freedom and stops us from becoming truly who we are.

The Authentic Gracious Self

When a person in the group process becomes aware of the negativity of shame and the destructive aspects of their own anger, such awareness gives them a yearning for a better life. It is amazing that as the group process matures, people who once seemed destructive and deeply hurt, rise up to become aware of wanting to release their anger and pain. This awareness sometimes happens suddenly, but often, it takes time. For example, in one case, a young lady was in the group for about six months. Although one could see the tears streaming down her face and her body tense with her pain and shame, there was nothing from her mouth. Finally, the time came when she was able to burst forth. At this point, when one becomes aware of the inner pain, one has to be intentional about confronting it. As André Chappelle would always say, 'you cannot conquer what you do not confront'. This confrontation is never easy and sometimes involves internal crying and sadness or it may burst out in a powerful catharsis. At that point, the person has to be willing to surrender the shame, pain and wounds of a lifetime. In the Family program, we describe this by saying that metaphorically, the psyche or heart is like a sponge. Originally, in our early life, it is filled with love. But as we become older, our experiences of hurt and shame fill the sponge and blocks the flow of love. In the Family group, as we squeeze the sponge of the hurt and pain, we release the hurt and allow the love to flow. This is a beautiful process to observe because as the pain and shame leaves the body, a calming, peaceful process occurs. This is done by people being encouraged to share their stories.

Sharing our story is not a simple process. It involves first of all a cognitive process where we tell our story, giving others the impression that even though the story is about us, we are not there. As the process deepens, we share our story effectively, and you could feel it resonating with people in the room, because that which is most personal is also universal. Finally, the deepest level of sharing our story is when we are able to give our life as our story. This produces a deep silence, empathy and attention in the group as the wounds of a lifetime are released and one could feel the love flowing in the group as persons are either meditating, praying or crying in empathy with the person. Surrender is always followed by a deep peace, what I like to call a 'still point', where chronological time is intercepted by Kairos, or the fullness of time. The still point is the present and the Presence is always in the present. From our experience, when the still point occurs, healing always results. This is not a one-shot deal, because in this veil of tears, we may experience our Authentic Selves, but before long, the pervasiveness of our hurt trail and vulnerability throws us back into our False Self. Fortunately, we don't stay there because we now have a vision of our Authentic Self, based in love, community, forgiveness and gratitude. So one has to keep on committing to the intention to move to the vision of the True Self and only as we practice and commit ourselves to that, we experience the Authentic Gracious Self (Figure 4).

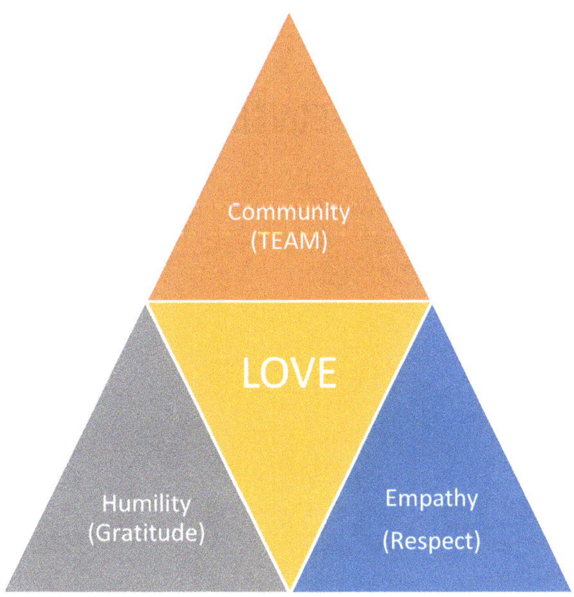

Figure 4 - The Authentic Gracious Self

The Contemplative Transcendent Self

Many persons, who have experience the Authentic Gracious Self in therapy or through self-exploration, have been struck by the awe and beauty of the experience of transcendence and the sense of oneness with the universe. It may happen within a religious setting, in nature, or as a result of acts of kindness and love. When persons have this experience, they seek out a power greater than themselves. Within the theory, we see it more as a gift resulting from deep commitment and faithfulness. The Contemplative Transcendent Self does not develop by psychotherapy alone, but requires a spiritual discipline including such practices as prayer, silence, solitude, sacred reading and the doing of good works. The life of love, manifested in the Contemplative Transcendent Self, involves dying to the kingdom of the ego False Self and the Shame Self. Love connects us to all life, making us accountable. Nelson Mandela portrays this in his autobiography, The Long Walk to Freedom when he wrote that his freedom was inseparably connected to the freedom of the South African people. According to Mandela, "freedom is indivisible" (Mandela, 1994). Love is who we are and not something we do. It is a sense of deep joy from within that characterizes the Contemplative Transcendent Self and leads one to hope. The Apostle Paul hints at the Contemplative Transcendent Self when he says, "I have been crucified with Christ. I (False Self Ego) no longer live, but Christ lives in me" (Galatians

2:20) .The mystery of this experience is that one experiences God as the transcendent source of their subjectivity and the small 'i' of our identity is swallowed up in the infinite love of the great 'I AM'. This results in a life characterized by love, manifested by deep solitude, compassion and communion with God, self, neighbor and the cosmos. This deep aspect of the human experience represents a creative ecstasy that absorbs chaos, exudes calm and instills hope.

CONTEMPLATIVE DISCOVERY PATHWAY THEORY

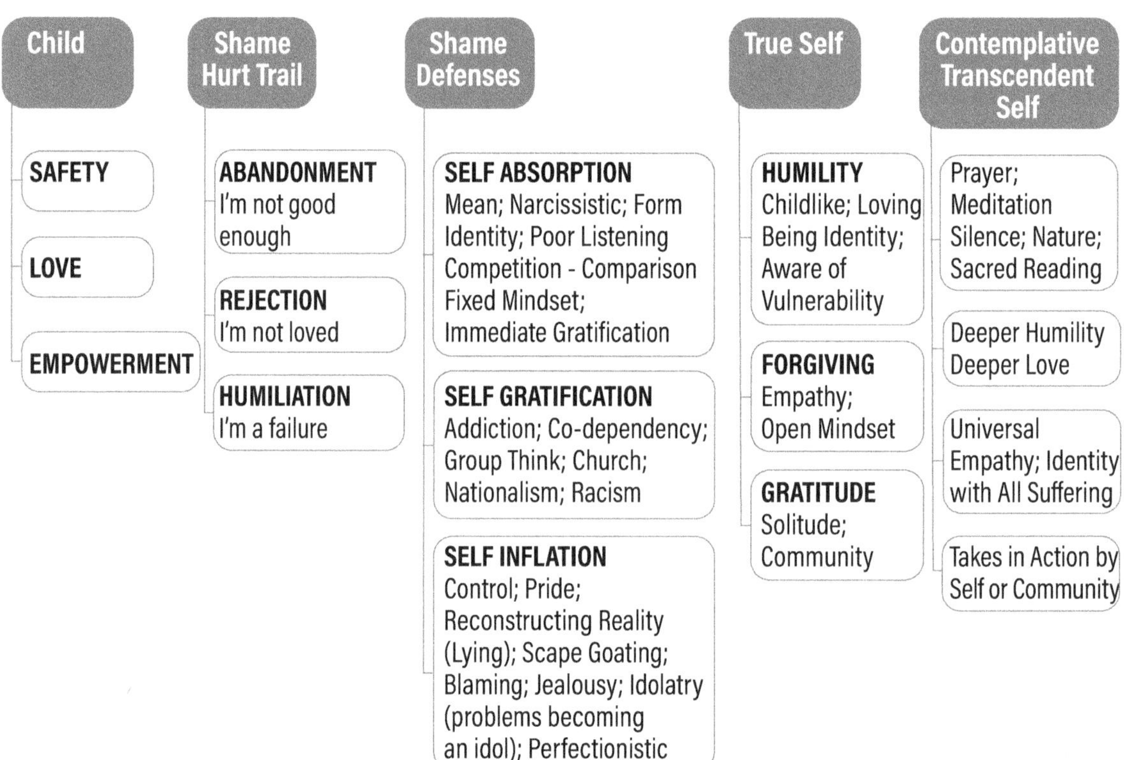

Principles of Treatment involved in CDPT

CDPT embraces all aspects of the internal and external world of the individual and motivates clients beyond recovery to experience Discovery. Discovery is the process in which an individual makes the challenging journey from being a victim of their shame, false self, based in fear and anger, to experience the freedom of their Authentic True Self based in love, gratitude and healing community.

CDPT involves the following:

a. Whole-person Process – this treatment is a whole-person process and not an event. It represents an ongoing process designed to address multi-dimensional aspects of a person's life and their shame core or hurt trail. By whatever name we give it, the heart, psyche or inner life, is like a sponge. We certainly absorb the many kind acts of love throughout our life. But as we experience impacted hurt and the development of shame, our internal sponge absorbs the hurt and shame which eventually blocks the entrance of love and self-compassion. I find it helpful to use the metaphor of the sponge because as we share our stories and release our pain and shame, we are emptying our sponge and making space for deeper awareness and the experience of love. Our experience is that we can be surrounded by readily available sources of love, but if our heart or psyche (sponge) is full of hurt and shame, we will not be able to appreciate the love that is available to us. This point is illustrated by the story of a young man who visited India in search of enlightenment. After listening to the man's expression of his desire for fulfillment, the healer he approached said "Sir, your heart is so full of you that there's no space for the enlightenment of love". Another metaphor is to imagine we did not empty our kitchen waste paper basket for 10 years. It would be impossible to live in the house. Yet, sadly, some of us have lived 50 or 60 years and have never made the journey to our heart to empty the waste basket of shame. As a result, we are unable to appreciate the availability of love and creative opportunities right before us. This has been one of the saddest experiences of our work. People have described that they are so deeply hurt that they feel they are a dead, living person. A young man said that while coming to therapy, he noticed a dead dog being pulled along the road by the Humane Society vehicle. He reflected, 'I am like that dead dog. I don't feel a part of my life or culture. I'm just being pulled along, not knowing where I'm going'. Releasing our shame through sharing our story awakens us to move beyond our limitations to open to our potential.

b. The Development of Awareness - insights from treatment are not static events. They require repetition, re-visitation and constant practice. Psychotherapy, like physiotherapy, requires continuous massage until the knot or cramp disappears. The healing of the mind is similar, requiring repeated massage, learning and working through our conflicts of shame and pain in order for growth to occur. The challenge is finding someone to share our deep stories involving our shame. Our experience is that if a therapist has not worked through their own shame, they would find it very difficult to help another person work through theirs.

By listening deeper and longer, I have learned that I tend to respond defensively to compensate for my own shame issues. For example, a very attractive and highly qualified young lady came for an assessment interview. After hearing her list of achievements, I said, "you have accomplished a lot. Congratulations". Becoming extremely angry, she shouted at me, 'Why does that matter?'

The truth is, she was shame-based and had worked very hard to compensate for her inadequacy. When I drew her attention to the compensation for her shame, she unleased her anger on me. The more successful shame-based persons are, the angrier they become when complimented. When the therapist is able to create an environment of stability, consistency and predictability, the therapeutic alliance, though fragile and labile, will slowly develop.

One of the most difficult things to confront is destructive anger because of the underlying compounded resistance and defenses. Much understanding and patience is required to work through the resentment, bitterness and hardness of heart. Care and caution is necessary because when shame-based affect or feeling is released, the therapist becomes the target. The therapist working with shame has to be willing to carry negative interjects and painful affects to allow persons to see through their bondage of shame and open to the freedom of love.

Psychoanalyst Janet Gibbs who I taught with for many summers at the Chautauqua Institution in New York warned of storming a patient's defensive barrier. Like the story of the Trojan horse, it is best to be invited to enter through open doors or to very subtly and wisely infiltrate the barrier of resistance. Ms. Gibbs warns that shame-based clients are able to infuse the therapeutic relationship with different counter-transferences, dropping us into the pit of despair and making us feel deeply inadequate.

c. Experiencing vulnerability – vulnerability is a universal phenomenon of all human beings. Human beings have a natural fear of vulnerability. When fear is combined with vulnerability, it produces shame involving abandonment, rejection and humiliation. But vulnerability plus love leads to empathy. There is no healing unless vulnerability is experienced in the presence of love. Vulnerability is not a weakness but rather a willingness to accept uncertainty, risk and emotional exposure. When this is done in a contemplative environment of acceptance, love and nonjudgmental listening, vulnerability gives rise to empathy, giving us the courage and commitment to face the most painful reality. Our level of defensiveness blocks vulnerability and reflects the client's fear of disconnection and shame. Once vulnerability through love gives rise to empathy, it results in compassion, combatting shame and enables us and others to feel valued and respected. Empathy can only result if one is willing or has the courage to be vulnerable. Once empathy develops, we are able to project ourselves into the feelings of others, yet be ourselves and treat them like we would wish to be treated if we were them.

d. Forgiveness and Letting Go – As patients surrender, they have to decide to let go the hurt and shame feelings, whether they were caused by themselves or others. Letting go does not mean trying to change the person who has shamed us but accepting what has happened. It is releasing fear and opening to love, not changing the past but deciding to not let it strangle us. Letting go is a willingness to face our truth, regardless of its pain. Forgiveness and letting go is a decision to live in the freedom of the present and grow into the future. It's not about who is right or wrong but willingness to learn and grow in self-understanding. So often, however, in letting go, we have to learn to live with the questions in order to grow into the answers. Forgiveness is making the perceptual shift from the negative attitude of fear to the positive virtue of love. Forgiveness is the only process that can heal a wound from the past that cannot be changed. It is a deeply personal experience of leaving the prison of our hurt to work through our feelings so that when the painful memory comes to consciousness, it loses its sting and does not affect us. Forgiveness means we can have a better tomorrow different from our yesterday. In forgiveness, we have to realize the enemy is not the other person but the doubt we harbor about ourselves buried deep within our souls. As human beings, we tend to forgive when we are ready to be healed.

e. Addressing the cognitive components of shame – it is a fact that what we think or focus on, we become. In fact, we don't see things as they are but as we are. So when our hearts are filled with cynical, gloomy, shameful thoughts, we are filled with negative feelings. For example, the shame of failure produces negative thoughts that create a vicious cycle of self-fulfilling prophecies, increasing the likelihood of failure, poor self-image and alienation. Our clients are instructed that shame-based thoughts and labels encourage self-sabotage because the person (because of the Shame False Self) would tend to over-personalize events and experiences. This often leads to the negative consequences of being judgmental, blaming others and refusing to take responsibility for our lives. This makes us passive victims of our fate, destroying the mentality that makes constructive change possible.

   Connected to this theme is the destructive power of emotional reason. For example, a gentleman who had been in the state hospital for many years said 'I am hopeless and my life is a disaster'. I replied 'You said you are hopeless?' He said 'Yes, there's no help available for me'. I said to him, "The sun, the light-giving power of the Universe, rose this morning and will set this evening. Neither you nor I had anything to do with it. Thus, there must be a power greater than us. You may feel hopeless but because you are not the ultimate power, you cannot say you are hopeless You can only say 'I feel hopeless.' And because you feel hopeless doesn't mean you are hopeless." To my surprise, a beautiful smile broke out on his face.

f. Sharing our Story – telling our story is not a simple process. Initially, when we tell our story, it is very cognitive and many times reflects what we have been told about ourselves. Because shame forms in the early part of our development, it is not released just because we tell our story. Guilt is 'I made a mistake' and shame is 'I am a mistake'. In telling our story, we may touch on some aspects of guilt but we will find it very difficult to release our deep shame core. But as we continue to work in therapy and our insight and ability to open our inner life deepens, we begin to share the emotional aspects of our story. At this point, shame burps out as we release some of the inner secrets of our painful experience. This process takes time and when we encounter resistances like the look on a therapist's face or the transference from the therapeutic environment, we shift back into the cognitive aspect of our story. But as we continue to work on the deeper aspects and uncover previously unknown parts of our story, we tend to arrive at a place where we give our authentic story, regardless of the cost. When this happens, that which is most personal is universal, creating a powerful ripple of healing that produces an 'ah-ha' reaction. At this point, the therapy moves to a very deep level, reflected in the changes in a person's life and relationships. The authentic sharing of our story takes time, patience and often requires a contemplative environment of love, silence (mindfulness) and non-judgmental listening..

g. Humility – research in the field of health psychology shows that gratitude, forgiveness, humility and love are the key ingredients to healthy interpersonal relationships and can reduce an individual's risk of internalizing psychiatric disorders such as depression and externalizing disorders such as substance abuse (Kendler, et al., 2003) (Tsang, McCullough, & Fincham, 2006) (Westberg, 2010). Related to forgiveness are the character strengths of humility (Powers, Nam, WC, & Hill, 2007), which is the placing of one's needs second to those of another, and love, which is the ability to build strong attachments to others in which both parties feel understood and valued (Allport, 1997) (Meyers, 1999). The road to humility is paved with stones of humiliation and shame. But when we choose to be healed, it is humility that allows us to release our shame and open up to love, forgiveness and gratitude.

h. Humor – The ability to laugh at ourselves is a powerful antidote to shame. Humor is a self-transcendent experience providing a sense of mastery. As we laugh, it's a form of surrender, freeing us from the entrapment of our essential being by shame and other negative influences. Professor Sophie Scott, Deputy Director of the University College London Institute of Neuroscience, shared that laughter is a non-verbal expression of emotion, liberating us from repressed fear, anger and other feelings. Laughter is a signal of affection and affiliation improving socialization. For example, mutual laughter can diffuse an uncomfortable situation (Contreras, 2017). In a very deep sense, humor reflects love, transcending our painful feelings of hurt and shame.

i. Gratitude – Thomas Merton reminds us that to be grateful is to recognize the Love of God in everything He has given us...Gratitude therefore takes nothing for granted." When we make the perceptual shift from fear to love, forgiveness follows. When we experience the healing of love, our defenses drop, pain is released and we develop an attitude of gratefulness. Receiving a gift is one thing, but when we say thank you, we give of ourselves. Gratitude means that the shame core has been impacted and, like the butterfly leaving the cocoon, we experience a discovery of the true self.

Increasingly, descriptive research is establishing gratitude as being strongly associated with both physical as well as psychological well-being (Emmons, 2004) (Emmons & McCullough, 2003) (Gordon, Impett, Kogan, Oveis, & Keltner, 2012). Although gratitude has been said to be "one of the few things that can measurably change people's lives" (Emmons 2007), the effect of promoting gratitude as part of psychosocial interventions has received comparatively little attention.

At the end of his life, Henri Nouwen's last words were, "Tell them I am grateful". Gratitude is the crowning splendor of life lived as the beloved of God. When a person starts to show evidence of gratitude in the therapy sessions, it is a clear sign that the healing of shame or pain is occurring. I was taught this reality by a very challenged, severe chronic crack cocaine addict who said, 'Dr. Allen, in the crack house, when a person says they are grateful for one day sober, they are on their way to healing their addiction'. When I first heard this, I marveled as this has been my experience in working through the issues of addiction and the deep elements of shame.

j. Aspects of Neuroscience – Quoting Dr. Daniel Siegel's work, Dr. Curt Thompson explains that 'an important part of how people change – not just their experiences but also their brain – is through the process of telling their stories to an empathic listener. When a person tells her story and is truly heard and understood, both they and the listener undergo actual changes in their brain circuitry. They feel a greater sense of emotional and relational connection, decreased anxiety and greater awareness of and compassion for others' suffering'.[3] Neuroscience offers novel ways to think about the benefits of CDPT. Our mind should be understood in terms of what or how we think. According to interpersonal neurobiology (IPNB), the mind regulates the flow of energy and information.

    a) Energy is the literal, electro-chemical communication between neurons.
    b) Information is the meaningful perceptions, whether conscious or unconscious, that are running through our lives every moment and are correlated to neuro-biological energy.

Shame disrupts the process of regulating the flow of energy and information by disconnecting the various functions of the mind from one another, leaving each domain of the mind cut off from one another as we feel ourselves disconnected from other people. Thus, the goal of the mind is to cause us to thrive and live effectively. Shame has the ability to undermine, in fact, disrupt this. Shame undermines God's intended creation of goodness and beauty in the world. The mind is a fluid, emerging process which is embodied and relational whose task is to regulate the flow of energy and information.,[4]

In his book 'Brainstorm', Siegel claims that we interact with the world in two views of reality: the physical world of objects and mindsight. Sadly, modern life has become more dependent on physical sight than recognizing the importance of our mind connection. This is challenging because without the mind connection, people can treat others without respect or compassion.

CDPT is based on mindsight where we help individuals to develop their internal world to relate more effectively to themselves and others. According to Siegel, focusing our mind on multiple interactions such as telling our stories, listening, singing, meditation, and social action, helps us build new circuits in our brain enabling us to adapt creatively to new experiences while increasing our health and developing harmonious relationships. Mindsight includes three fundamental skills: insight, empathy and integration. Insight is our ability to appreciate our inner mental life, helping us to understand the present, past and future. When we reflect on things going on inside of us, we develop mindsight mapping of the brain, activating our pre-frontal circuits where the inner and interpersonal experiences are coordinated and balanced. Empathy is the ability to sense the inner life of another person, enabling us to see them from our perspective and imagine what it is like to walk in their shoes. The gateway to compassion and kindness, empathy is the key to social intelligence, allowing us to understand the intention and needs of others. In this light, relationships can be defined as the sharing of energy and information between persons. Insight and empathy cultivate integration empowering us to coordinate our relationships with each other. Sadly, when integration is blocked, chaos results in our internal and external relationships, developing a powerful rigidity which destroys individual and community development. These neuroscientific insights validate the effect of The Family where people share their stories of pain and shame in a contemplative environment, creating mindsight (insight, empathy and integration) in the participants leading to coordination, balance and self-regulation (Siegal, 2013).

k. Contemplative Prayer – spirituality reflects a relationship with a higher power grounded in compassionate love. True spirituality includes expressions of awe, reverence, peace, joy, meaning, value, purpose, hope, humility and gratitude. Therapy associated with spiritual development incorporates contemplative practices (e.g. personal accountability, silence, prayer, mindfulness, sacred reading, community and the doing of good deeds). This process leads to the formation of the Contemplative Transcendent Self and can help to move a client from recovery to a discovery mindset.

The Role of the Therapist

Shame is difficult to treat because it is ubiquitous, evasive, deeply internalized and hidden. Unlike other emotions released by catharsis, shame is difficult to admit, express and discharge. Shame is difficult to identify because it has few associated verbal and non-verbal expressions. But, shame does manifest itself by blushing, the turning away of the body, downcast eyes and a muted voice (Vick, Waller, Parr, Smith Pasqualini, & Bard, 2007). The identification of shame requires a keen alertness on the part of the therapist to pick up the subtle signs of its manifestation.

Developing a meaningful therapeutic alliance with a shame-based client requires patience, understanding and compassion. As the client releases deep-seated shame feelings, with anger, the therapist becomes the disavowed object of hate, rejection and disgust. Accepting the negative introject in a loving manner with a sense of containment, respect and a non-judgmental attitude is a special skill.

Treatment in this model presupposes that the therapist should have already faced their own hurt or shame before working with the inner hurt and shame of others. In reality, some therapist-client relationships may contribute to the addition of multiple layers of self-absorption, self-gratification through pride and anger. This fortification of the False Self and blockage of the development of the Authentic Gracious Self (True Self) occurs when the client learns skills but does not face his or her shame and work through the defenses of the Shame False Self.

A Case Study – Coming out of the Water

A well-known C.E.O. of an international company made an appointment for a three-day, intensive psychotherapy session for himself and his wife. He said that he tried his best to care for his family, in spite of his tremendous demand at work. However, he felt he failed because his wife became depressed, withdrawn and dissatisfied with him. As are result, their relationship was strained and challenged. He felt they needed help as soon as possible. I chatted briefly with his wife by telephone and she agreed with what he said and admitted that she felt trapped, angry and frustrated.

During the first session, the husband shared particulars of his work and admitted that his heavy schedule placed a terrible strain on their marriage. He said he tried hard to create a space for his wife to work along with him. She did a good job but felt limited and was left feeling unfulfilled. While he was sharing his story, his wife, who appeared tired and very sad, zoned out. When I asked her what was wrong, she said she had heard it all before and had enough. As a result, she was at the end of her rope. She said she did everything in her power to make the marriage successful, raise the family and support her husband in his work. In spite of all this, she had arrived at a place in her life where she felt empty, had no purpose or direction. She hit a brick wall. As a result, she was extremely frustrated, tired and unable to push on with the marriage and the work. Listening intently, the husband empathized with her and apologized profusely for his contribution in making her life so miserable. He told her he would do anything in his power to make things better. Obviously, she had heard this many times before and the more he talked, the more distant she became. She was hurting deeply, very depressed and filled with internal hostility. At that point, it was evident that we needed to work individually to deal with her issues. Her husband agreed and said he would be available to come into the sessions whenever she desired.

After describing the nature of my work, I shared with her that the most important thing was to give her a chance to share her story in a contemplative environment of love, acceptance, silence and non-judgmental listening. I told her that I would be listening intently as she talked but reserved the right to interrupt to ask for clarification or challenge something that appeared inconsistent to the rest of the story. I explained that sharing one's story takes time because we have to move from the cognitive to the emotional, to arrive at the authentic reality of our experience. This is extremely important because much of the pain in our life occurred before speech and our ability to describe it. The right brain forms earlier than the left brain and therefore houses much of our early pain which is nonverbal, visual spatial and intuitive. As we become comfortable in the therapeutic relationship, the right brain delivers information into the left brain which seeks to put it into a logical, linear and language form which is easier presented. But I stressed to her that many deep issues in our lives defy logic and language and present themselves as groans, grunts, or body responses. At those particular times, I would stop and ask her what she thought the nonverbal expression or the body language was saying. She had a deep desire to be healed and so she was prepared for our sessions and moved immediately into telling me her story.

After listening to her for about two hours with a break in between, she asked me if I had any feedback. I shared with her that my assessment was that she was facing some type of internal shame which had occurred earlier in her life and may have blocked her development. Surprised at this, she asked me to explain. I shared that shame is a deep, hidden feeling that results from the shattering of cherished dreams, wishes and expectations. As a result of this, it is manifested by such powerful feelings as boredom, anger, feeling trapped, emptiness, addiction to limitations, fear of potential and of being known. The sad thing about shame is that it often rejects the love it craves and turns in against itself. I continued to support her by letting her know that we can only get at these dynamics by creating a safe environment to share her shame and pain openly. Getting in touch with our individual stories is not a simple process. We have to move beyond telling our story, which is mostly cognitive. As we become more trusting, we begin to share the emotional aspect of our story and release some of our deep emotions of shame and pain. As the story becomes more coherent to the reality of our inner life, more shame is released and we eventually give ourselves authentically with our story. However, this takes time, patience and often repetition. So often in our stories we come across blocks which, like kinks or cramps in our muscles, which require constant massaging for the muscle to function effectively. As I was explaining my psychotherapeutic approach, her eyes became heavy, her face looked down and her body withdrawn, demonstrating a posture of shame.

After a period of hesitation, she said she came from a loving family where her mother and father worked hard to give her and her siblings a good life. As a childhood prodigy, she was industrious and excelled in her spiritual, academic and social life. She was deeply committed to her church and took her faith in God seriously. She worked hard at school, participating fully in class and did her homework assignments on time. She was the 'teacher's pet' and the children looked up to her because of her outstanding achievements. As a result of her hard work, she received many rewards from the church and school. At that point in her life, she was riding high. Everything was going her way. As a result, her parents, teachers and friends had great expectations for her future.

In her teen years she became pregnant. She was deeply ashamed because she let down her parents, her church, her teachers and all those who thought so highly of her. With tears in her eyes, she said her world collapsed. Deeply hurt, the joy had gone out of her life. She was particularly upset by some of her teachers who now looked down on her with disdain. She felt alone, terrified and hopeless. She began to weep.

After a period of silence, I asked her what it would be like for her to make contact with her younger teenaged self. She was terrified and somewhat resistant. But I encouraged her to realize that her younger self was an intimate part of her life and if not related to, could contaminate her future development. She eventually agreed and we sought to make contact with her inner self using a role play where I became her younger, teenage self. I asked her to talk to me and tell me what she thought of me. She became very distant and finally burst out, 'I hate you! You messed up my life!". I replied that I was sad and disappointed because I felt that when she became an adult, she would take time to connect with me, comfort me and understand my pain. But like all the other adults and some of my friends, she avoided me and was ashamed of me. As a result, I felt lonely, afraid and a hopeless failure. But more than anything, I felt unlovable and that no one would ever want me. She tried to connect with me in the role play, but found it very difficult.

In our work together, we also used a series of letters. I asked her to write from her teen self to her adult self and vice versa. Using the role play and the letters, we were able to pin point the pain and shame of her younger self and how that experience had shamed her deeply and blocked her development, leaving her vulnerable and afraid. I shared that if we could open to a loving, accepting and non-judgmental relationship, the vulnerability plus love would allow her to develop empathy for her younger, inner self. This empathy and insight would release the feeling of shame and open her to experience her authentic self. As she developed more insight into her life, she described that since the time she made the mistake in her early teenaged years, she was forced to live "under water". This allowed her to hide and be invisible to people she felt would further shame and dislike her. I asked her what that was like. She said 'I had to live in hiding and be careful when I came up to breathe because I was terrified of people'. She explained that in order to catch her breath, she determined to do all she can to please others so they may love her.

As a result, she has been a pleaser most of her adult life. She went on to explain that this desire to please others was accompanied by a painful attempt at perfectionism which drained her, leaving her hostile, afraid and empty. In her marriage, she was appreciative of her husband who she felt loved her in spite of her shameful past. Lacking education, she felt blocked because she could never rise to his standard. The result was the powerful codependency of pleasing and perfectionism in raising her family and being a chameleon to fit into everybody's needs to hide her deep shame. Then she started crying profusely, saying, "I can't do it anymore. I just can't do it anymore. Even though I believe my husband loves me, when I come up out of water, unconsciously, he pushes me back down. I have no choice but to accept my prison of shame. I can't go on. I feel like I'm going to explode!"

As we came to this part of the therapy, I invited her husband to sit with us. A loving and compassionate person, he was tearful and sad to hear the pain and shame in his wife's story. He was particularly struck to hear that she felt she was living under water and she felt that when she came up for air, he was pushing her back down. He apologized profusely and reinforced that she did her best to help him in his work, did a great job as a mother and a wife.

When the client reaches a point of where they are in touch with their deep inner shame and pain, healing is on the way. "God, the Eternal Healer, is close to the shame-based or broken heart and will never destroy a crushed spirit" (Psalm 34:18). I was conscious of the Still Point, where her chronological shame was intercepted by the Kairos, the eternal healing of the love of God. After finishing our sessions, we had a time of prayer and allowed ourselves to just rest in the contemplative silence and stillness of God's love.

From the airport on their way home, my client called me. In the airport lounge, she had just seen a large painting of a woman coming up out of water. She said this was a God-moment which validated her therapy. I knew the painting well. It was done by Brent Malone, one of our most distinguished Bahamian artists, who toward the end of his life, had a miraculous experience of coming to faith in Christ.

Returning home to the United States, my client completed her Bachelor's and Master's degrees in psychology and became a licensed therapist. She now has a successful psychotherapeutic practice where she brings healing to individuals, couples and families.

In preparing this chapter on the Contemplative Discovery Pathway Theory, I asked her to list some of the principles she found helpful in our psychotherapeutic work together. Here is her response with my explanation or further elucidation of the principles.

1. Understanding and facing shame – she described shame as the powerful undercurrent that keeps us hidden and under water. She said it was not just the psychological understanding of shame, but how the shame interrupts our basic human functioning and also blocks us from ourselves, others and a deeper relationship with God. God shows up to be with us but in our shamed state, we avoid Him. For example, when God came down in the cool of the day to spend time with Adam and Eve. He asked 'Adam, where art thou?' Adam replied 'we were naked or ashamed and cannot meet with you' (Genesis 3:10). The point is that God, in love, came down to meet with them but their shame blocked the love that was theirs to receive. In an atmosphere of acceptance, love and nonjudgmental listening, she claimed she was able to release her shame and pain. She particularly expressed the joy of realizing that it was not too late to make up for a mistake she made at sixteen years old and take steps to change the course of her life.
2. The whole process required a deep humility and accepting herself as she was. This meant letting go of the pain and shame to accept not what could or should have been but what she was. Recognizing God's forgiveness and love, she intentionally forgave herself, her husband and her family of origin for the pain she experienced. After the therapy, it took years to complete the acceptance and healing of her broken life. She said forgiveness was a critical step for her. This is so important because in my experience, we only forgive when we are ready to be healed!

3. Facing her unhealthy boundaries or her crippling codependency, she stayed under water because she was afraid and ashamed of herself and other people. As a result, her whole life was about pleasing others with the hope that they would love her. At the same time, though failing miserably, she tried to be perfect so that she could fit in. But the more she tried, the more difficult her life became. Staying under water was one way she could remain invisible. She realized that she blamed everybody else, including her husband, for keeping her under water. But the insight from the therapy was it was her own shame and desire for invisibility which kept her under water. Blaming others and judging them made her feel better but it could never heal her. She said 'I had to learn that having boundaries is healthy which means learning to say 'no' in a loving and affiliative way'. She agreed that this is not an easy process but it depends on the commitment to continue working at it in spite of often failing and being discouraged.
4. Facing one's shame exposes deep vulnerability. Vulnerability is part of our human existence. That's why we wear clothes and seek to defend ourselves. But as we open to our deep shame of abandonment, rejection and humiliation, our fear of ourselves and others turns our vulnerability into further shame. This is dangerous because it can propel us into a murderous rage or what is described in this book as the Evil Violence Tunnel (Chapter 4) where we become destructive to ourselves, family and others. In other words, hurt and shamed people hurt themselves and those they love. On the other hand, when vulnerability is exposed in a loving environment of acceptance and nonjudgmental listening, empathy develops and this produces insight and a powerful integration of well-being and the healing of self and others.
5. As we move into the Discovery of our Authentic or True Self, we become aware of our vocational creativity in which we care for ourselves and look for outlets to help others. This reality brought her back in touch with her innocent childhood curiosity and with continued right brain work, she sorted out the deeper hurts from her past using such creative influences as art, music, gardening, interior decorating and creative writing. Obviously, these developments led her to finish her education and express them in her vocation as a distinguished therapist. In fact, she said returning to school was a growth experience by helping her to put together many pieces of the puzzle of her life. Describing herself as a 'lifelong learner', she is involved in the discipline of learning to listen to her life and the lives of others to understand and become aware of her vocational purpose.
6. Helping Others – when a person really experiences the Discovery of their True Self in love, they have a desire to be known not as they could or should be but as they really are. This quality is a powerful healing grace to others. She wrote,

> 'After our time together, I took your advice to volunteer with pregnant 16-year-olds and love them. It was an early step to understanding and loving myself. Now

as a therapist and trauma healing facilitator, helping others in their pain continues to bring meaning to my life'.

7. The building on the Discovery of the True Self using the spiritual disciplines of prayer, meditation and inspired reading and good works validated God's love for her. This resulted in her releasing the need to control or please others and opening to the freedom of love, humility, forgiveness and gratitude. In fact, she is beginning to touch the highest development of the self, which is the Contemplative Transcendent Self.

8. She has made excellent progress but it is important to realize that in life, even though we open to our True Self in love, we often fall back due to mistakes or other shameful practices and reencounter our Shame False Self. But the continuing vision of our True Self in love prevents us from staying there. Instead of being addicted to our limitations, we reach forth toward our potential, in spite of repeated setbacks.

Additional Comments

As a young child,, the client experienced a meaningful love story in which her basic instinctual needs of safety, connection and empowerment were met. But sadly, as she entered the early teen years, her dream of love was shattered and she was catapulted into the dungeon of shame involving abandonment, rejection and humiliation. This is so painful to the human psyche, that the brain, through a series of neuromechanisms, develops a Shame False Self involving self-absorption, self-gratification and control to block the destructive elements of shame. The sad thing about the False Self is that it is a perverse rescuer and that our being, the Immortal Treasure, which is a gift of God's love, becomes attached to our life's situation. Thus, instead of our being I Am who I Am, the beloved of God, we become I am what I fear, do, possess, etc. This makes our life precarious and often we spend time hiding from our potential and our vocational creativity or as described by her, 'keeping under water'. But as we work through our life story, releasing the shame and pain that has blocked our development, the False Self unravels, opening us to the Discovery of our True Self with its solitude, humility, love, forgiveness and gratitude. This results in the detachment of our Immortal Treasure of our being from our life situation so that we become the Beloved of God and form healing community. This is the deepest freedom of our being in that we come from love, to love and will one day return to love.

The diagram below (Figure 5) describes the CDPT, moving from the Natural Self to the Shame S False Self to the Authentic Gracious and Contemplative Self.

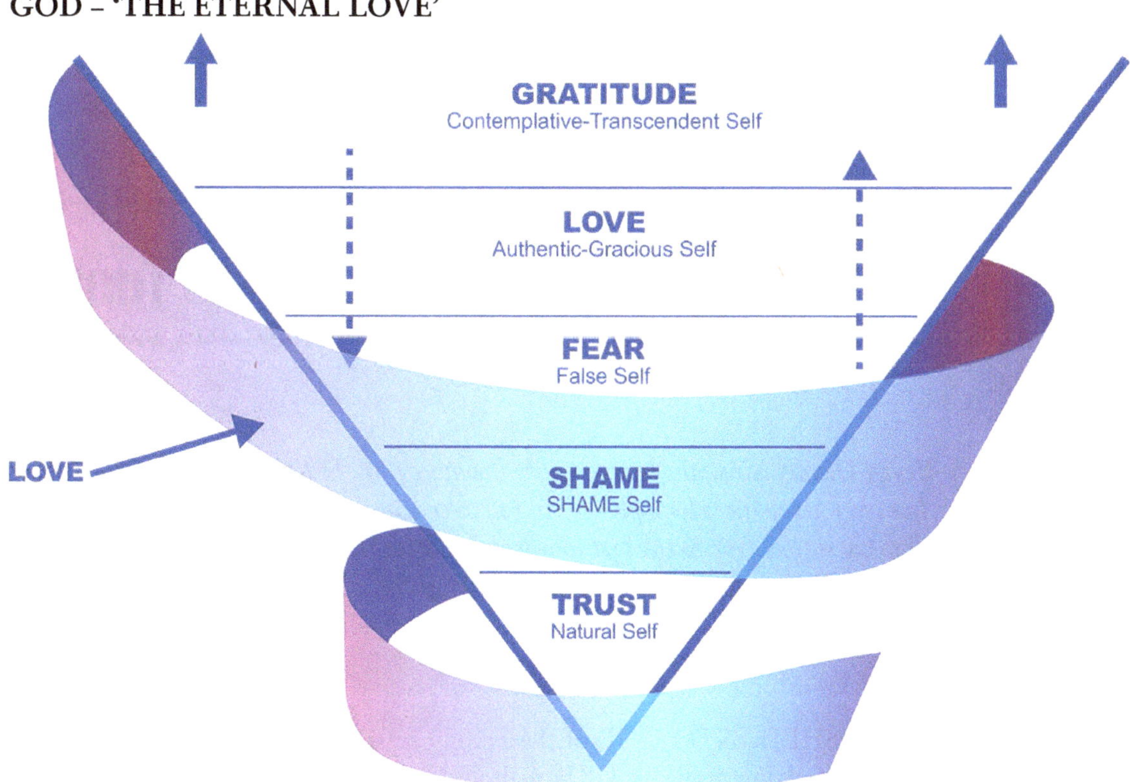

Figure 5 - The Contemplative Discovery Pathway Theory

REFERENCES

Masterson, James. The Search for the Real Self (New York: Free Press, 1988).
Emmons, R. Thanks! How practicing gratitude can make you happier. 2007.
Thompson, C. Anatomy of the Soul. (Carol Stream: Tyndale House, 2010).
Siegel, Daniel. The Mindful Brain (New York: W.W. Norton, 2007) 4-5.

CHAPTER 4
The Evil Violence Tunnel

"Of the Seven Deadly Sins, anger is possibly the most fun. To lick your wounds, to smack your lips over grievances long passed, to roll over your tongue the prospect of bitter confrontation still to come, to savor to the last toothsome morsel both the pain you are given and the pain you are giving back – in many ways, it is a feast fit for a king. The chief drawback is that what you are wolfing down is yourself. The skeleton at the feast is you." [1]
— Frederick Buechner

A YOUNG LADY RUSHED INTO ONE of the Family sessions shouting, "They killed my brother and I want revenge! I'm going to kill somebody today!" She said she had a machete in the car and came to the Family because someone told her to visit the group before she did something destructive. As the young lady screamed profusely, the Family group was shocked and silent. After about 10 minutes, an older lady approached her and said, "I understand how you feel. They killed my son a year ago. Like you, I was deeply hurt, and I wanted revenge. But as time went on, the feelings of revenge poisoned my whole being and I found myself being destroyed. I realized that if I didn't get help, I would either do something destructive to myself or someone else. In the Family, I've been able to express and release my feelings of hurt and revenge." Hugging the young lady, the older lady said, "I cannot tell you what to do. But, if you do not let your feelings of revenge go, you will have two murders to deal with: your brother who was killed and the psychological murder of yourself." The two continued to cry together as the Family group listened. Finally, the group ended and people left quietly. Walking out together, the two ladies exchanged telephone numbers. A few days later, I received a letter from the young lady saying that the Family group, especially the older lady, had prevented her from committing murder. Looking back, she recognized that she was in an uncontrollable state and realizes now that she had to let the feelings of revenge go.

This young lady was in a murderous rage and had entered the Evil Violence Tunnel, where she could have been destructive to herself or another person. Thanks to the intervention of the Family and especially the older lady who understood her plight, she was able to calm down and later thanked the Family for helping her to prevent a murder.

The Evil Violence Tunnel is first described in the story of Cain and Abel in Genesis 4. Cain was the eldest son of Adam and Eve and may be described as very entitled. He was an agriculturalist or farmer by profession. Abel, his younger brother, seemed less endowed and was a humble shepherd of sheep. When the time came for them to make sacrifices to God, Cain made a sacrifice of the best fruit and produce from his farm. On the other hand, Abel made a smaller sacrifice of some pieces of meat from a young lamb. To Cain's surprise, God chose Abel's sacrifice over his. As a result, Cain was extremely angry and shamed. According to Genesis 4:6 'his countenance was down and his face was enraged' meaning he was ashamed. God warned him that 'evil was standing outside his heart's door and intended to master him.' He warned Cain that he must master it (Genesis 4:7). Cain was so angry, hurt and ashamed that God's warning fell on deaf ears. He asked Abel to go for a walk in the fields and murdered him. When God asked him where was Abel, Cain replied 'Am I my brother's keeper?' (Genesis 4:9). As anger becomes the predominant emotion throughout our world, we need to remember that it is a portal into evil or destruction. "Do not let the sun set on your anger in order to give the devil a foothold" (Ephesians 4:26).

In a recent article in *The Guardian* of the United Kingdom, Dr.Aaron Balick, a psychotherapist and author, says "I think for sure anger is more expressed. What you see of it is a consequence of emotional contagion, which I think social media is partly responsible for". Psychologically speaking, the important thing is not the emotion but what you do with it, whether you vent, process or suppress it. Neus Herrero, a researcher at the University of Valencia, found that there is a hormonal response to anger. Cortisol, a stress hormone, increases instead of decreases. Testosterone, heart rate and arterial tension also increase. Herrero was surprised to discover that anger has a 'motivation of closeness'. That is, we show a natural tendency to get closer to what made us angry to try eliminating it (Williams, 2018).

Shame and the Evil Violence Tunnel

In the Contemplative Discovery Pathway Theory model, the developing hurt trail leads to the deprivation of basic instinctual needs such as survival-security (safety), affection-esteem (connection) and power-control (empowerment) leading to shame (Self-Hatred Aimed at M.E.). Shame (including feelings of abandonment, rejection and humiliation) is toxic to the human psyche. As a result, the brain, through a series of neuromechanisms, compensates by forming a powerful defensive shame false self, involving self-absorption, self-gratification and control. Shame is a master emotion with a mixture of negative feelings resulting from the shattering of highly valued wishes, dreams or expectations. Hidden in nature and attached to our family secrets, shame is manifested in society by many forms of social fragmentation such as anger, violence, addiction, family disintegration and revenge. According to James Gilligan, criminal violence can be understood as a desperate attempt to ward off shame (Gilligan, 1996). This is further validated by Robert Brenneman in his book, *Homies and Hermanos* (2012) :

> Although the experience of shame is a deeply personal experience, the sources of shame can be traced to the institutions and policies that perpetuate endemic poverty, weak

> schools and precarious family systems. . . .In effect, the concept of shame represents the intervening variable between these negative social phenomena and a small army of youth who have chosen to abandon traditional pathways to economic stability and respect in favor of the dangerous and frequently violent shortcuts offered by the gang.[2]

If deeply hurt persons have the opportunity to share their stories of shame in an empathic environment, it leads to healing and the development of their authentic self involving the positive emotions of love, humility, forgiveness and gratitude. However, if the deeply shamed person is confronted by more hurt, a powerful murderous rage develops, transcending the defensive ability of the shame false self resulting in the Evil Violence Tunnel (Figure 1). The internalized murderous rage splits off the shamed or inadequate part of the person and either (a) introjects it to act out against the self, leading to self-injury or suicide or (b) is projected onto another person, leading to the hurting of others or homicide. Regardless, the end result of the Evil Violence Tunnel is catastrophic with devastating consequences.

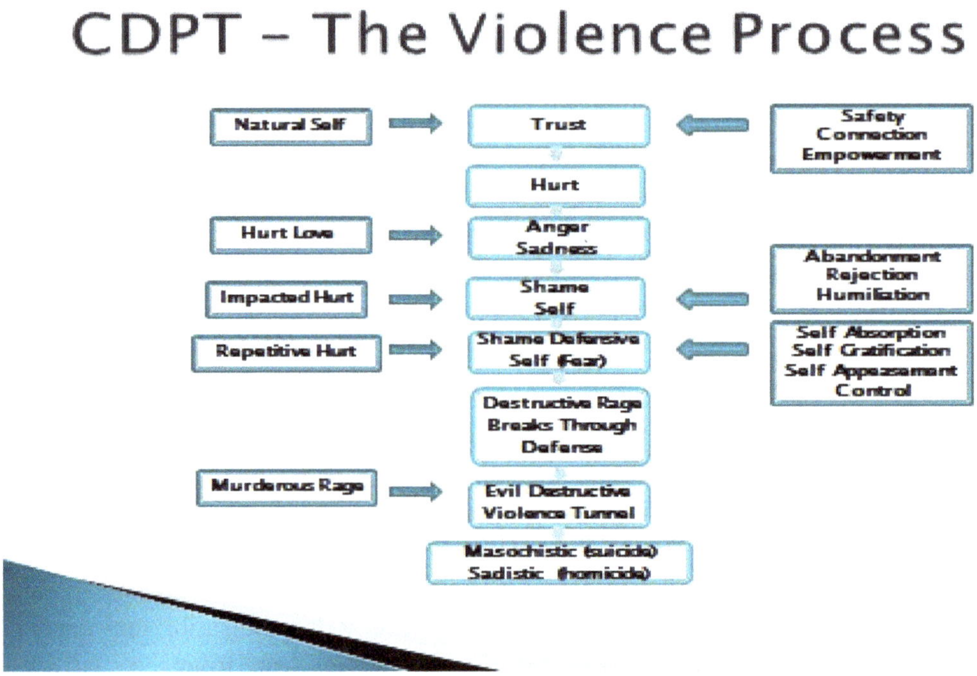

Figure 1 - The Violence Process according to the Contemplative Discovery Pathway Theory

Methodology

The conceptual framework of the Evil Violence Tunnel was developed as a result of the pilot study carried out in 2012, discussed in Chapter 1. This study was then followed up with a grant from the Templeton World Charity Foundation to further examine the findings, testing the effectiveness of The Family: People Helping People Project over time. Although this work came out of the pilot study and the ensuing 3-year study, the major thrust of understanding the Evil Violence Tunnel syndrome evolved out of the qualitative analysis of the praxes reports of individual Family groups in marginalized areas, the adult prison and juvenile detention facilities. Particularly helpful in understanding the syndrome were the comments and analysis of persons serving time for murder and other violent crimes.

Dynamics of the Evil Violence Tunnel

The nervous system is driven by survival and is primed to respond to threat and pursue reward. Nerve connections between the cortex (the cognitive portion of the brain) and the amygdala (early warning portion of the brain) process sensory information, and interpret stimuli such as potential threats. At the amygdala, the situation is compounded because the destructive stimuli are met with stored memories and knowledge from the hippocampus. The periaqueductal gray (PAG), a small structure located deep in the brain, serves as the final common pathway where emotions and behaviors come together to promote survival. A specialized group of neurons, gives rise to different emotions and behaviors when activated (George, 2013). When a person moves toward the Evil Violence Tunnel, they experience changes in appearance, voice, and attitude. When acute, it may result in violence (i.e., road rage or murder). If chronic, it is manifested by bullying and controlling behaviors, resulting in hostile relationships.

Early life traumas are catastrophic (Figure 2) for "footprints on fresh cement last a long time." These traumas inhibit or disconnect the pathway between the higher centers of the brain (cortex) and the feeling part of the brain (amygdala), making the individual more vigilant and anxious. As a result, individuals become prone to the fight–flight or shut-down aspect of the brain to enhance interaction with the environment and ensure survival. It may be hypothesized that persons vulnerable to entering the Evil Violence Tunnel experience this disconnection between the cortex and the amygdala. Posttraumatic stress disorder (PTSD) may be a powerful precursor or trigger to the Evil Violence Tunnel. Angry people have hair-trigger tempers and become involved in destructive acts to people and property. Persons with serious anger problems have overwhelming emotions resulting in impulsive actions. Lacking insight into their mental state, they rationalize their behavior and blame others. Anger is a personal warning signal to address our internal dynamics. Often, anger is "Sad's bodyguard", meaning that the person who is angry is deeply hurt and wounded. Studies of violent anger have indicated persons with specific traits, including: (a) a genetic component (Coccaro, Kavoussi, Berman, & Lish, 1998), (b) different levels of neurotransmitters in the brain (George et al.2001), and (c) differences in brain structures such as volume, glucose metabolism and communication signals in critical areas (Schiffer et al., 2011).

The Evil Violence Tunnel is associated with murder, domestic violence, revenge attacks, bullying, road rage, emotional battery and so forth. Men and women have similar prevalence for anger, but men tend to be more destructive. This has been validated by a report from the

National Violent Death Reporting System, where in 2004, there were 144 incidents of homicide-suicide. More than half of the victims (74.6%) were females and most of the perpetrators (91.9%) were males. Moreover, in 2005 in Canada, 1 in 10 homicide cases were homicide-suicide. Almost all of the incidents (97%) were cases in which female victims were murdered by their male spouse (van Wormer, 2008). The phenomenon of the Evil Violence Tunnel has similarities to the well-known murder-suicide phenomenon relating to romantic relationships. However, in our experience, the Evil Violence Tunnel may occur in persons who are not romantically involved or closely interrelated. Our impression is that the experience of the Evil Violence Tunnel Syndrome is equally distributed between males and females. However, in the Bahamas, males tend to be more severely destructive in committing suicides and homicides. In fact, according to a report by Bethell and Allen, the rate of suicide among males (3.7) was more than seven times higher than the rate of suicide among females (0.5) (Table 1; Bethell & Allen, 2014).

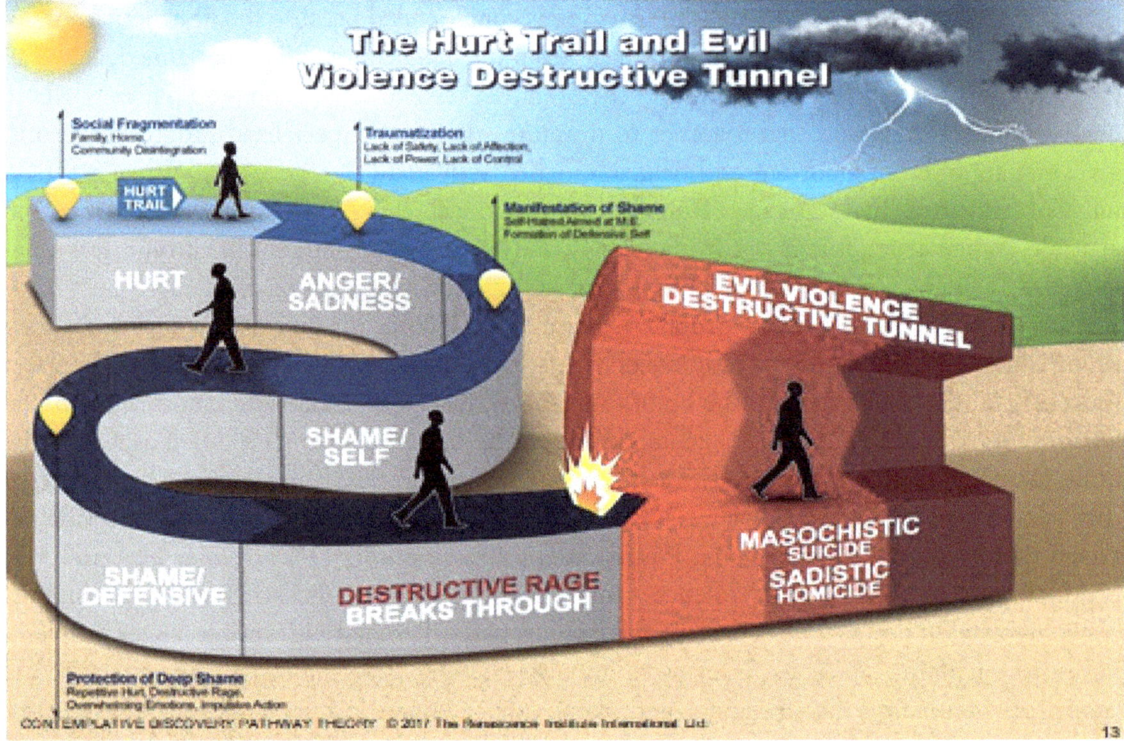

Figure 2 – The Evil Violence Tunnel

Table 1 – Crude Suicide Rates in the Bahamas by Gender (2000-2013)

Gender	**Population (combined)**	**Number of Suicides**	**Rate of Suicide**
Male	2,260,800	83	3.7
Female	2,382,400	13	0.5
Total	**4,643,200**	**96**	**2.1**

Precursors and Triggers of the Evil Violence Tunnel

The Evil Violence Tunnel has a number of precursors and triggers as listed below.

1. Early childhood trauma leads to impacted hurt, resulting in shame, which is a powerful precursor to violence and the Evil Violence Tunnel. Scheff (1988) described violence as a form of avoiding shame. Dorothy Lewis and associates at the Yale Child Study Center made a powerful connection between severe childhood abuse and vicious murders in late teenage years (Lewis, 1998). Persons who have experienced serious early trauma tend to develop PTSD in later life and may experience epigenetic changes, which could be transmitted to the next generation. Persons with PTSD may be more susceptible to the Evil Violence Tunnel.
2. Mental dysrhythmias (e.g., bipolar disorder, major depression, partial complex seizures) may trigger violent outbursts.
3. Persons vulnerable to destructive anger and the development of the Evil Violence Tunnel feel out of control and use alcohol and drugs to modulate their feeling. But the more they use, the more they need to calm their internal chaos by decreasing tolerance and preventing withdrawal. Alcohol and drugs depress cortical pathways accentuating murderous rage and the Evil Violence Tunnel (American Psychiatric Association, 2000).
4. Provocation, involving intense criticism, contempt, demeaning speech and behavior, acts as a trigger of the Evil Violence Tunnel.
5. Loss and grief unexpectedly may explode into the Evil Violence Tunnel. Losing someone is sad, but the parallel feeling of anger at the loss may be destructive.
6. Fatigue—HALT (Hungry, Angry, Lonely, Tired) is accepted as a trigger for relapse in addiction. Fatigue particularly is a powerful trigger for the Evil Violence Tunnel, especially if alcohol is involved.
7. Persons with borderline and narcissistic personality disorders may be more prone to enter the Evil Violence Tunnel.
8. Intermittent explosive disorder triggers the Evil Violence Tunnel, especially in domestic violence, which is always complex because of the denial and resistance of the perpetrator and the victims (Coccaro et al.,1998).

Stages of the Evil Violence Tunnel

Interviews with persons with serious suicide attempts or who were involved in destructive or homicidal acts have enabled us to categorize the six stages of the Evil Violence Tunnel (Figure 3). Inmates in our Family project at the prison have validated the stages of the tunnel as true to their experience in real life (see the section "Additional Note—Prison Inmates' Description of the Evil Violence Tunnel").

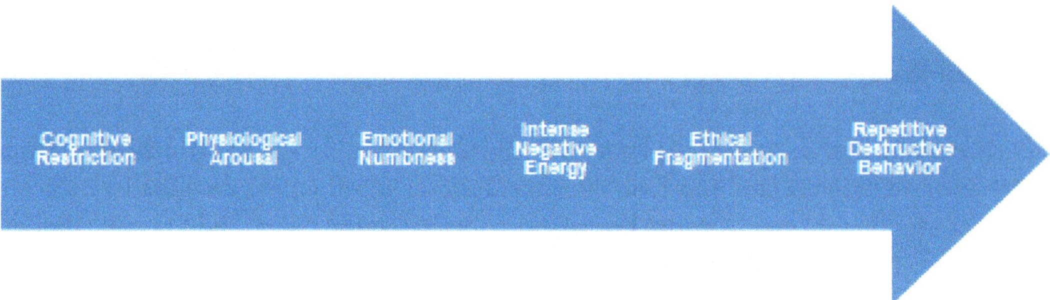

Figure 3 - Stages of the Evil Violence Tunnel

1. Cognitive Restriction

In this state, persons claim their mind is fixated on the hated person. As a result, they are unaware of other perspectives, creating a sense of being in a tunnel. At this time, there is an outpouring of the sympathetic neurotransmitters, noradrenaline, adrenaline and so forth and the person is unable to benefit from helpful interventions. This severe tunnel vision inhibits the person from taking advantage of other options and projects them into a downward destructive spiral. For example, a father reported that he was shocked after his daughter drowned herself with her two young children. She left a note claiming she had no place to stay. The father said that this surprised him because he had space available in his home that he would have gladly shared with her and her children.

2.The Physiological Arousal

The person is in a very hyper aroused state, with increased heart rate and blood pressure and is usually sweating profusely. As the anger increases, the arousal blocks the input from the higher thought centers of the brain, lowering the IQ, and making them act differently than when in a relaxed state. Persons who attempted suicide, claimed that in this stage, they were resistant to any type of intervention. It is interesting to note that a number of persons who failed to carry out a serious suicidal attempt claimed they were interrupted by a still small voice, encouraging them not to do it. The question is, Why would some people hear this voice and others not?

3. Emotional Numbness

With cognitive restriction and in the hyper aroused state, the person experiences emotional numbness. Losing all sense of fear, they throw caution to the wind and become a danger to themselves or other people. Persons in the Evil Violence Tunnel have alexithymia, where they repress their deep hurt feelings and shift directly from the thought of being hurt to destructive behavior. This phenomenon contributes to emotional numbness, making them even more destructive. For example, a young man stabbed his girlfriend multiple times because of alleged unfaithfulness. When asked why he kept stabbing her, he replied, "I wanted her to feel what I was feeling." When asked what he was feeling, he replied, "I do not know."

4. Intense Negative Energy

In repeated interviews, numerous persons shared that in the state of murderous rage, they felt influenced by powerful negative energy, propelling them to destruction. An inmate stressed that while in the Tunnel, "There's nothing positive towards the person/thing in our thoughts at all." In one case, a group of law enforcement officers shared that while investigating a murder scene, the accused confessed that before the murder, he felt overtaken by negative energy empowering him to be destructive. Another person who had killed three times shared that on each occasion, he was influenced to make the negative rather than positive choice. During his rehabilitation, his mother's love and influence intervened in his life, enabling him to receive forgiveness and change his behavior. He shared that when threatened now, he finds it easier to make the positive choice rather than to give in to the negative or destructive alternative.

5. Ethical Fragmentation

As the person goes further into the dark tunnel, they experience the fragmentation of their values and ethical formation. As a result, the constitutive principles of non-injury, truth telling, and caring become nonexistent. Another way of describing this is that the pathways to the higher centers in the brain, dealing with thought and positive decision making, are blocked and the person is more open to their lower or animalistic instincts. Numerous persons claimed that after committing the destructive act, they have an intense awareness that they have done something that was ego-dystonic or not in keeping with their value system. The question is whether the ethical fragmentation in the Evil Violence Tunnel is a fragmentation of values or the repression of them during the murderous rage.

6. Repetitive Destructive Behavior

At this point in the Tunnel, persons said that they found themselves being repeatedly destructive by stabbing, shooting or hurting themselves or others. During the interview, sometimes the person became very sad and wondered why they could not refrain from the destruction directed at the self or projected onto others. The Evil Violence Tunnel is like a wave that rises slowly, accelerates toward the peak and then collapses in destruction. After the destructive act, some individuals claim they felt a powerful release, leaving them exhausted, to such extent where they lie down to rest or fall asleep. However, later on, when their pathways to their higher cortical centers of thought and understanding are opened, they become agitated and remorseful when they realize what had occurred. The repetitive destructive behavior appears to occur when a person enters a zone where they lose control. For example, a young lady shot her husband because she was constantly provoked by his refusal to come home at an appropriate time. Shocked, she said, "I'm not a murderer. I did not mean to kill him. But I couldn't stop myself, and now, how do I forgive myself for what I've done?"

Additional Note—Prison Inmates' Description of the Evil Violence Tunnel

One of our major Family groups is located in the local correctional facility in Nassau, Bahamas.

We shared with inmates our research concerning stages of the Evil Violence Tunnel, dealing with violence toward self and particularly others. They were very interested in this. However, they said they did not like the psychological language or what they call the 'psychobabble'. After hearing us describe the stages, they said we were extremely accurate. They were so interested that they took the paper and said they wanted to spend time amongst themselves putting it in their own language. They told us that there are special things that trigger killing or wounding other people. From their point of view, the major triggers are: (a) somebody stealing your drugs, (b) somebody purposely damaging your car, (c) someone who disrespects you in front of your girlfriend or makes a pass at her, (d) somebody who has tried to hurt you in the past. In their world, revenge is seen as 'macho'. If you don't seek revenge, you are not respected by your colleagues; (e) someone who has told a lie or shared a very confidential secret, which could lead to you being hurt or even killed, (f) a betrayer, that is, a person who tells you one thing and tells another person a different story. In the kind of life they live, this is the most dangerous thing that could happen.

The following are the stages of the Evil Violence Tunnel that the inmates described:

1. They did not like the phrase 'cognitive restriction'. Instead, they described the first stage as fixation on the person who they wish to harm. Once that decision is made, you may even take drugs or do anything else to enhance or prepare for the action.

2. They described that their bodies undergo physical and chemical reactions which destroy any kind of rational thinking. Obviously, drugs and alcohol play a part in this as well.

3. They described the emotional numbness as purely the loss of feeling, particularly fear or compassion. At this point, you have to get yourself 'psyched' to be rough and tough.

4. They did not like the phrase 'negative energy'. Instead, they said you become overwhelmed with anger and powerful feelings of destruction. You then have abnormal, aggressive feelings. Some of the inmates said they prefer to see it as 'the devil enters the picture' and all you can do is hate and destroy. They went on to describe that any kind of sensitivity of doing something different than hurting or killing the person is quickly eliminated in one's mind.

5. The breakdown of their value system where they do not consider or care about right and wrong regarding harming the person. You become psyched in thinking only of how you can harm or destroy the person. At this point, there's no turning back.

6. A continual push (pressure) to stab, shoot or strike the person without any awareness of the consequences.

The inmates agreed that after the act is done, there's a let-down or a calm. In some cases, the drugs or alcohol wear off or you may fall asleep. To prevent yourself feeling regret or hurt, your friends encourage you to drink strong alcohol like Hennessey or brandy along with smoking marijuana and using ecstasy or cocaine. In a study carried out by van Wormer (2008), it was found that the intense impulse to kill is associated with a powerful sense of self-destruction, as well as the desire to hurt those once loved. The inmates did not seem to agree with this. They said that when they hurt somebody else, they have no intention of wanting to hurt themselves. It seemed that their anger and action is 'other' directed rather than toward themselves.

Intervening With the Evil Violence Tunnel

This phenomenon of the Evil Violence Tunnel has been encountered repeatedly in our work. The question is, 'What can be done to prevent it?' When questioned, persons who experienced the tunnel reported that they could not envisage what type of intervention would help. The Evil Violence Tunnel is like a wave, and our only hope of intervention is at the onset of the entrance into the tunnel. This means when people become aware of their anger or threatening thoughts, they must learn to walk away, not only once, but repeatedly. According to D. T. George et al. (2011), when a person is very angry and particularly under the influence of alcohol, the amygdala processes stimuli at 30 milliseconds outside of our conscious awareness. As a result, by the time a person thinks about it, they have already reacted. This makes walking away sometimes unrealistic. In some cases, Prozac, a serotonergic reuptake inhibitor may be helpful by (a) making persons less angry, that is, mellow and (b) giving them an extra second to think, which may enable them to walk away. It must be stressed however, if the person is under the influence of alcohol, the Prozac is ineffective (George et al., 2011). In our experience, at a certain point, the tunnel is addictive and has a seductive quality. It's hard to move away from the hated object or person when the wave is at its peak. In light of the prevalence of this phenomenon, we developed a technique called the Family Perceptual Shift, which has proved helpful to numerous persons with serious anger problems. The stages of the Family Perceptual Shift are listed below.

1. **Walk away, take time out.** Recognize when the provocation is producing shame and rage in us. At that point, we have to change our activity and walk away. We call this "taking time out." A number of people who have experienced the Evil Violence Tunnel, either in suicidal or homicidal attempts, shared with us that if they had taken time out or moved away from the situation, it would have prevented the destructive act.

2. **Process the hurt and shame.** In reference to our theory (CDPT), impacted hurt and anger produces shame, involving abandonment, rejection and humiliation. After taking time out, if we could process the hurt and shame by reflection, writing, or telling our story to an empathic, nonjudgmental audience, the shame can be reduced. According to Hariri, Bookheimer, and Mazziotta (2000), groups help people to label their feelings, which activates the cortex and

serves as a top down control to calm the amygdala. This has been our experience in The Family: People Helping People project, where a number of persons have shared their stories of either being close to or in the tunnel and have learned to manage their anger. Shame is diminished when shared or expressed. Conversely, if repressed or withheld, it leads to destructive consequences (Allen, 2010).

3. **Deep breathing.** Deep breathing, with gaps between inspiration and expiration, relaxes the body. In breathing with our eyes closed, the brain secretes alpha waves, which produces a deeper relaxation. This relaxation and slowing down militates against the development of anger and shame (Tolle, 2005).

4. **Silence.** Silence, a fast disappearing entity in modern culture, is one of the best antidotes of hurt and shame. In silence, as we allow our thoughts to sail through our mind, we become present to ourselves. As a result, new perspectives develop and what we perceived to be a serious issue may be just a passing thought. Emotions are feelings in motion, so if we can let them pass through, they will not have a deleterious effect on us. Sadly, because of our shame core, we become addicted to our negative thoughts, compounding our shame, pushing us toward murderous rage and the Evil Violence Tunnel (Allen, 2004).

5. A prayer or pledge. The brain works by substitution. Instead of saying, "do not be afraid or angry," we seek to replace the fear with a simple pledge stating, I pledge that in times of darkness, fear and anger, I will choose to love and be kind. I will choose to be humble (that is, accept myself and circumstances as I am). I will choose to forgive those who have hurt me and also forgive myself for the wrongs I have done. Most of all, I will choose to be grateful for all that I have been given.

6. **Opening to the streams of love in our life.** When we cannot reach the source of love, we can open to the streams of love in our life. All love is interconnected. In times of deep hurt and anger, if we focus on persons who loved us unconditionally as a child, (e.g., mother, father, grandparent, priest), the streams of love flowing from them soothes us. The person may be dead, but the stream of love continues to flow because love is stronger than death (Allen, 1993).

7. **Open to thin spaces.** Opening to thin spaces in our lives means reflecting on memories of places where we felt truly loved and at peace. In the Bahamas, this is often the beach, where the beautiful aquamarine waters transcend imprisonment in time and open us to the eternal mystery. The intersection between chronological time (Chronos) and the fullness of time (Kairos), is the still point where we experience the interconnectedness of all things accompanied by peace, love and gratitude.

8. **Gratitude.** Gratitude is the most effective neutralizer of anger and shame. In gratitude, we

open to love and recognize that life itself is a grace. The highest evolution of being human is to express love and gratitude. We encourage persons to write down three things for which they are grateful. This completes the shift from fear and shame to love and gratitude (Emmons, 2007).

Case Vignettes

1. A young lady with her little boy was waiting for her husband to pick her up after work. When he arrived, she noticed that her husband smelled of alcohol, making her apprehensive. On the way home, the little boy asked his father for the toy that was promised to him. When the father replied that he had forgotten, the little boy became angry and shouted at him. Intervening, the mother told the son she would get the toy for him. But her intervention was too late because the father was enraged. Slamming on the brakes, he shouted obscenities at the little boy and scolded him for speaking so disrespectfully. Shocked by the tone of the father's voice, the mother and child were terrified as the father drove recklessly home. At home, the mother and the son quickly left the car as the father drove away in a rage, screaming violent threats. The mother and child were afraid, not knowing what would happen. Arriving home that night, the father went to bed but was unable to sleep. The next morning, he was despondent and said he was ashamed and remorseful for his behavior. He said he deeply loved his son but was shocked that something came over him, making him feel numb and out of control. He eventually asked his son to forgive him and promised it would never happen again.

2. A 27-year-old male shared that he was enraged when he found out that his girlfriend cheated on him. After a few alcoholic drinks, he rushed over to her apartment, where an argument ensued. Extremely angry, he took a knife and stabbed her repeatedly. He thought she was dead and panicked. Fortunately, the next-door neighbor heard the screams for help and called the police and the ambulance. Taken to hospital, the young lady was treated and was eventually discharged. During the interview, the perpetrator was calm and puzzled that he could be so cruel to someone he loved so deeply.

3. A young lady shared that her husband was repeatedly unfaithful and eventually, she could not take it anymore. Angry and hyperventilating, she put her three children in the car (ages 4 years, 2 years, and 9 months) and drove rapidly toward a high pier overlooking a deep part of the ocean.

   Approaching the pier, she called her husband, saying "I'm giving you what you really want...goodbye." Accelerating the car, she drove toward the edge of the pier. Just before reaching the edge, to her surprise, the 9-month-old child, who could not talk, shouted "mummy, mummy, stop!" Surprised and shocked, she slammed on the brakes, stopping about six feet from the precipice. Calming down, she reversed and drove to a friend's house where they stayed for a week. Discussing the incident with her, she was able to identify all the stages of the Evil Violence Tunnel. Sadly, she said that in her hyperactive, destructive state, she was not aware of any type of successful intervention. This case correlates with a homicide–suicide study conducted in the United Kingdom, which indicated that women who killed themselves would often kill their children as well (van Wormer, 2008).

4. Grief is a powerful precursor of anger. When we lose someone, we feel sad, but we are angry that they're gone. A gentleman described that when his mother died, he and his sister went to the funeral home to pick out a casket. Bullying him, the sister told him to make the undertaker change the casket they had chosen. Overwhelmed with grief, he refused. Enraged, the sister pushed him and viciously slapped him. Even though he was grieving deeply, the gentleman said that he could feel a powerful wave of anger coming over him. Deeply shaken, he was about to lose control and attack his sister. To counteract this, he sat down immediately and started to cry for his mother, praying not to lose control and hurt his sister. After a while, he calmed down. On reflection, he said he knew he was entering a powerful destructive state (the Evil Violence Tunnel). He was surprised that at this most sacred and sad time of his life, he could feel so violent.

5. An older brother was jealous of his younger brother because he was more successful in attracting young ladies. One evening, after picking up his younger brother from a party, he felt discouraged. The younger brother teased him and told him he needed to find a girl. The older brother became angry, took out a knife and repeatedly stabbed the younger brother. Arriving home, the family took the younger brother to the hospital, leaving the older brother terrified about what had occurred. Describing the incident, the older brother said he felt that when his younger brother teased him about not being able to attract girls, a powerful rage came over him. He did not remember stabbing his brother and was surprised to see the blood in the car.

Conclusion

It was a quiet Tuesday morning and my clinic was very calm. The receptionist called to say an older lady was there to see me. Welcoming her into my office, I asked her to sit down. Pulling her chair close to me, she said 'Doctor, this is a serious visit and it wouldn't take long'. She continued

"I have encountered pain greater than I can handle. I have been a very committed Christian for most of my adult life, serving as a missionary, teaching Sunday school and volunteering to help the poor. But now I feel I've come to the end of my road. I've experienced a deep pain of betrayal by my husband and I have decided to kill myself. I bought a gun and I planned to do it earlier this week but I called a friend in Florida and she said 'promise me, before you kill yourself, go and see Dr. Allen because I've just finished his book 'In Search of the Heart'. I believe he can help you.'"

Looking at my sadly, she said 'Doctor, I don't believe you can help me, but I'm only here to grant a last wish to my friend'. At that point, the pain in her heart was so deep that it affected the atmosphere in the room. Having worked with the devastation and pathos of serious crack addiction, I had encountered deep tragedy and pain in the heart which affected the atmosphere of the interview. I felt the same way with this dear lady. Continuing, she said 'you have no medicine which can work for me. You have no Bible verses which I don't know. I am finished and I plan to shoot myself after I leave this session'. Feeling somewhat apprehensive and shocked, I found myself calling her 'mother'. I said 'Mother, you've been a very faithful woman and done the best you could for your family. I recognize that it's very little I can say or do if you are determined to kill yourself'. Interrupting me, she said 'I know it's wrong. But because I have tried to be faithful to my God and family, I believe God would understand and forgive the old lady'. Recognizing that she was determined to carry out her plan, I found myself bowing in silent prayer. I asked God for grace, wisdom and more than anything else, the right words to say to this dear lady but I remembered Isaiah 50:4 which states "The Lord God has given us the tongue of understanding that we may know how to sustain the weary one with a word". Feeling somewhat fortified through the Holy Spirit, I said to her 'Madam, do you know about the cross?' She said 'Dr. Allen, I know everything about the cross. As a little girl, I made a decision to receive Christ as my personal savior and serve him the rest of my life. The cross of Christ has been my guiding light throughout my whole life. But now, my faith is shattered.' I then said to her 'I know you understand the cross as a means for eternal salvation but do you understand the power of the cross as a means for life's management?' She looked at me puzzled and said 'what do you mean?' I replied 'yes, our Lord did die for our sins and eternal welfare but more than anything else he went to the cross because he knew there were certain things in life which were too heavy or painful for us to carry'. In fact, it says in Isaiah 53:4 "surely he has bourn our griefs and carried our sorrows". I asked if she understood what that meant. She said vaguely, but it was not clear to her. I asked if she would receive my interpretation. She said 'of course'. I then proceeded to tell her

"For me, the cross is for eternal salvation. But as a person who has struggled in the pathos and hopelessness of crack addiction and all its horrors, I have found the cross a source of management for my life. This means that when I encounter pain bigger than me, I have to let Christ on the cross carry that, because I am unable to do so."

There was silence. She said she was very angry because of the betrayal. I knew that she was in the Evil Violence Tunnel and therefore in danger of self-destruction. I asked her 'would you be willing to allow Christ to carry your pain and shame on his cross?' She looked at me and said 'I don't think it'll work but I will try it'. As she left the office, I felt deeply warmed and blessed by her presence. I saw her weekly for three months. I noticed that she seemed to be getting stronger and had moved away from the Evil Violence Tunnel of suicidality. We came to the point where we discussed termination. We agreed to have one last session. I admit I was anxious and apprehensive about the last session. But paradoxically, I also felt at peace. The receptionist rang and said the old lady was on her way to the office. When she entered, she was carrying a croc-a-sack with large pieces of wood sticking out of it. This was puzzling because I didn't know what was going on. Putting the sack on the desk, she took out two crosses, a large one and a small one. With tears in her eyes, she said, "The day after our first session, I went into my field and I made a large cross and placed it in the corner of my room. Every morning and every night, I prayed to God, telling Him 'the old lady can't carry this shame of betrayal and pain'. Because I know He loves me, I asked him to please let Christ his Son carry it on the cross for me. I continued to give Christ my cross daily, according to Isaiah 53:4. The miracle is that God delivered me. I am able to forgive my husband and I no longer want to kill myself."

In other words, she moved out of the Evil Violence Tunnel. She went on to say that she brought two crosses. The larger one was for me to keep in my home and the smaller one was to stay in my office. She told me that when people came to see me with shame, anger or hurt bigger than themselves, she would be happy for me to tell them the story of the old lady and the cross. These two crosses have proved a tremendous blessing to me and my family as well as others who I've had the chance to help deal with the Evil Violence Tunnel.

Greek mythology reminds us "whom the gods will destroy, they first make mad." Anger can be creative, but beyond a certain point, it is one of the most destructive forces in the universe. On the other hand, if we could work through the anger and shame in our heart, we release the hurt and pain and make space for love. Each person's life is a challenging journey from being a victim of their shame and false self based in fear and anger to surrender to the discovery of their authentic true self based in love and gratitude. In The Family: People Helping People Project, we have seen many persons recover from the perils of the Evil Violence Tunnel and learn to appropriately manage their anger and move on to positive self-development (i.e., resocialization). However, there are many unanswered questions and the concept of the Evil Violence Tunnel requires more research, especially as it relates to murder, domestic violence, road rage, bullying and other destructive behaviors.

REFERENCES

1 Buechner, Frederick. "Anger" in Wishful Thinking: A Seeker's ABC (San Francisco: HarperSanFrancisco, 1993) 2.

2 Brenneman, Robert. Homies and Hermanos (2012) 107.

CHAPTER 5:
The False Self: The Internal Saboteur

Life batters and shapes us in all sorts of ways before it's done...
The original, shimmering self gets buried so deep that most of us hardly end up
living out of it at all. Instead, we live out all the other selves which we are constantly putting on
and taking off like coats and hats against the world's weather. —Frederick Buechner[1]

THE FALSE SELF IS A COPING mechanism to deal with shame, which promises relief but delivers more pain. According to Dr. James Masterson:

> *It is the nature of the false self to protect us from knowing the truth about our real selves—keeping us from penetrating the deeper causes of our unhappiness and from seeing ourselves as we truly are: vulnerable, terrified, and unable to let our authentic selves emerge.*[2]

Created early in childhood, the false self defends us from the painful reality of shame that often stems from:

- **Abandonment** ("I am not enough"),
- **Rejection** ("I am unlovable"), and
- **Humiliation** ("I am a failure").

In facing the harsh realities of life with its woundedness, the false self helps a child negotiate the painful transition from the hurt of childhood to adulthood. According to Thomas Merton, the false self is "an illusory, self-centered identity, constructed and driven by the desire for pleasure, experience, power, and recognition. . . .It is the mask we wear based on our desires and illusions about ourselves"[2](p.28), The false self seeks external validation through achievements and experiences, creating an excessive network of defenses that distort our true selves and block intimacy with God, with others, and even with ourselves.

Brennan Manning, a Catholic priest and recovering alcoholic, describes poignantly the birth of his own false self:

"When I was eight, the impostor, or false self, was born as a defense against pain."

The imposter within whispered, "Brennan, don't ever be your real self anymore because nobody likes you as you are. Invent a new self that everybody will admire, and nobody will know". So I became a good boy–polite, well mannered, unobtrusive, and deferential. I studied hard, scored excellent grades, won a scholarship in high school and was stalked every waking moment by the terror of abandonment and a sense that nobody was there for me. I learned that perfect performance brought the recognition and approval I desperately sought. I orbited into an unfeeling zone to keep fear and shame at a safe distance. As my therapist remarked, "All these years there has been a steal trap door covering your emotions and denying you access to them." Meanwhile, the imposter I presented for public inspection was nonchalant and carefree."[3]

Living in the clutches of our own false self, we become terrified of being who we truly are. No one willingly gives up their false self unless they feel safe and loved. In the story of The Velveteen Rabbit, when the rabbit asks, "How do we become real?" the old skin horse replies: "You need to find someone who loves you. Then you become real." Similarly, as we share our stories in a contemplative environment of love, acceptance, empathy, and nonjudgmental listening, we can release our shame and open ourselves to our authentic self in love. But this is not always easy. As children, overwhelmed by fear and anxiety, we often cover our hurt with defenses, such as the belief "little boys don't cry", and in doing so, we bury not only our pain but also our true self.

Therefore by the time we reach adulthood, our false self has multiple layers, like an onion, that shield us from our woundedness. Sadly this inner shame pushes us to remain hidden and unknown. It is as if we go under water to make sure we are not seen. This hidden, painful state creates a powerful vulnerability that terrifies us. But as Brené Brown has taught us, "the same vulnerability can be the birthplace of shame, weakness and scarcity, but if we are loved, the same vulnerability can become the birthplace of courage, love, and meaning."

The Origin of the False Self

The false self is a *perverse rescuer*: it promises relief but delivers pain. Rooted in fear and anger, it will drive us to sacrifice our very lives to make us feel better in the moment. But this experience is short lived and we end up feeling worse. In childhood, for example, when we wanted a cookie but were told we could not have it, the false self whispered, "Take it." We took it, perhaps even lied about it, and justified it to ourselves. The false self convinced us it was acting in our best interest. Even though in the end we received some type of punishment and received some type of pain or rejection.

James Masterson in his book *The Search for the Real Self* explains that the false self plays a deceptive role: it pretends to protect us but is programmed to keep us fearful, fearful of being abandoned or of not being able to be alone. Thomas Merton, in *Seeds of Contemplation*, sees the false self as "an illusory person who seduces us to live a life of pretense and illusion, only to be shattered by it."[4]

The three basic needs of a child are safety, love, and empowerment. When these needs are unmet, hurt and loss give rise to shame, manifesting as:

- **Abandonment** ("I'm not good enough")
- **Rejection** ("I am not loved"), and
- **Humiliation** ("I am a failure").

The false self compensates for the deprivation of our instinctual needs through various defenses:

a. **Self-Absorption** – a defense against abandonment.
b. **Self-Gratification** – a defense against rejection.
c. **Self-Inflation** – a defense against humiliation.

1. Self-Absorption

Feeling abandoned and alone, we become absorbed in ourselves and isolated from others leading to defenses such as

a. Fearfulness and defensiveness which lead to isolation and intimacy dysfunction.
b. Emotional "rollercoasters", elation followed by depression, due to dependency on external experiences for purpose and meaning.
c. Extreme defensiveness: denial, blaming, projecting, or making others the problem.
d. Craving compliments and a strong desire to be noticed.
e. Identity fused with possessions, achievements, or connections ("I am what I own, know, or control").
f. Narcissism and disconnection from real feelings, intuition, and insight.
g. Lack of empathy and reciprocity, making sharing and intimacy impossible.
h. Difficulty praying or worshiping because self-preoccupation turns everything into "me, myself, and I."
i. Discomfort with silence, externally and internally because silence confronts the false self with its own nothingness.
j. Identity based on a utility/disutility ratio: "As long as I'm useful, I'm okay. When I'm not, I'm nothing."
k. Chronic loneliness from distrusting others and overvaluing self-sufficiency.

2. Self-Gratification

This defense used to block the pain of rejection leads to

a. **Addiction**: An insatiable desire for drugs, alcohol, sex, gaming, anger, work, or other stimulants. Weak boundaries lead to excess, and we prefer to remain in weakness rather than change.
b. **Co-dependency**: A powerful drive to please others in the hope that pleasing will earn love, only to discover that a lifetime of pleasing still leaves us unloved.
c. **Contra-dependency**: Isolating oneself while secretly wanting others to reach out. It is like living in a castle surrounded by a moat—wishing for visitors but never lowering the drawbridge, and feeling hurt if they stop knocking.
d. **Cultural adaptation**: Thriving only within familiar cultural surroundings; without

them, feeling lost and disoriented.

e. **Groupthink:** Needing the identity of a group to feel secure—changing behavior based on who is watching. Examples include nationalism, racism, or denominationalism.

3. Self-Inflation

This is a desire for absolute control to avoid feeling vulnerable,

a. **Pride:** A sense of invincibility; a cloak for shame.
b. **Reconstruction of reality:** Lying to reshape events.
c. **Scapegoating:** Projecting our shame onto others to make them feel inferior and ourselves superior, or vice versa.
d. **Illusion of permanence:** Believing things will never change, ignoring life's realities of loss and transition.
e. **Idolatry:** Making problems our "god" or giving people godlike status.
f. **Perfectionism:** A false belief in flawlessness, covering shame and inadequacy.

A beautiful example of the false, self manifested in self-absorption, self-gratification and self-inflation, is Jesus' teaching in the parable of the rich man (Luke 12:15-21):

He (Jesus) said to them, "Beware, and be on your guard against every form of greed, for not even when one has an abundance does his life consist of his possessions. And He told them a parable, saying, "The land of a certain rich man was very productive. And he began reasoning to himself, saying, 'What shall I do, since I have no place to store my crops?' And he said, 'This is what I will do. I will tear down my barns and build larger ones, and there I will store all my grain and my goods. And I will say to my soul, "Soul, you have many goods laid up for many years to come; take your ease, eat, drink and be merry." But God said to him, 'You fool! This very night your soul is required of you; and now who will own what you have prepared?"

In our adolescent program for teens referred by the court, we don't necessarily use the term "False Self", but the dynamics are prevalent. Susan was a 16-year-old female who was continually in trouble in school. Her father was abusive to her and her mother As a result, Susan took out her anger against her father by fighting young men in her class.

Susan was suspended numerous times and threatened with expulsion from school. Because of her reputation, she was given the nickname "Fight." After a particular fight where she hurt a young man in her class, Susan was sent to the Adolescent Court Referral Program for troubled teens. Based on a carrot/stick approach, if the teen took advantage of the counselling program, their legal issues would be forgiven. But if they failed to attend, their legal charges would be upheld. Because of Fight's history, the therapists and program staff felt pessimistic about her success in the program.

Susan's therapist was Dr. Deannie Fountain, a skilled adolescent therapist who has helped numerous teenagers with troubled histories. Dr. Deannie took a special interest in Susan. After doing a thorough history and developing a treatment plan to impact Susan's behavior, Dr. Deannie held a special conference with her. Looking Susan in the face, Dr. Deannie told her she would no longer be referred to as "Fight" in the program. She would be called "Miss Susan" and would be treated as a young lady who is respected by the staff and others in the program. Surprised, Susan was shocked because she had never been treated with loving support and respect. Dr. Deannie told her that she would not be viewed as someone who is angry and wanted to fight boys, but seen as a young girl who was deeply hurt by her father. Dr. Deannie was making the perceptual shift by seeing Susan as a hurt young girl appealing for love. Looking Susan in the face, Dr. Deannie said in a loving voice, "Miss Susan, I love you. I want you to remember me by seeing me smiling at you and saying I love and respect you. When you feel threatened by boys in your class, instead of fighting, stop and remember that I love you. And you will not have to fight."

In the program Susan came to accept Dr. Deannie's love and approval. She calmed down, had a positive attitude, and participated fully in the program. The staff realized Susan was working hard to make changes in her life. After completing the program successfully, Susan was able to return to school. The first few weeks went smoothly. But one Friday, a young boy in her class teased her and threatened her. Picking up a chair, Susan threatened to throw it at him. Observing the interaction through a slightly opened door, the headmaster was deeply disappointed. To his amazement, as she was about to throw the chair at the boy, Susan put the chair down. The headmaster came in the room and asked Susan, "What happened?" Susan told him, "I was about to throw the chair at the boy when I saw Dr. Deannie's face smiling at me and saying, "I love you, you don't have to fight anymore." Feeling better, I put the chair down." The good news is that Susan went on to graduate and now has a job.

I need to stress how the false self weaves its way through our whole personality and life experience and will do anything to help us defend against pain. The false self will negotiate even our own death or the death of another to make us feel better. But it is an illusion with no substance. It aims to provide emotional programs for happiness to counteract our sense of abandonment, rejection, and humiliation; but in the end it seduces us, exploits us, abandons us, and even destroys us. The Bible reminds us that "there is a way that seems right to a man, but in the end it leads to death" (Proverbs 14:12).

The false self is only diminished when we feel loved. Whenever we feel safe in the love of someone who really cares for us, we let down our defenses and open up to face our deeper selves, our true selves. Psychotherapy involves grieving or working through our childhood trauma. As we penetrate the defenses of the false self, and expose our real, hurt selves, this in turn leads us to our deeper selves. Spirituality involves responding to God's invitation to move beyond our false selves to our true selves in God.

According to the Apostle Paul:

"I [my false self] have been crucified with Christ and I no longer live, but Christ lives in me. The life I [the true self] live in the body, I live by faith in the Son of God, who loved me and gave himself for me." (Galatians 2:20)

Christ put it this way: "If anyone would come after me, he must deny himself and take up his cross and follow me" (Mark 8:34). As we work to transform our false selves, we will face our pain [our cross], but Christ is with us every step of the way.

The concept of the False Self has long been recognized by followers of Christ. Saint Bernard of Clairvaux, a 12th century mystic of the Cistercian order, described the concept of the false self. In the twentieth century, Thomas Merton and Henri Nouwen have discussed it. The writings of Father Thomas Keating and Basil Pennington have brought it into further prominence. More recently, the concept of the false self provides a bridge between psychiatry and theology. James Masterson, a psychoanalyst, has written extensively about the false self, and his work has helped to develop insight into the nature of a person from a psychological perspective. From the work of Keating, Pennington, Merton, and Nouwen I have gained many insights in my own psychiatric practice.

As I travel along my own spiritual journey, I have learned that only when I feel safe with God do I truly feel safe with myself. In other words, to really know God is to know oneself. As we look for a deeper understanding of ourselves, we move into the foundation of our being. Knowing God allows us, like the prodigal, to run to the caring, compassionate father so beautifully depicted in the parable of the Prodigal Son (Luke 15:11-32) The father receives us, asking no questions, allowing us to trust ourselves to his care. As we open to our true selves, we come to realize that our own woundedness is also a source for the healing power of God through ourselves to others.

REFERENCES

1 Frederick Buechner, *Telling Secrets* (San Francisco: Harper/SanFrancisco, 1991), 45.
2 James Masterson, *The Search for the Real Self* (New York: Free Press, 1988) 53.
3 Brennan Manning, *Abba's Child: The Cry of the Heart for Intimate Belonging* (Colorado Springs, Colorado: Navpress, 1994), 51.
4 Thomas Merton, *Seeds of Contemplation* (New York: New Directions, 1949), 28.

CHAPTER 6
The Still Point: The Healing Of Silence

"Be still and know that I am God..." (Psalm 46:10)

IT WAS A BEAUTIFUL MORNING IN the Bahamas, July 5, 2012. The sea was calm and a light, balmy breeze was blowing. All was quiet and still. Rising early, we helped my wife Vicki and her sister Kathy prepare for their special journey to Staniel Cay to dive at the famous James Bond underwater Thunderball cave in the Exumas. This had been a long-term wish of Kathy who lives on a farm in Virginia and Vicki was going along with her. The small plane left Nassau for Staniel Cay at 7:00 am. I went to my office and sat in contemplation and prayer as I thought about the events for the day. Around 9:30 am, the receptionist called to say that my brother-in-law, Douglas Kay, was on the line. Doug, usually calm and collected, was upset as he told me that he had just received news from his wife Kathy that Vicki, my wife, had drowned. Shocked and stunned, I hung the phone up and sat quietly in my office chair as many thoughts and questions cascaded through my mind. 'How could this happen? I just dropped them to the airport two hours ago!' There was such an excitement in the home about their trip. Still shocked, I continued to sit in the silence which turned to a deep stillness.

We tried to reach the government medical clinic at Staniel Cay but our efforts were in vain. My heart sunk as I thought of the worst case scenario. Even if she could be revived, Vicki, my loving wife and mother of my children, would be brain dead. I decided to drive home. Although my home is close to my office, the drive seemed long, torturous and extremely difficult. Entering the house, I felt nervous, anxious, fearful and sorrowful. Going immediately to our bedroom, I sat down in my favorite chair. Looking at our bed, my wife's closet...I just couldn't believe it. By now, more than a half an hour had elapsed. I had images of me pushing my wife along in a wheelchair if she was brain dead. I feared Vicki was gone and I just couldn't believe there could be such an abrupt end to her life and our life together. My children, Marie and David, appeared and apparently, unknown to me, I was groaning deeply. In my heart however, I was praying for a miracle.

My office manager called to say that she was able to reach the clinic but from what she was told, things did not look good. The nurse, who was busy with resuscitation, said she would call back in a few minutes. In a short but what seemed like a long wait, I just sat silently in the stillness. Eventually, the phone rang. The nurse shared with me that Vicki was found floating face down by an American tourist who jumped off his motorboat after hearing Kathy scream for help. Joined by a friend, they pulled Vicki's body out of the water on top of the cave entrance where Kathy pleaded with God and screamed, "Don't take my sister! Don't take my sister!" Finally, the two young men were able to put her in a little boat and head to shore. They continued trying CPR to resuscitate her but as time went by, it appeared more hopeless. Arriving at the beach, she was transported to the clinic in an open truck. The nurse said they had given her oxygen and continued resuscitation but there was little to no response. My heart sunk because I felt that hoping against hope, she would be revived. The nurse said, 'Excuse me, Dr. Allen, I'll call you right back'. Again, the moment of waiting in the quietness and stillness was heart-wrenching. Finally the nurse called and said that an anesthesiologist from California who was on holiday noticed the flurry of activity at the clinic and came in. As they continued the resuscitation efforts, he asked the nurse to give her an injection of the diuretic Lasix, even though it didn't look good. The nurse told me that before she gave up, she wanted to try one last thing. She said she would put the phone to Vicki's ear. I shouted 'Vicki, this is David and I love you'. At that point, the nurse said 'wait Dr. Allen, I think I noticed a breath'. I waited and then there was silence. The nurse came back on the phone and said, 'I think she's starting to breathe very lightly'. I felt relieved but was afraid to let myself feel positive. The nurse asked me to organize an air ambulance so that Vicki could be taken to Nassau as soon as possible. With the help of my office manager, this was organized.

Within the hour, Vicki arrived in Nassau. We waited expectantly and nervously for the ambulance to arrive at the hospital. While waiting, the housekeeper called saying that Kathy had called the house from the plane and said that Vicki was relapsing and she wasn't sure she would make it. I felt terrible and faint, but in prayerful meditation, in silence and stillness, I waited and hoped against hope. Finally, the ambulance arrived and Vicki was taken into the hospital. She was seen by two leading medical consultants, a neurologist and a cardiovascular surgeon. After examining her, they came out and said felt she would be fine. I was shaken but relieved. She spent the night in the Intensive Care Unit.

The next morning I received a call from the American tourist and his friend who rescued my wife. They asked me if they could come to Nassau to visit my wife in the hospital. They shared with me that they were still in shock because they were sure that she was dead. They felt that her survival was a miracle. When they arrived in Nassau, they called me and I drove to Paradise Island to pick them up. I was surrounded by their relatives and friends from California who kept shouting 'miracle, miracle, miracle'. At the hospital, they reiterated their experience in finding Vicki face down and the difficult time they had dragging her dead weight out of the current onto the jagged rocks of the reef. Arriving at Vicki's bed, they were surprised to see her doing so well. Shaking their heads, they just said, "Mrs. Allen, we've never seen anything like this in our life". They went on to say that they had come from a loving family but they don't believe in God. However, this experience showed them the importance of living in love and not anger. They said that after hearing that Vicki was alive, they talked together with their family and friends and shared what they believe was their first involvement in a miracle. After some hesitation, they asked Vicki if they could look at her back because they said they had to pull the dead weight of her body on the prickly, jagged coral reef which tore up her bathing suit. To their surprise, when we showed them my wife's back, there were no scratches, cuts or bruises. Looking at me in consternation and surprise, they said 'This had to be a miracle'. We all remained silent and still. Of course, I gave thanks for the goodness of God's grace toward my wife, myself and my family. Returning home, I spent some time in contemplative prayer and was led to a scripture 2 Corinthians 1:9 "indeed we had the sentence of death within ourselves in order that we should not trust in ourselves, but in God who raises the dead." I found myself sitting in silence. In some strange sense, my wife was saved but in a deeper way, I came to know a little bit about the healing of silence. I also came to understand Romans 8:26-27 when Paul writes that 'the Holy Spirit prays in us with groans or words that cannot be uttered'. I was reminded by what my daughter said when she saw me sitting in my room. She said all she could hear was a deep, repeated groaning coming from me. In spite of my helplessness, another force was at work in the situation. I now understand the meaning of Exodus 14:14, when God tells the Israelites, "I will fight for you if only you would be still".

Silence and Stillness

> The endless cycle of idea and action,
> Endless invention, endless experiment,
> Brings knowledge of motion, but not of stillness,
> Knowledge of speech, but not of silence.[1]
>
> -T.S. Eliot

Silence is a disappearing commodity in our present world. A cacophony of noise assaults us everywhere...in the home, restaurants and even the church. Most sadly, the noise of our obsessive, continuous internal dialogue harasses our mind and neutralizes the possibilities of any harmonious joy in our hearts. Father Henry Nouwen, who I was blessed to know at Yale Divinity School, was a friend who taught me about the value and healing of silence. Nouwen bemoaned the fact that in our modern lives, the noise in our head drowns the healing voices of the singing of angels. He often reminded me, "It's hard to live without hearing the singing of angels". Howard Thurman, an African-American Theologian Philosopher, said that we should always be able to hear the angels sing. He reminds us

> There must be always remaining in everyone's life some place for the singing of angels, some place for that which in itself is breathlessly beautiful, and by an inherent prerogative, throws all the rest of life into a new and creative relatedness, something that gathers up in itself all the freshets of experience from drab and commonplace areas of living and glows in one bright white light of penetrating beauty and meaning – then passes. (Thurman, 1951)

Soren Kierkegaard, the nineteenth century Danish philosopher and theologian, warned us that 'the present state of the world, the whole of life, is diseased. Create silence. Bring men (people) to silence. The words of God cannot be heard in a noisy world'.[2] Kierkegaard's admonition is validated by the ancient prophets, 'Be silent before the Lord' (Zechariah 2:3). 'The Lord is in this Holy Temple, let all the earth be silent before Him' (Habakkuk 2:20). John of the cross says that silence is the language of God, and it is only in silence we hear it. Ammonas, the disciple of Anthony, reminds us:

> Behold, my beloved, I have shown you the power of silence, how thoroughly it heals and how fully pleasing it is to God. Wherefore, I have written to you, to show yourselves strong in this work you have undertaken, so that you may know that it is by silence that the saints grew, and that it was because of silence that the power of God dwelt in them, because of silence that the mysteries of God were known to them.[3]

A room is silent. It has no choice. But a room where people choose not to speak or move is still. Silence is a given, the silence of stillness is a gift. Exterior silence leads to interior silence. Interior silence opens us to stillness. Stillness opens us to infinite spaciousness, the united field of consciousness where we experience the interconnectedness of all things and learn that our life is not a puzzle to be solved but a mystery to unfurl. According to Eckhart Tolle,

> "When we lose touch with stillness, we lose touch with ourselves. When we lose touch with ourselves, we lose touch with the world."[4]

In the stillness of silence, our False Self melts and we discover the authenticity of our True Self. It is in this stillness and spaciousness that King David could say 'Thou prepares a table before me, even in the presence of mine enemies' (Psalm 23:5). In stillness, we experience the Eternal Mystery and open to the love which never lets us go and the face which never turns away. The prophet Zephaniah explains this when he said 'the Lord is with you. He delights in you and he quiets you (gives you the stillness of spaciousness) with His love. He rejoices over you with singing' (Zephaniah 3:17).

According to Thomas Merton,

> Not only does silence give us a chance to understand ourselves better, to get a truer and more balanced perspective on our own life in relation to the lives of others: silence makes us whole if we let it. Silence helps to draw together the scattered and dissipated energies of a fragmented existence. It helps us to concentrate on a purpose that really corresponds not only to the deeper needs of our own being but also to God's intentions for us.[5]

God is love and, in His presence, our defensive Ego Addictive False Self and shame melt away revealing our true identity as the beloved of God. The stillness of silence is not the absence of noise, but the absence of our Ego False Self blocking us from our true essence.

A day of Silence
Can be a pilgrimage in itself.

A day of Silence
Can help you listen
To the Soul play
Its marvelous lute and drum.

Is not most talking
A crazed defense of a crumbling fort?

I thought we came here
To surrender in Silence,

To yield to Light and Happiness,

To Dance within
In celebration of Love's Victory!
-Hafiz, "Silence"[6]

Stillness is the awareness or the unified field of consciousness in which life is not a puzzle to be solved, but a mystery to be unfurled. We do not have a thought or see a flower. We are the awareness in which the thought is had and the flower is seen. There is an intimate connection between *being* and the *now*. The *now* is not only what is happening at the moment, but it is the unified field of knowledge in which life happens. Unfortunately, the constraints of humanity limit fully understanding the *now*:

> "*Now* we see but a poor reflection as in a mirror; then we shall see face to face. I know in part; then I shall know fully, even as I am fully known." (1 Corinthians 13:12)

Transcending intellectual, psychological and cultural forms, stillness is formless. Jesus said, "The words I have spoken to you are spirit and they are life" (John 6:63). Stillness is related to the presence of the *Eternal Being*. "Be still and know that I am God" (Psalm 46:10). "In quietness [stillness] and confidence will be your strength" (Isaiah 31:15). "He leadeth me beside still waters" (Psalm 23:2 KJV).

Be still my soul
The Lord is on thy side
Bear patiently
The cross of grief or pain.

Leave to thy God
To order and provide;
In every change
He faithful will remain.
Katharina Von Schlegel, "Be Still My Soul"

Stillness is the Gap Between Stimulus and Response

Labeling, naming or interpreting before we really see, destroys the essence of what is seen. The sea becomes a body of salt water; the rose becomes a piece of vegetable matter; mountains become mounds of dirt and rock. Unable to adequately express the essence of reality, we label the things as though to point at them. My mentor, the late Dr. Gerald May, used to say, "Pointing at a tree is not the tree!"

The main thing is, knowing how to see.
To see without starting to think,
To see when you see,
And not to think when you see...
Thomas Merton [7]

In our anxiety-laden culture with its time pressures, stillness evades us. Almost before seeing we start to label. As a result, we are "ever hearing, but never understanding; ever seeing, but never perceiving" (Isaiah 6:9). How can we look at the Bahamian sea with all its myriad colors and not be grasped by its beauty? Between seeing and naming, between hearing and interpretation, is stillness. The longer we cultivate the gap between stimulus and response, the deeper the stillness, being and presence. This is the essence of contemplation: being in the very presence of God.

Losing our true human connectedness, we create a world of bland familiarity and distance. As a result, parents no longer see children; husbands are not present to wives and vice versa and friendships become shallow. No longer grasped by awe, beauty and mystery, we create a world where strangers walk as friends and friends as strangers. Stillness means taking time to see before thinking, hearing or interpreting. As Georgia O'Keefe says. "Still—in a way--nobody sees a flower--really—it is so small—we haven't time—and to see takes time, like to have a friend takes time."

Faith starts with awe and begins with a mixture of wonder and fear we all feel toward mystery (Cox, 2009). But awe only becomes faith when it gives some meaning to the mystery. Novelist Flannery O'Conner claims that mystery is a great embarrassment to the modern mind. Awe and mystery are basic and universal human emotions. In 1917, Rudolf Otto, a German scholar, published a book called the *Das Heilige*, which was translated in English as *The Idea of the Holy*. The stillness of silence generates a deep sense of awe and mystery which opens us to the Holy Other. "Be still and know that I am God" (Psalm 46:10). The Apostle Paul states "great is the mystery of godliness" (1 Timothy 3:16). As we open ourselves to the depth, awe and mystery of silence and stillness, simultaneously, we open ourselves to the experience of faith, which is the substance of things hoped for, the evidence of things not seen (Hebrews 11:1). The proof of this faith is the expression of our love to God and our commitment to our fellow human beings.

Stillness is *knowing* and *being known*. Turning doubt to faith and fear to love, the silence of stillness instills courage making our weak legs strong. When the priest Zachariah was told that his wife would have a baby in her old age and his name was to be John, he scoffed in unbelief. God shut Zachariah's mouth to get his attention by introducing him to the silence of stillness. When the child was born, in the transformation from unbelief to enlightenment, Zachariah wrote, "His name is to be called John" (Luke 1:13).

Deep listening always involves the silence of stillness in acceptance and obedience. The word stillness is derived from the same Latin root *audiens* which means to listen intently. The silence of stillness allows us to listen, obey and follow the voice of love in our life. "Holy, holy, holy, Lord God Almighty, heaven and earth are filled with His glory" (Isaiah 6:6).

On the other hand, the word *absurd* is derived from the Latin word *absurdis* meaning *deafness*. Life is absurd because we become deaf to the meaning and beauty of life. Without the silence of stillness, the voice of love is faint, and it is difficult for us to appreciate the awareness of God's presence.

Dr. Rob Norris, my former pastor and a respected theologian, wrote concerning the deeper meaning of stillness:

> "There are times when, like the Apostle Paul, [we] can see neither sun nor stars and life seems beset with tempests. Then there is only one thing [we] can do and only one way forward. Reason cannot help; past experiences offer no light. Even prayer brings only limited consolation; then [we] must put [our] soul in one position and keep it there. [We] must stay [our] soul upon the Lord; and come what may – winds, waves, thunder and lightning – no matter what, [we] must lash [ourselves] to the helm, and hold fast [our] confidence in God's faithfulness, His covenant engagement, His everlasting love in Christ Jesus."

Resting in God involves the inward silence of stillness in which He calls us gently and quietly, saying,

> "Come to me, you who labor and are overburdened and I will give you rest. Shoulder my yoke and learn from me, for I am gentle and humble in heart and you will find rest for your soul, my yoke is easy and my burden light" (Matthew 11:28-29)

Life Experience

In my journey of Psychiatry in the U.K., Africa, South America, U.S.A. and now back in the Bahamas, the light and healing of the Still Point is a powerful source, refurbishment and courage through God's eternal grace and spirit. During experiences which challenged my life and love,

I was comforted by the hope and presence of the Eternal Spirit. I've come to realize that in the deeper meaning of life, non-dualism transcends the destructive dualism of our Ego False Self.

This means learning to recognize that my adequate and shame parts are always together and cannot be separated. I have my strengths and weaknesses and they are one. It counteracts the dualistic concept that we split off our inadequacy and project it on to others, giving us a sense of self-righteousness and superiority. But this is pure hypocrisy, because there is no righteous or totally together person. All of us are wounded and carry with us our strengths and woundedness, our victories and failures, our virtues and sins. This dynamic counteracts the common defense mechanism used by our shame False Self, in which we seek to scapegoat others by splitting off our shame parts and projecting them on to others so that we can feel better about ourselves in a form of what I call 'sadistic scapegoating'.

Similarly, we can also split off our adequate selves and project them on to others, feeling sorry for ourselves and living a martyr complex. This too is narcissistic, destructive and a way of expressing a false humility. The fact is, the cross reminds us that the vertical and horizontal poles are together and cannot be separated. This gives us a sense of peace, hope and courage. Thus, I am who I am with all my strengths and weaknesses, and you are you with all your strengths and weaknesses. It is only as we come together to accept this reality, we can experience the healing and hope of true community.

The Still Point and the Family Meetings

During the Family meeting process, the sharing of the pain of such tragedies as murder, violent crime, rape, abuse or the ravages of natural disasters, have led us to experience the power of the Still Point. One quiet Wednesday afternoon, the East Street Family group process was moving along, with people expressing their trials and challenges. Then a young lady shared that her boyfriend who she had just seen, was murdered. Crying, she also shared that her brother was murdered. As we tried to digest the pain of this quiet, reserved person's story of violence and fear, another lady shared. She said that in the recent Hurricane Matthew, the roof of her house blew off. Terrified, her four children, ranging from 11-15 years, huddled around her. In their own way, they sought to protect the mother they loved while at the same time, sheltering themselves through her love. The mother shared that she received the news the next day that her eldest son, who was present with her during the storm, was shot and murdered in a nearby empty building. At that point, the atmosphere was filled with sadness, fear and angst.

Recognizing the powerful state of distress and hopelessness, I called for the Holy Moment. In the Family, when the Holy Moment is called for, it means that we are at the Still Point, where the painful experience of our chronological existence is being met by the hope and triumph of the Eternal Love. In response to the palpable pain, some people were crying, others praying and meditating, while many were just in awe and overwhelmed. At the Still Point, the miracle is that the silence of stillness is able to absorb the pain and fear more than any words can express. In a contemplative moment, we take a long, loving look at the reality of the unseen grace, peace and healing which descends on the room. Producing a sense of oneness, calmness comes over the room, radiating the development of a healing community, where the group becomes one. We are comforted with knowing 'God will not ignore the broken hearted or crush the overwhelmed spirit' (Psalm 34:18). At the appropriate time, when the group seems settled, a short verbal prayer is said. As the group ended, we sang the spiritual

> "Sometimes I feel like a motherless child, a long way from home. Sometimes I feel like a fatherless child, a long way from home."

In a mysterious way, we are comforted by the recognition that God is our home, giving us a sense of peace and renewed hope to continue on.

The Still Point

> At the still point of the turning world. Neither flesh nor fleshless;
> Neither from nor towards; at the still point, there the dance is,
> But neither arrest nor movement. And do not call it fixity,
> Where past and future are gathered. Neither movement from nor towards,
> Neither ascent nor decline. Except for the point, the still point,
> There would be no dance, and there is only the dance.
>
> *Burnt Norton* T.S. Eliot

In the mystery of the stillness of silence we experience the Still Point where our chronological daily experience in this vail of tears is intercepted by Kairos, the eternal time, in which the mystery of love unfolds. At a talk given at New Providence Community Church in Nassau, I said that the cross represents the point where human struggles and limitations are intercepted with the joy of eternity, culminating in the hope and triumph of the resurrection. The cross, a symbol of our spiritual journey, is our anchor to help us overcome the woundedness and tragedy of life. The cross is our eternal hope.

The vertical pole of the cross, signifying the love of God, is with us in sickness or health, in life or death and time or eternity. At the intersection of the vertical and the horizontal poles of the cross, pain is met with joy, despair, hope and death, life. In my clinical and research work in the drug world, I was deeply challenged by the pathos, cruelty and sometimes hopelessness of life. But the greatest motivating factor for persevering and struggling in those difficult moments was seeing life through the lens at the intersection of the horizontal and vertical poles of the cross (the Still Point).

To my surprise, Tyrone Ferguson, an internationally known sculptor who was present at the lecture, made a steel cross with a circular opening at the intersection of the horizontal and vertical poles and delivered it to my house weeks later. I have been particularly blessed during my meditation and contemplation of looking through that opening at the intersection of the cross, into the beautiful, blue ocean, the glorious clouds and the clear blue sky above. The Still Point is where I find myself, but in a deeper way, experience the Presence of God. "Heavenly Father, thank you for the cross. It is where I find my joy and shame but where I also hear the angels sing, bringing hope, courage and faith beyond fear".

"Cross" by Tyrone Ferguson

Forgiveness

The mere thought of you
Fills my heart with anger
And cold shivers of hurt
As fresh today as when
I first experienced them

And In the recesses of my mind
I wonder if you feel the pain I feel
Or whether I am but a speck
Of insignificance on your horizon

And so I retreat in fear
For the pain of abandonment
Is beyond endurance
And I am left to hold onto my rage
Or feel the dreaded, empty nothingness of my existence

And there I stay
For a week, a month, a year, a lifetime
Unable and perhaps unwilling to seek redemption
And release from such needless suffering

And there I will languish
Unless...unless...unless
I seek forgiveness
Not mere platitude
But soul-searching, gut wrenching acknowledgement
That I am a prisoner in my own house
You are not the enemy
The enemy is the doubt I harbor about my worth which lies buried in my bosom
At the very core of my soul

I have given you the most precious gift I have
My own healing power
And it is painful to realize

That this gift belongs to no one else
It is mine!

And with the gift of my own value and worth
I can separate myself from you
And be complete
Just as I am

And it is this wholeness
Which allows me to be free
To see you as you are
And ask that you be accountable for your deeds
Rather for my worth and well being
As I will be accountable for mine

I know now, I have a choice
If I accept my gift of autonomy and authenticity
I need not be doomed
To be forever vulnerable to life's vagaries
I can finally accept life's invitation to grow

And if by chance we are able to meet anew
And honor our hurts
In the spirit of acknowledgement and forgiveness
Then we may be blessed to feel
The full measure of our being
And resume our journey secure in our discovery that
We can only be who we are

And if such a meeting is no longer possible
I need not despair
I am still free
To settle our accounts
Within the sinew of my bones
And reclaim the raw awesome power of my own true being

Richard U. Rosenfield
April 23, 1997

REFERENCES

1 Eliot, T.S., "Two Chorus from the Rock". *The Wasteland and Other Poems* (Toronto: Harcourt Brace Jovanovich, 1962). 81.

2 Spoto, Donald. *In Silence: Why We Pray.* (Boston: Penguin 2005), 193

3 Spoto, Donald. *In Silence: Why We Pray.* (Boston: Penguin, 2005), 190

4 Tolle, Eckhart . Stillness Speaks (Novat, CA: New World Library, 2003), 3

5 Merton, Thomas. Contemplative Prayer (New York: Image, 1971), 42.

6 Hafiz, "Silence" *I Heard God Laughing: Poems of Hope and Joy.* (Boston: Penguin, 2006), 67.

7 Shannon, William H., *Seeds of Peace: Contemplation and Nonviolence.* (NY: Crossroad Publishing Co, 1996), 53.

CHAPTER 7

Discovery: The Freedom To Be Fully You

"The real voyage of discovery consists not in seeking new landscapes, but in having new eyes."
Marcel Proust

THE BAHAMAS EXPERIENCED A COUNTRYWIDE COCAINE epidemic in the 1980s. During that period, I tried to treat a young 16-year old teenager from Lyford Cay who had become addicted to crack cocaine.

Descended from a wealthy family, André Chappelle had everything going for him, but he said, "When I tried cocaine, it was the key that fit my lock." After a number of attempts at recovery, André would do well for a few months and then relapse. Despite treatment at some of the best rehabilitation centers around the world, André's addiction morphed into a chronic, relapsing pattern. During periods of sobriety, he worked on his recovery. He was creative and blessed many people with his talents, insights and mechanical gifts. Even while living on the streets of Nassau, he helped students at the College of the Bahamas with their homework and counseled persons about life. Instead of attaining the positive reinforcement of the high, as a chronic addict, he was now seeking the negative reinforcement of the drug to block the descent into the paralyzing depths of cocaine depression, anhedonia and despair. André succumbed to homelessness and vagrancy. He was beaten severely on numerous occasions.

In spite of his dehumanized state, André comforted and encouraged many persons, including myself. Sitting with him, I remember him saying to me, "Doc, I know you tried to help. But you did not fail. It's just that I loved cocaine more. It is my life". The downward spiral of his life continued for more than 20 years as he became enveloped with shame and despair. But in spite of his grotesque appearance, André was polite and willing to lend a helping hand. He was particularly helpful to ladies in trouble. For example, he sought to protect them if they were attacked, changed their flat tires and in some cases, even repaired their cars. He also acted as a volunteer security guard for a number of businesses, warning staff of potential threats.

In this state of chaotic degradation, André said that he would never discuss two things: his faith in God and his family. Asked to explain, André said he came from a religious family that helped him to develop a strong faith in God. Even though he failed miserably because of his addiction, he believed that Jesus loved him and would eventually deliver him. Secondly, when asked about his family, he became silent and tears streamed down his face. Looking at me deeply hurt, André said, "My mother couldn't take my addiction and she died of a broken heart." He said his father was extremely disappointed in him because he failed to take advantage of many opportunities afforded him. Finally, unable to cope with the situation, his father left the homestead, moved to another country and shortly afterwards, passed away. While talking to me, André suddenly stopped. Looking through his unkempt beard and almost hidden face, he said, "Not too good, aye? That's a lot for a man to carry! The only thing that eases this deep pain and shame is a good hit of cocaine." Feeling sad and helpless, he looked at me and said, "You got it now Doc?" I replied "I'm trying to understand".

André's story is a metaphor of my own country. When I was appointed head of the National Task Force on Drugs in the 1980s, I was shocked at the ravages and violent destruction of human life that occurred in the national crack cocaine epidemic. As a result, many members of my family, friends and fellow citizens were deeply hurt and destroyed. I found myself descending into a deep sense of despair, but found solace through friends and academic colleagues who joined me from other countries to assist in the war on drugs. The reality is that André, like many others in my journey, was able to recover from cocaine addiction. But many times they were so miserable and depressed, they relapsed. There was something lacking. I came to believe that the treatment of addiction must go beyond recovery (stopping the use of the drug) to move to Discovery.

Discovery

Discovery is the challenging journey from being a victim of our Shame False Self, based in fear and anger, to our Authentic True Self based in love and gratitude. Moving beyond recovery, Discovery involves breaking apart the hardened shell of repressed hurt and shame of our false self to expose the Immortal treasure of our redeemed True Self made in the image of God who is love. As we release our shame and woundedness, we experience our authentic self in love. However, according to the Apostle Paul, "We have this treasure in earthen vessels that the power may be of God and not of us" (2 Corinthians 4:7). Yet our being, this Immortal Treasure, gives us meaning. Dignity. Identity and value (MDIV), a God given purpose for each of our lives.

The child at birth contains the immortal treasure (the spirit and the soul) which is the seed of his/her Authentic True Self. According to the Contemplative Discovery Pathway Theory, shame and its defensive False Self, blocks and inhibits our journey towards authenticity. Shame (Self Hatred Aimed at M.E) is a deep, internal, painful feeling resulting from the shattering of our most cherished dreams and expectations. Our basic instinctual needs for safety (survival/security), connection (affection/esteem) and empowerment (power/control) are not just the results of our being hardwired for love with cravings for self-esteem, intimacy and respect, but are the very substance of all our dreams in life. When a dream shatters, a lie is born. The shattering of the dream of safety leads to feelings of abandonment accompanied by the lies "I am not enough. I am hopeless" .Similarly, the shattering of the dream of connection leads to deep feelings of rejection, accompanied by the lies "I am unlovable. No one wants me." When dreams of empowerment shatter, the resulting humiliation gives birth to the lies, "I am a failure. I am helpless."

Discovery of our True Self.

Discovery has seven major components: (1) taking time out, (2) awareness (3) confrontation, (4) surrender, (5) commitment, (6) vocation and (7) facing death. These stages do not necessarily occur in sequence and they repeat themselves over and over again in the journey of the Discovery of our authentic freedom.

1. Time Out

Discovery involves breaking the pattern of our life to take time out for reflection to think about our thoughts and feelings. In our busy lifestyle, this is not easy, but if we are too busy to take time out, we are just too busy. Taking time out requires intentionality. Contemplative mindfulness is helpful. As we allow ourselves to breathe deeply, we find ourselves opening to a contemplative atmosphere of being loved, accepted and nonjudgmental thinking. Time out allows us to make space to become present to our lives and to invite God to be the presence in our present.

On Christmas Eve 2009, Andre was all alone. He realized that his niece whom he had last seen as a baby was now 19 years old. As multiple thoughts cascaded through his mind, he was reminded that so much time had passed and so many opportunities had been lost. This shocked him into the awareness that he must come to grips with his life.

2. Awareness

Awareness is a deep sense of consciousness beyond the control of our body, thoughts or sense perceptions. It is the recognition that we are loved by the great 'I AM' We could never be outside the presence of God, but we can block the awareness of his presence by the False Self and its obstacles to authentic freedom.

Awareness, like contemplation, is a gift of God involving the transformation of Consciousness to open us to His unfailing love. In our experience, the person arrives at that point when their life is totally broken. They do not know what to do or where to go. They recognize the utter helplessness to deliver themselves the deep cry of their heart is simply, "Help!" Awareness may occur through psychotherapy, the tragedy of deep loss or a transcendental force of nature. A gentleman shared with me that he had to go through illness to learn stillness. Awareness may also occur through spiritual awakening by inspired sermons, readings, deep prayer and meditation and the serving of the poor. Awareness, though often prefigured by a piercing and terrifying loneliness, leads to a deep sense of solitude, where we are alone with the Alone. According to Henry Nouwen,

> "Solitude is the furnace of transformation... [It] is the place of the great struggle and the great encounter — the struggle against the compulsions of the false self, and the encounter with the loving God who offers himself as the substance of the new self" (Barton, 2004).

This solitude is often manifested by a deep sense of presence, being loved. Sometimes, there's a unitive experience of being at one with people and nature. It is experienced with vulnerability, which is translated into empathy with the pain of our own story and the story of others. As a result, we move from a sense of anger to compassion and from resentment to forgiveness. This numinous experience is described by some people as if they are being carried toward the light. The solitude invites external silence which leads to interior silence followed by stillness and spaciousness. The result of this is an overwhelming sense of gratitude resulting in the recognition of deep love and grace that is present in all aspects of life.

André Chappelle became aware that he was lost, which had a riveting effect on him. On Christmas Eve of 2009, he watched people going about their final preparations and he remembered his sense of isolation, degradation and failure. At 2:00 am Christmas Morning, he found himself lying in an empty parking lot of a fast food restaurant. He could not get out of his head the image of the 19 year old niece contrasted with the little baby he had seen when she was a few months old. Forced to take an inventory of his life, he remembered painful events such as when he was beaten for three hours with a baseball bat, left unconscious and his arm disfigured. He was stoned by children who would make fun of him. Many times his own family and friends rejected him because they could not cope with his degradation and vagrancy. On this particular morning, Andre said he experienced a deep, piercing loneliness that he had never felt before. He was shattered and totally hopeless. With tears in his eyes, he said he recognized, for the first time in his life, that he had come to the end of his rope. There was nowhere to go but into further destruction. Feeling lost and empty, he fell on his knees and begged God for help and forgiveness. In his own words, he said "Jesus showed up and said let's go." Andre said he knew at that point in time, that his addiction and vagrant life were over.

Appearing at the office of his family lawyer, he told her that he was finished and wanted to change his life. After giving him some money, she told him if he was serious, go get a haircut and come back to her office with two of the same pair of shoes. He told her 'I will' and did so. Within a few days, she made arrangements for his criminal records to be expunged and by the end of the week, he found himself at the airport going to visit his sister in America. Even though he had periodic cravings for cocaine, he said that he felt the inner presence of God gave him strength. He finally decided to return to Nassau, his home, because he felt that was the place of his mission. He spent some time living at Teen Challenge, working with a friend Eric Fox, where he helped others caught in addiction.

One day, Andre showed up at one of my Family meetings on Blue Hill Road. Looking well put together, in his right mind, he smiled when he saw me. I was shocked. He said 'Doc, what are you up to now?' I described to him the Family project and how it worked. He listened to people sharing their stories and became intensely involved. After the meeting, he asked me for the reading material and our publications describing the theory behind the Family. He read everything I wrote and really started to practice the Contemplative Discovery Pathway Theory. He claimed this had a powerful impact on his life and came at the right time. Being a mystic, he spent much time in silence, meditating. He lived a very sparse lifestyle, eating minimum food and leading a very contained life. As he and I grew closer, I began to see a powerful awareness of healing and spirituality radiating through his life. But I must admit, having spent so much time in the past trying to help him, I lacked faith, and in some sense, found myself waiting for the relapse. To my surprise, he kept chasing me, wanting to hear more and more about the Family and the theory. He would even come over to my house at night and present questions about the research and papers he had read. Eventually, André Chappelle became the essence of the CDPT. His story pierced the hearts of young and old, but in it all, there was a deep sense of mystery. It was impossible to be with him and not recognize the transcendent power of God that produced the change in his life.

After completing the Facilitator Training Course, he became a very competent facilitator in a number of groups and brought healing and hope to many persons who were in despair and had given up on their lives. His very appearance and presence in a group was a healing power. As one of the young men in prison said to him, "If you could heal and change, then there's hope for us all."

3. Confrontation

As we confront our shame and painful experiences, we often feel anxiety, fear and sadness manifested by a deep sense of grief. As we become aware of the deep hurt that operates through our life like a red, hot, pulsating electric wire, we recognize that to move from where we are, we have to let go of the past and open to the present. Sadly, many of our painful issues, though inflicted upon us, have their origin from some of our own narcissistic and self-destructive tendencies. As we become aware of this, there is a prevailing sense of sadness, regret and often foreboding. But at the same time we start to see things in a new light. This is Discovery, where we open to the vision of our True Self, not as we are, but as we could be.

As André came to understand the theory and attended more Family sessions, he said something that I'll never forget. He said 'awareness is important, but there's no healing unless we're willing to confront the shame and pain of our life. What we do not confront, we cannot conquer." He said his understanding of the Contemplative Discovery Pathway Theory is that there are two streams in life:

(a) The love story of forgiveness
(b) The hurt trail of shame and fear.

He went on to say our heart or psyche is like a sponge. In our younger years, it absorbs the love from our love story, but as life becomes more complex and we experience the woundedness of life, the sponge of our heart absorbs the hurt, shame and pain. This shame and pain clogs the sponge and prevents love from being further absorbed. As a result of this, many of our hearts are hurt and even though love surrounds us, we cannot appreciate it. André said the Family is simply a place where we learn to squeeze the sponge of our heart to release the shame and pain and make space for love. He particularly liked the metaphor of how it would be if we had not emptied our kitchen garbage for twenty years — the stench would be revolting! He said many of us live and die and have never emptied our heart or psyche of the hurt and wounds of a lifetime.

He said he had learned during his meditation and attending The Family sessions how to squeeze the sponge of his heart and release the pain and shame of his life.

4. Surrender (Letting Go)

The transition from the False Self to our True Authentic Self (involving intimacy and freedom) is a process of letting go, which sometimes occurs instantly but other times is an up and down prolonged process. The Bridges Transition Model (Bridges, 1995) is helpful in examining the stages of surrender. According to Bridges, surrender or letting go involves the following:

a. Disengagement from our previous lifestyle — we let go of our dependence on the temporal, external reality or form to open ourselves to the eternal, formlessness and joy of the inner life.
   "Therefore, we do not lose heart, but though our outer persona is disappearing, yet our inner persona is renewed daily...we look not at the things which are seen, but at the things which are not seen, for the things which are seen are temporal (form), but the things which are not seen are eternal (formlessness)." (2 Corinthians 4: 1618)

b. Dis-identification— as discussed previously, in our Shame False Self, our being, that is, the I am, instead of resting in the Eternal Love, becomes attached to our life situation. This becomes our predominant reality, where our 'I am' becomes what I feel, do, think, possess, etc. Surrender means breaking this identity to open up to our true being, the Imago Dei or Immortal Treasure which is in love and God.

c. Disenchantment — in our False Self, we are nurtured from our self-absorption, self-gratification (things, money, position etc.) and our ability to control our life.
   Surrender involves breaking free from the nurture of these temporal, transitory realities to rest in the freedom of our Authentic True Self based in love and gratitude. Thus, we are no longer nurtured by what we feel, think, do or possess, but rest in the freedom and dwelling of the great I AM.
   "He who dwells in the shelter of the Most High rests in the shadow of the Almighty." (Psalm 91:1)
   In this deep sense of peace, we are able to forgive those who have hurt us and ask forgiveness from those we have hurt.

d. Disorientation —as we go through the process of surrender, we experience anxiety and ambivalence as we endeavor to let go of the past to open up to the new reality of Discovery. This sense of disorientation is terrifying for so many of us that we withdraw from the process of letting go, preferring to live in the past.

As these four processes occur, we pass through what may be described as the 'zone of chaos'. It's like a trapeze artist waiting to take hold of a new baton. To grab the new baton, he has to go through the four stages and for a while, be stranded in midair (the zone of chaos) before grabbing the new baton and swinging to the new paradigm. This new paradigm, called the authentic intimacy and freedom of the True Self, involves four major components: love, humility, forgiveness and gratitude. These are accompanied by a new sense of freedom where we see and hear things differently. Some have called this "seeing with the third eye" or "hearing with the third ear". The first eye/ear being the physical reality, the second the cognitive / emotional (that is, causation or how to fix it) and the third eye/ear being the contemplative experience of communion, where there is a space between stimulus and experience. Instead of naming, categorizing or claiming, we look beyond thought and description and are grasped by the beauty and awe of the universe.

Surrender is a process, not an event. It involves letting go of the False Self with its fear and anger and opening to love, humility, forgiveness and gratitude of the True Self. Surrender also involves changing direction. That is, giving up the false programs of happiness of the False Self involving power, pleasure, position and possessions, to follow the dictates of unfailing love. Thus, the False Self and its restricted freedoms, relate to circumstantial happiness. The True Self, on the other hand, is based in joy, which is the internal transformation produced by love, manifested by authentic freedom to live.

André said that once he confronted the pain, he had to learn to surrender. He had to let it go. He said this is a process. Every time more pain came to consciousness, he had to keep letting go. Sometimes, this is very difficult and at times, he would feel somewhat disoriented. Other times, he would long for his old identity of being on the street, where he had no responsibility. He had to surrender afresh and let the thoughts go. André shared with me that as he began to squeeze his heart of the pain and surrender it, his faith in God became more vibrant. This renewed faith was manifested by a deep reality of God's love and also a heartfelt gratitude for his being spared through his years of tragic living. Perhaps the most revolutionary insight he gave me was that the same love he had for a class mate in the eighth grade, Kim, returned. As a result of that, they came together and were married. In talking with his wife Kim, she shared that in eighth grade, she also loved André and would write her name as 'Kim Chappelle'. André said his surprise was that the deep love he felt for her in eighth grade must have been present while he was homeless on the street. But his heart was blocked with pain, shame and addiction and he could not appreciate it. After surrendering his pain, he said the love for Kim came rushing back, like his love for God. This led to their marriage. André claimed that the love they experienced in those three years was the deepest love he had ever known in his life.

5. Commitment

Discovery requires a commitment to understand the deeper meanings of our life story.
This results in the release of the shame and pain hidden in our right brain and covered up by our addiction to logic, argument and naming. Life is wounded. In our sojourn in this vale of tears, we are often thrown back to grovel in the dust of our Shame False Self. But having experienced Discovery, we no longer stay anchored in our False Self. We continually seek to move in the per-

ceptual shift from the shackles of shame and fear to the freedom of love and gratitude. This requires a commitment to practice the psychological and spiritual disciplines, e.g. psychotherapy, contemplative mindfulness, prayer, study and meaningful actions of social justice. Commitment is a learned behavior that demands continuous, persistent practice, like playing the piano or being fluent in a foreign language. Discovery is a dynamic process involving the continual emptying or kenosis of our inner pain and shame to open to a deeper love with ourselves, others, God and the world. This is a revolutionary metanoia in which we move from our egocentricity or selfish heart to the transcendent experience of love, humility, forgiveness and gratitude. In so doing, we become a faithful missionary and student to understand our heart and inner life.

André was deeply committed. He spent much of his time studying and examining how the insights of the Contemplative Discovery Pathway Theory applied to himself! For example, in the midst of Hurricane Matthew which was passing through the Bahamas, André joined me at my office. I couldn't wait to spend time with him and share our mutual concerns and interests about our experience of meditation, spirituality and inner life. I welcomed him gladly. But, to my surprise, he immediately went into a back office and closed the door. I followed and sought to enter the room. Looking at me, André said "Doc, I love you but I need to be alone to meditate, read and pray". He implied he was missing fellowship with God and wanted to be alone with the Alone. I backed out of the room. I realized that André had a deep commitment to the Discovery of the eternal mystery of love which changed his life. But I also realized something else. In most of our discussion, we talked about moving from the Shame False Self to our Authentic True Self in love. But on that day, I became aware that André had moved beyond the True Self to experience the mystery and depth of the Contemplative Transcendent Self in God. This is the highest evolution of the human spirit involving gratitude and living a contemplative life in the presence of God. In a quiet and humble way, I realized that André walked with God.

Commitment to our journey to Discovery also involves community. André attended three Family groups a week and was active in developing the Discovery training program. As a result, he blessed many persons who came to hear him and learn about the miraculous change in his life. Referring to André, one lady told me 'When he speaks, he is a direct window into God". This touched me because even though she did not know him, she validated my own understanding of this friend whom I was close to yet in a deep sense, maybe did not fully know.

6. Vocation

Discovery opens us to our vocation to experience God's transcendent love for all life including persons, nature and things. But the vision of transcendent love is validated by commitment and action to the mission of that love in the world. The two poles of transcendent love, the vision and mission, are inseparable. The vision of love without the mission is an empty sentimentality divorced from reality. The mission of love without the vision is a prescription for burnout and frustration. Moses went to the mountaintop, but he had to go down the valley and serve the people. David was a man after God's own heart, but he had to struggle in being a missionary to his own family, particularly Absalom. Peter enjoyed being on the Mount of Transfiguration, but he had to come down and go through the painful journey of the crucifixion. And so we too may experience miraculous events of Discovery, but they are count as nothing if they do not lead to loving action.

As our shame and pain is released through Discovery, our being, the Immortal Treasure, is liberated from our precarious life situations. This opens us up to our vocation and life purpose to be co-creators with God of the world of goodness and beauty. For example, King David served God's purpose in his generation (Acts 13:36). Many of us have a career. But sadly, the busyness, noise and multiple distractions of our career often choke our vocation and purpose. Our vocation is not only expressed in action, but as Milton so poignantly wrote, "they also serve who only stand and wait" (When | Consider How My Life is Spent).

I spent my formative years at the old, classical University of St. Andrew's in Scotland. This was a meaningful experience because I met many older persons who mentored me and introduced me to the dynamics of the inner life. I remember an old man coming up to me after a church service saying. "Young man, God has more to do in you than through you." I have never forgotten this. It has been a powerful guide throughout my journey. Another example was a gentleman in Edinburgh who claimed he was offered a lucrative, international job where he would have to spend much time away from his family. He said this job was excellent for his career But it would be disastrous for his vocation. I was impressed when he said that through his prayer and meditation, he was led to say no to that job because he wanted to consolidate his vocation.

As I came to experience the miraculous revolution in André's life. I found him to be a man of contemplative solitude and meditation. He was very aware of his vocation to share his experience of God's love in all aspects of his life. For example. | remember him saying 'Let's start a Family in the prison'. | was totally confused by this because [did not know how the inmates would react. But following André's lead. We went to the prison. When the inmates saw him, they said 'Welcome home'. Apparently. André had been incarcerated five times. They had heard of me, but they did not know me. They felt as though André was one of them. As a result, our Prison Family group became one of the most cohesive Family groups in the program. The inmates call it 'The Free Your Mind Group®' because like Victor Frankl, they have experienced the freedom of choosing their attitude in spite of their circumstances. André introduced me to the inmates' art and suggested that we put their work on public display. With the agreement of the Minister of National Security, the first Family Inmate Art Show was held at New Providence Community Centre in May 2014. This was a tremendous success. The public loved the works of art and especially appreciated the handbags, which were sold out. It was very exciting to see the male and female inmates demonstrating the pride of showing their work, organizing the show and collecting the money. Thanks to André, the event was a success and had wide public appeal.

7. Facing Death

Discovery not only opens us to the challenges of life but enables us to face the reality of death. The experience of the Immortal Treasure of our being opens us to the gift of God's eternal spirit which ushers us victoriously through the Valley of the Shadow of Death. J.B. Phillips explained «...it is significant that Jesus Christ on more than one occasion is reported to have spoken of "eternal life" as being entered into now...The man who believes in the authenticity of

His message and puts his confidence in it already possesses the quality of "eternal life" (John 3:36, 5:24, 6:47 etc.). [Concerning] physical death, [it is] not merely an experience robbed of its terror, but an experience [that] does not exist at all. [Jesus said] "if a man keep my saying, he shall never see death" (John 8:51)...the meaning that Christ intended...was that death was a completely negligible experience to the man who had already begun to live life of the eternal quality" (Phillips, 1978).

After three years of a loving marriage and the creation of many meaningful friendships, André developed an inoperable, terminal carcinoma. This was a great shock to him because he said in his 25 years on the street, he never went to a doctor. This painful diagnosis was puzzling. I came to realize the evidence of André's authentic self in that he lived in a nondual reality. As I sat with him, he would vacillate from saying 'Doc, I have to beat this™ but also admitting that 'Maybe this is the end of the road'. I visited him daily. He taught me much about the dying process as I sat and listened to his wisdom. He said when you visit someone who is dying, always come to go because no matter how close you are to them, the dying person must make that journey alone. At nights, I became accustomed to him saying 'Okay Doc. it's time to go'. We had many conversations and arranged consultations with various doctors. One night, while visiting him, André, with tears in his eyes, said 'Doc, this is it. This film will soon end and this story will be over'. This was extremely painful to me because André had become a soul friend. He encouraged and supported me and did many things that I could not do. Right to the end, he kept thinking of ways to improve the Family program. For instance, he had found a new container box building which he felt we could use to develop our program for the challenged young boys who would eventually need a home. While dying, André worked on a lecture which he presented at the Family Facilitator Training Session on September 24™ 2016 (see Epilogue). He spent a lot of time preparing this lecture. During our drives on Sunday afternoons, he would question me to clarify and organize his understanding of the theory. My last time with him was the night before he died when we sat outside under the moonlight and the stars with the trees and flowers which he loved dearly.

André looked very regal and stately. Stopping the conversation abruptly, he said, "Doc, this is it. Goodbye. Don't stop the work of the Family because people need a place to squeeze the sponge of their heart, releasing their hurt and shame. There are few places in our society to do this. The gift of the Family to me was it gave me the opportunity to share the deep, complex and even controversial sides of the story of my life. In doing so, much shame, pain and ugliness was released. But this revealed the beauty and love that was there all along'.

André asked me to speak at his Memorial Service. He said he had no fear about death, but what struck me was when he admitted 'there are many unknowns'. He reminded me that the God who was with him in the pain and the chaos of addiction and the healing Discovery was the same God who was leading his journey through the Valley of the Shadow of Death. He then asked me to leave and advised that I take care of my family. The next morning, Saturday December 16™, 2016, I was called to his house. His wife told me André refused to eat. I went outside briefly and she called me back in. She said that André sat up in bed, raised his arms and mumbled some words which she did not understand. He slumped back in the bed and died. This was very moving to me because I believe André had the Beatific Vision in which he saw the life beyond with his Lord and was welcomed home by the angels. His favorite scripture verse was, "He who began a good work in you will perfect it until the day of Christ Jesus. "(Philippians 1:6)

Epilogue

The War for Peace Within Ourselves*

*"Peace is not the absence of war or struggle...
Peace is the absence of fear in the midst of our struggle."*
-André Chappelle

Introduction

As we search for peace in our daily lives, our own hidden fears and their partner, anger, become the triggers which prevent us from experiencing tranquility and peace.

In the turbulent and chaotic world which swarms about our daily lives, all we want is a little peace, just a little sliver of a taste, where for a moment we can set aside the baggage of our life and escape into a world without care or concern--a place where problems are suspended, reality is ignored and we are at peace in ourselves and the world. If only everybody else understood the unwritten rules and abided by our unspoken wishes, we could hold on to this peace. But unfortunately, the car in front of us didn't get the memo, and in an instant, this peace evaporates into a hot button some fool just pressed.

Addiction

Behind every form of addiction is the desire to attain a feeling. Some chase the high, some chase the low, many want to just escape being ourselves because it's all about changing how we feel or don't want to feel. We take an external substance or activity to change the way we feel internally. This pattern develops and the behavior becomes a habit and the habit becomes an addiction which determines our priorities.

Even behaviors are addictive. For example, the angry, aggressive co-worker rules the roost through intimidating, well-timed, selectively targeted and measured outbursts. Notice the word "measured". Control is the objective and becomes the addiction, rewarding us with feelings of insatiable dominance. Our fix must be satisfied. The brain constantly brings to our remembrance feelings of euphoric recall of the highs, but never the devastating, painful lows.

*This is a transcript of the last lecture given by André Chappelle to The Family Training Institute September 24, 2016, at New Providence Community Centre.

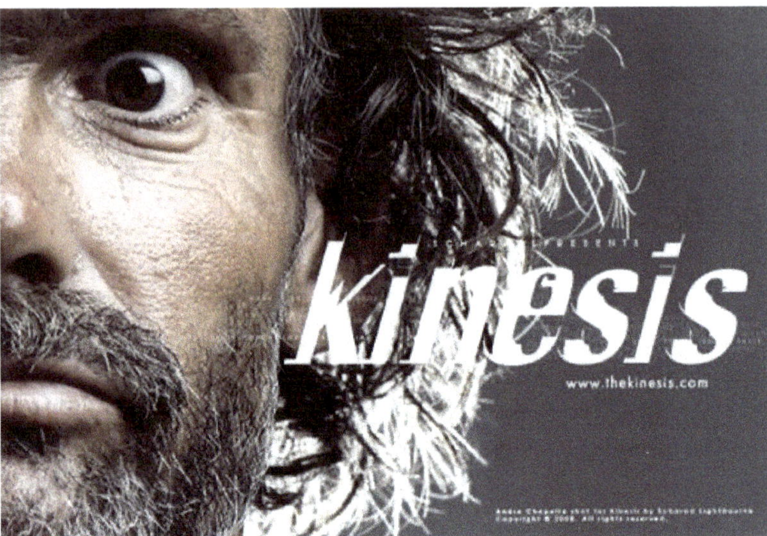

André Chappelle, on the streets Photo Credit: Scharad Lightbourne. Used with permission.

In that initial introduction to the reward of an external substance or activity, there is an overwhelming, euphoric pause of tranquility and peace. For this moment in time, all is well. It is for this euphoric recall that we will sacrifice anyone or anything to achieve again and again, where our head and our heart are in peaceful synchronization with each other. Temporarily devoid of fear, we are filled with nothing but hope at the possibilities of what could be. But the reality is, we find it unbearable to live with ourselves, so we need a break, a pause, a moment of peace, a moment of power, and our addiction provides instantaneous gratification on demand and never lets us down. This dynamic then governs our whole life.

With the introduction of cocaine to the Bahamas in the early 80's (Jekel, Allen, Podlewski, Clarke, & Dean-Patterson, 1986), our population discovered an immediate ticket to internal fulfillment and temporary inner peace. Cocaine filled the gap of our shame false self--the gap between the reality of who we really are and the dreams of our and others' expectations. Cocaine, alcohol, gambling, sexual additions, cigarettes, and even our cell phones or addictive shopping all give us the sense of well-being, that all is well with the world and for a moment we're at peace, enjoying ourselves.

Let's look at the state of our young men today. Their repeated exposure to abandonment, humiliation and rejection at an early age has left them hardened, as many have experienced so many disappointments that it's less painful to not feel (or love) than to allow themselves to be open and vulnerable. As fellow human beings, they also have this same inner desire for love, safety, trust and control or power, but today the drug of their choice that always delivers the feeling of adequacy is the GUN. The gun fills the gaps within their empty, unproductive, powerless, shame filled lives because when I have a gun, I have power, I can produce, and people do what I say. I am somebody, somebody whose voice wants to be heard. But when you only know how to communicate through physical action, if you can't hear what I'm saying, I'm willing to die trying to get my message of pain out. Thus the Bahamas does not only have a violence problem, but a serious communication problem!

At times, we have the ability to even fool ourselves by confusing inner peace with external happiness. And so the genuine pursuit of inner peace is hijacked as we learn to settle for moments of happiness. The problem with happiness is that it is always temporary and circumstantial: a song, a movie, a book, a person, an activity, a beautiful sunset, but in the end, how long does the happiness last? We take pictures of sunsets and sunrises, trying to capture the feeling it gave us, to prolong the feeling of happiness. Some travel the world to seek this happiness, only to find it evades their grasp.

Dr. Allen's Contemplative Discovery Pathway Theory (CDPT)

The Contemplative Discovery Pathway Theory (Allen, Mayo, Allen-Carroll, Manganello, & Allen, 2014) gave me a way to make sense of my life in dealing with the world around us. As we enter life in our natural state, we seek love, manifested by safety, connection and empowerment (Figure 1). But sadly, life is wounded. A smack on the behind accompanied by rejections and the world becomes a hostile place, leaving us to feel abandoned, rejected and humiliated (Figure 2).

And to protect ourselves from experiencing these feelings of shame and pain, we develop a false self, involving self-absorption, self-gratification and control based in fear to shield our vulnerable broken heart from being hurt again (Figure 3). Oh, but only if it were that easy, because so often, love masquerades as hurt, and sometimes what we think is love is just more pain. This cycle repeats itself until we become impenetrable, lonely, bitter, wanting to be loved but afraid of the risk involved with letting our guard down to become wounded again. So this False Self is a perverse rescuer. It seeks to block us from pain but tends to hijack our life in the wilderness of fear where we look for substances, behaviors and things to give us pseudo-happiness in developing addictions to block the fear. Sadly, the addiction takes over and our lives are destroyed. Fear now controls our life and it is most powerful because the fear of fear itself is so damaging. The silent voice of our fears play over and over inside our heads, propelling us, immobilizing us, restricting us because of the dreadful memories of humiliation and shame in front of those whose approval we so desperately seek.

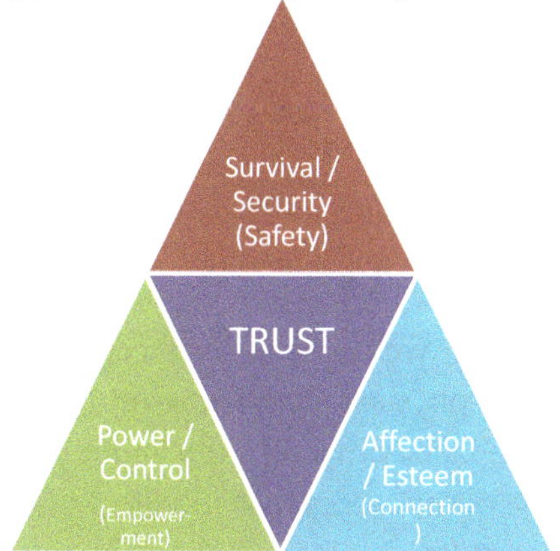

Figure 1 - The Natural Self

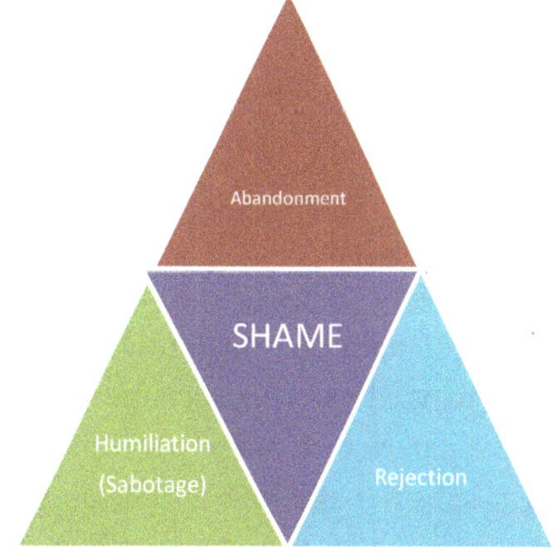

Figure 2 - The Shame Self

What Shall We Do?

Have you ever watched people who while in the midst of chaos are still able to exude calm? This is DISCOVERY, where we come to know the difference between what we can control and what we can't. At this point, how we respond to the chaotic situation is based on a choice. Our choice is based on the state of our heart. There are only two foundational emotions in life: fear and love. If our heart is based in the fear, the chaos continues. But if we can make the shift to open our heart to love, we move to experience authenticity (Figure 4). "There is no fear in love. But perfect love drives out fear" (1 John 4:18).

Our response is also predicated on our past. If there are emotional, stressful or traumatic events which have not been addressed, then how we respond is strongly influenced by our own unresolved issues. What makes us angry today is connected to where we were hurt yesterday. No one "makes" us angry...becoming angry is our choice!

Somewhere deep below, within the recesses of our heart, still resides the taste of peace woven into the fabric of our being, trying, desperately, to be connected back to its original, authentic source of love, whose byproduct is peace. But life has obstructed, obfuscated, prevaricated, and just plain led us astray from the very truth that would connect us back to our original selves.

The fact is if we take ownership of our truth, regardless how brutal it may be, it no longer has the power to dictate or dominate the emotional fate of our lives, and peace with ourselves is at our heart's door. Forgiveness and letting go are the keys which allow us to walk in peace (Figure 5).

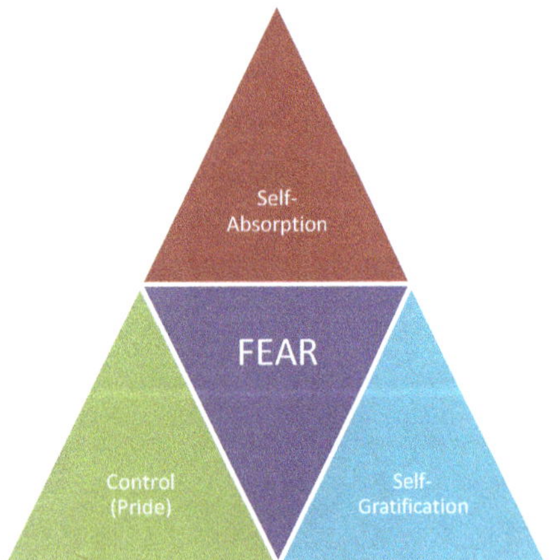

Figure 3 - The Shame False Self

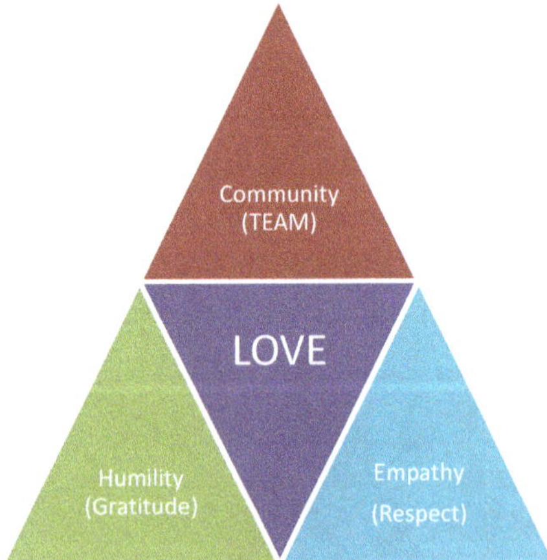

Figure 4 - The Authentic Self

Acceptance is a powerful moment of transformation, when we consciously accept what fate has handed us. This acceptance, especially when it involves physical pain, allows us to separate the exterior of ourselves from the interior. But when we face and accept our inner pain, the fear subsides and love and healing begin. Then there is the outer acceptance of who we are, what we look like, our hair, our face, our teeth, and the list goes on.

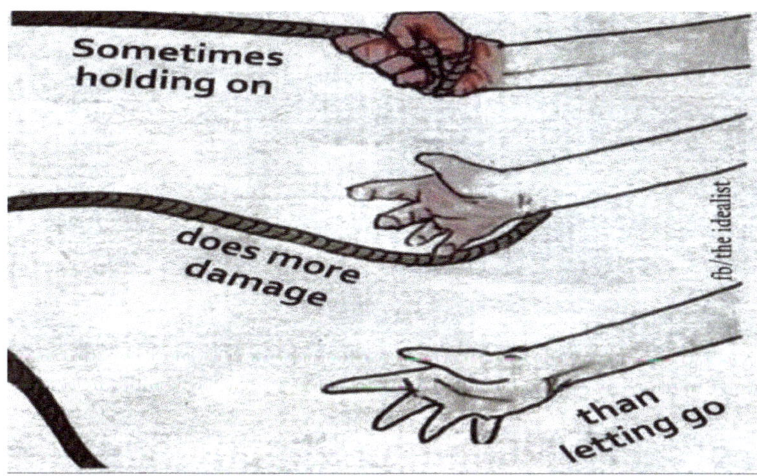

Figure 5 - Letting Go

I was once accused of stealing a battery from a pump house near Sir Sidney Poitier Bridge (Paradise Island Bridge). Three men came looking for me based on the words of another man. I was dragged to the pump house, tied to a chair, and beaten with a cutlass and a shovel handle for two or three hours. After a while the pain no longer mattered. It became a matter of mental endurance. There were also times when my tooth became so infected, that half my face would swell up and the only way I knew how to temporally alleviate the tooth ache was to bang my head against the wall. During these events the only inner peace I had involved drugs. But these experiences taught me how to separate what's going on outside from what's going on inside.

Once the fear of the physical pain passes there comes some semblance of inner relief, a calmness, even in the midst of the violence. There is no escape, no point in fighting, only acceptance that my fate lies in God's hands and with that understanding there is a place that I learned to go mentally, which allowed me to endure.

According to Marcel Proust "the real voyage of discovery consists not in seeking new landscapes, but in having new eyes". Once leaving the streets and making peace with myself and God, my journey of self-discovery began. The Family: People Helping People Project (Allen, Allen-Carroll, Allen, Bethell, & Manganello, 2015) (Allen, Bethell, & Allen-Carroll, A resocialization intervention model: The Family: People Helping People Project, 2016) and CDPT forced me to face what I feared the most about myself. **You will never conquer what you don't confront!**

There were deep scars of abandonment, humiliation, and rejection that I had run from my whole life and would never have admitted to anyone. But in The Family, I began to open up by telling my story and sharing my fears. The beautiful thing was, this was met by love and it produced peace within my heart. I came to realize that our heart is like a sponge. It becomes filled with the hurt, fear and shame of a lifetime, often blocking love and hope, pushing our life towards despair. When we can squeeze the sponge to empty the hurt and shame by sharing our

Photo Credit: Torell Glinton/eNueMAG. Used with permission

André Chappelle and his wife Kim.

story in a caring environment like The Family, we make space for love to enter our hearts and peace soon follows.

This peace I treasure and value and it acts like a barometer, for whenever I sense my inner stillness being ruffled, I check myself. I check myself because it's not what's happening on the outside that determines the state of my inner world, but rather it's the peace of God within me that allows me to determine how to respond. This is a choice: the choice to respond either from a heart of fear or a heart of love. You can either be a thermostat or a thermometer!

I don't know if gratitude is a fruit of peace or if peace is a fruit of gratitude, but I do know that they enhance each other. Without peace in my heart, the pace of this world doesn't allow me the ability to stop and smell the roses of life. To be grateful for a particular moment in time requires a peaceful slowing down in acknowledgement of the simplicity of God's creative beauty. Without either, the mystery and joy of life evades the living.

Thus the struggle to regain what was originally lost becomes a chase to replace an original with a counterfeit. The counterfeit is the temporary moments of peace, most often acquired through an external substance or activity. The casual cocktail at the end of a long day, brings that immediate sense of relaxation and the ability to unwind, but it's honestly just a false bus ride to that counterfeit peace.

Conclusion

As the old song says, "Everybody wants to go to heaven, but nobody wants to die." I have cancer. I am facing a big challenge in my life. It is not easy because there are so many unknowns. But my story will soon be over and my film will soon end. The person I need more than anybody now is Jesus and I have a personal relationship with him. I have chosen to look at my diagnosis, not as a death sentence, but rather a gift of life. Time is to be lived as time is the currency of life.

This presentation about peace was born in the midst of this extraordinary challenge to my life. But in spite of the unknowns, there is a loving Being greater than ourselves who wants to restore our heart back to its authentic state. What I want to leave with you is the reality that to achieve this authentic state, we must be willing to **squeeze the sponge of our heart of pain and shame by telling our authentic story and make space for love.** When this happens, fear slips away and the love story begins to reconnect within our heart and peace begins to flow.

Remember, **peace is not the absence of war or struggle. Peace is the absence of fear in the midst of our struggle!**

Thank you all for your support during my time on the streets, particularly around the Oakes Field area. I am also grateful for those of you who believed in me to make a comeback and experience my authentic life through God's healing grace. I ask your forgiveness for anything that I might have said or done to any of you that may have caused hurt, pain or fear. As I leave you, please remember, peace is possible, in spite of the struggle. Finally, I want to say a special 'Thank You' to my Princess Kim who has loved me with a love far deeper than I could have ever dreamed. Thank You All...Goodbye!

André Chappelle
September 24, 2016

REFERENCES

Allen, D. F., Allen-Carroll, M., Allen, V. S., Bethell, K. Y., & Manganello, J. A. (2015). Community Resocialization via Instillation of Family Values through a Novel Group Therapy Approach: A Pilot Study. Journal of Psychotherapy Integration, 289-298.

Allen, D. F., Bethell, K., & Allen-Carroll, M. (2016). A resocialization intervention model: The Family: People Helping People Project. Clinical Case Reports and Reviews, 491-495.

Allen, D. F., Mayo, M., Allen-Carroll, M., Manganello, J. A., & Allen, V. S. (2014). Cultivating Gratitude: Contemplative Discovery Pathway Theory Applied to Group Therapy in The Bahamas. Journal of Trauma and Treatment.

Jekel, J. F., Allen, D. F., Podlewski, H., Clarke, N., & Dean-Patterson, S. (1986). Epidemic free-base cocaine abuse. Case study from the Bahamas. Lancet, 459-462.

Memorial Service for André Chappelle

January 19, 2017 at 4:00 pm
New Providence Community Centre

Remarks by Dr. David F. Allen, MD, MPH

Distinguished Life Fellow – American Psychiatric Association
Founder & Principal Director, The Family Group Therapy Project

This is a very sad day for me because André was my friend and colleague, and really my right hand person. On the other hand, this is a happy day because we celebrate André's home going, to be with the One he loved so dearly, his Lord. He is now, after a really torturous journey of ups and downs, at rest. Today I would like to share with you what has resonated in my heart for the past few months—how André's life has become a symbol of hope. According to Carl Jung, a symbol is "a poet of our dreams and a bridge to unseen shores." Andre's life was poetry and introduced us to a deeper meaning of this life and hope in the life beyond.

First, André was a symbol of hope for the field of addiction.
Addiction is one of the world's most difficult illnesses to treat and is growing exponentially. Exposed to cocaine during a time when The Bahamas was undergoing a massive crack cocaine epidemic, like many of our young, bright, beautiful people, André succumbed to the illness of cocaine addiction. While I had the privilege of being with him at this time, I must say that I failed to help him stay off the drug. Even though he had periods of recovery in which he was extremely creative, I was unable to halt the onset and development of that terrible disease. I watched him plummet from the wealthy and secluded community of Lyford Cay to live as a homeless vagrant in the Bain Town and Oakes Field areas of Nassau. Periodically, I would meet him. He would say, "Doc, you didn't really fail. It's just that I loved cocaine more." It seemed as if he was seeking to encourage me, even though he was suffering from the devastation of addiction.

Because of the resources at his disposal, André had the opportunity to be treated at some of the world's leading addictions recovery centers. During intermittent periods of recovery, he was very creative. For example, one Sunday afternoon, he and Clint Kemp stopped by our home. At this stage, I want to mention that Clint befriended and mentored André and many other broken characters.

Clint and André sat down and shared that they had a vision for a church with a difference in the west. I was shocked. After I recovered, I said," That's a great idea!" In my head, I was thinking, "Well, that should be a swinging place!" The truth is that we are meeting today in the very place they envisioned.

During his time on the streets, while undergoing what I call malignant addiction, André was always decent. As one lady said to me, "Dr. Allen, he dignified homelessness." He was a volunteer security guard at McDonald's in Oakes Field. He was also a skilled mechanic, helping people fix their cars. He was a part-time tutor. Many members of our Family program have reported that André tutored them through their courses at the (then) College of The Bahamas. And at the same time, he was an entrepreneur. Apparently one gentleman was stuck on the line at McDonald's, lacking 17 cents. André asked, "Sir, would you let a homeless man help you by giving you the 17 cents?" Relieved, the man was able to leave happy with his meal, but he returned the next day to thank André for coming to his rescue. As a reward, he gave André a dollar, to which André replied, "Very good, you're a good gentleman. I like this deal very much. Suppose I give you 17 cents every day and you bring me a dollar the next day?" They both laughed. That was André—he made people laugh.

Even in the degradation of his addiction, André was a counselor. One gentleman in our Kemp Road Family claimed that while buying something at McDonald's, he got into a conversation with André. He was so blown away by his wisdom that he returned weekly to meet with him to discuss his problems and listen to André's wisdom. This gentleman is now helping to run The Family program at the prison and the youth court referral program which André helped to develop.

But back on Christmas day, 2009, around 2:00 in the morning, André faced one of the great crises of his life. As he later told me, "Doc, I had never felt so lonely. There was no one around. Earlier that day I'd seen my niece. She was now 20 years of age. I realized that I had been on the streets from the time she was a baby. I had been in this place for a very long time." As the night wore on, André's loneliness worsened. In his own words, he said, "I finally got on my knees and cried out to God." He told me, "Jesus showed up and said, 'Let's go! This is over'." Some people call this an epiphany, but I want to use the words he did, and I knew him very well. To me, the proof of this encounter is in what followed.

Over the next few days, he found another local heroine, Attorney Diane Stewart, who helped him to sort out his legal affairs and clear his criminal record. Then Cecil and Earla Bethel brought him into their home for several weeks. He entered a faith-based addictions recovery program at Teen Challenge and the rest is history. I failed, but God passed.

In early 2013, Andre began attending the Family group on Blue Hill Road. He shared his story and it was obvious to me, that he had really changed. Asking me for information, he read everything I had written on the Contemplative Discovery Pathway Theory (CDPT). He eventually went through the facilitator training and became an indispensable helper in the development of the Family program. He said that as he began to share his story, he began to release the pain and shame which had blocked his heart from the love around him. He described the theory simply by saying there are two streams in life: the love stream and the hurt/shame stream. "Our heart is like a sponge. Over the years we absorb the hurt that blocks the love, leading to anger, addictions and other destructive behavior." As he began to squeeze the hurt and shame in his heart, the love he had longed for all along became real to him. This led to the recommitment of his life to God and the marriage to his childhood sweetheart, Kim whom he called Princess. Andre opened his true self to love and moved from recovery to discovery.

Secondly, he was symbol of hope for prisoners.

Arriving at the prison with my team in 2012, I wondered how my Family Group Program would fit in. As the inmates filed in, they assessed us: "We know you're Dr. Allen, but we know André Chappelle. He is one of us." They said to him, "Welcome back home." In this moment, I felt assured that our program was off to a good start.

Week after week, these men and women would pour out their hearts and their hurts. André would share that being in prison was an opportunity to explore who they are and find the freedom still inside them. In other words: two men behind bars; once saw only the bars, the other saw the stars. Andre's work touched the inmates so deeply eventually they named it the "Free Your Mind" Group.

Then one Wednesday while at the prison, André said, "Doc I want to show you something." He led me along a detour away from the guards, opened a side room, and showed me some beautiful straw work. Calling the gentleman in charge, I asked about the beautiful purses on display in the room. André mused, "Maybe we need to do a Prison Art Show." Right in this room where we sit today, the art show was held, and thanks to the Hon. B. J. Nottage, Minister of National Security, nineteen inmates attended the opening and demonstrated their spectacular designs. The women shoppers just grabbed up the purses. They stood at the display tables next to their selections and would not sit down when I called the meeting to order, as they wanted to hold their prospective purchases.

Again, André saw all this and said, "Doc, this should be an annual event." The inmates were extremely well behaved, accompanied by only one overseer. It was pretty dark outside, and I was apprehensive about what could go wrong since it was on my watch, but the event went smoothly.

André helped me to see the talent of persons in prison—that they are still a part of us, and we are part of them. This vision has impacted development of a new parole program to help former prisoners reintegrate into society.

André became a symbol of hope for our country.

Recently André and I attended a briefing with law enforcement agents. As they discussed crimes of the previous few days, an officer turned to me and asked, "Do you see any hope for our crime problem?" I said, "Yes—look at André...I failed, but God passed."

And I could look at so many other men and women with whom I had failed. But with persistence, by being there when God was ready to work and they were ready to respond, I was able to see many miracles. André represents that. Eric Fox, head of Teen Challenge, represents that. William Lunn, who was homeless for many years and is now one of my right hand men, represents it as well.

Why is this day so meaningful for me? We are celebrating the life and the home going of a distinguished Bahamian. But I also sense that we have been given an opportunity to uncover in André's story a treasury of hope for our country. As God produced revolutionary miracles for André, Eric and William, I am profoundly encouraged that the same hope is available for anyone in our country who is ready to seek the Love of God.

Finally, André symbolizes hope for the journey, through faith, from time into eternity. Over the past six months, I had the chance to walk with André as he traveled the corridors of pain and death. We would go for rides on Sunday afternoons, when he would share his intimate feelings. He spoke often of how the Contemplative Discovery Pathway Theory that anchors our Family meetings had really helped him to open up to his true self. During this period of time, André developed the thinking expressed in his final lecture at The Family Training Institute, "The War For Peace Within Ourselves".

In our talks, I asked André to describe "the theory" in his own words. He said, "Doc, it's simple. Our heart is like a sponge. Over the years, it absorbs all of our shame, pain and hurt. For many of us as Bahamians, our sponge is so full that love can't get in, so we end up with addiction, violence and self-destruction. In The Family as I began to share my story and empty my heart of the hurt, shame and pain, God's love came in a special way, leading me not just to recovery but to discovery of myself as a person capable of receiving love. And this led to my reconnection with my childhood sweetheart, Kim, and to a beautiful marriage in which I experienced love in a way which I had never known." He said, "Doc, don't stop The Family, because there are very few places you can go to squeeze out your heart. You can't do it at church, you can't do it at home, and you can't do it at work. The Family is a place where people can come to empty their shame. They may have to cry or scream out their pain and hurt, but then they can open their hearts to the Love that will never let go."

In my last interview with him, two nights before he died, we sat outside under beautiful clouds, surrounded by the tropical plants he loved. André said, "Doc, this story is nearly over. This film is nearly ended. Thank you for being there for me. You have to go on. All I need now is Jesus, and I have him." But looking at me intently, he said, "Doc, there are still a lot of unknowns, you know. This journey is a mystery."

Then he said, "Okay, I have nothing else to say. The time for psyching me out is over now. Why don't you talk to me? How do you feel?" he asked, folding his arms mischievously. I told him, "I feel sad. I'm really going to miss you." We both cried. Then he said, "Okay, it's time to go. Go home to your wife." I answered, "Okay...I came to go."

So I was left with the impression that although we were very close, he knew that he had to make this journey alone with his Lord, and that this time I couldn't go there with him. The next evening, I sat for half an hour, watching him and Kim. She was sleeping. One dog lay across Kim's neck, the other on her lap. André looked at them wordlessly. I watched the deep love between them. The silence said more than words could ever express. With tears in my eyes, I left.

The next morning, after spending some time with them, I left to do an errand. Five minutes later, Kim called to say, "He's gone." Hurrying back, I was struck by what Kim shared with me. She said André told her he didn't want food anymore. He lay down, weak and tired. All of a sudden, he raised his head, sat upright, stretched out his arms and looked to the beyond. His lips were moving, but she could not hear what he was saying. Then he slumped back and died.

Having encountered André as one who was filled with the power of the Holy Spirit, my interpretation of this experience was like Stephen the New Testament martyr. André had a beatific vision of the Cosmic Christ, standing with God the Father, welcoming him home to his eternal rest.

Though he is gone, he left us with a mystery. Who was this man? In the final analysis, for me he became a symbol for the life beyond. Notwithstanding the rough course of his life, he finished well! I believe he heard the words, "Well done, good and faithful servant...welcome home, beloved son."

It is my hope that you too will encounter Jesus who rescued André from addiction, walked him through recovery, empowered him to help the broken, comforted him in cancer, helped him say his painful goodbyes, and ultimately welcomed him home to eternal Love. This Christ is our hope.

Appendix
Published Articles

Epidemic Free-Base Cocaine Abuse: Case Study from the Bahamas. *The Lancet Ltd*, 1986;1:459-462.

Nine Years of the Freebase Cocaine Epidemic in the Bahamas. *American Journal on Addictions*, 1994, 3:14-24.

Cultivating Gratitude: Contemplative discovery pathway theory applied to group therapy in the Bahamas. *Journal of Trauma*. Treatment 3(3) 2014

Cocaine Addiction: The Nemesis of Modern Culture by David F. Allen, MD
Presented at the Jack W Provonsha Lectureship for the Alumni Postgraduate Convention on March 3, 1997

Adapting Group Therapy to Address Real World Problems: Insights from groups offered in the Bahamas. *International Journal of Group Psychotherapy* 68 (1), 17-34 2017

A Resocialization Intervention Model in the Prison - The Family: People Helping People Project, *Sociology International Journal*, October 16, 2017

Spirituality and transformation in a community-based group in the Bahamas Mental Health, Religion & Culture 2019

A social intervention for court-ordered adolescents—The family people helping people project. Examining social identities and diversity issues in group therapy Routledge 2020

Community-based treatment of suicide through the family: people helping people project *Japan Journal of Medical Science* 2025

Epidemic Free-Base Cocaine Abuse
Case Study from the Bahamas

JAMES F, JEKEL
HENRY PODLEWSKI
SANDRA DEAN-PATTERSON

DAVID F. ALLEN
NELSON CLARKE
PAUL CARTWRIGHT

Department of Epidemiology and Public Health, Yale University, School of Medicine, New Haven, Connecticut, USA; Community Psychiatry Clinic, Nassau, Bahamas; National Drug Council, Nassau; and Sandilands Rehabilitation Hospital and Sandilands Hospital Drug Clinic, Nassau

This article was first published by *The Lancet*, March 1, 1986

Summary

Beginning in 1983, a sharp increase was noted in the number of new admissions for cocaine abuse to the only psychiatric hospital and to the primary out-patient psychiatric clinic in the Bahamas. For the two facilities combined, new admissions for cocaine abuse increased from none in 1982 to 69 in 1983 and to 523 in 1984. Although there was some evidence for a rise in cocaine use during this time, as the drug became cheaper and more available, a primary cause of this medical epidemic seemed to be a switch by pushers from selling cocaine hydrochloride, which has a low addictive potential, to almost exclusive selling of cocaine free base, which has a very high addictive potential and causes medical and psychological problems. Although the use of free cocaine base is rising around the world, this is the first report of a nationwide medical epidemic due almost exclusively to this form of the drug although similar problems are reported with smoking coca paste in South America.

Introduction

The past decade has seen an increase in the use of cocaine in the United States and UK. This drug is not generally perceived as being harmful as heroin. 1-4 However, data are accumulating to suggest that cocaine is indeed a very dangerous drug.5-8

Data from the US National Institute Drug Abuse point to a 91% increase in cocaine-related deaths between 1980 and 1983. 9 Kleber and Gawin7 have suggested that certain drugs have a low productivity for producing compulsive-addictive behaviour, so that, say, less than 15% of people using such drugs become addicted; examples are alcohol and marijuana.

At the other extreme are drugs such as heroin and nicotine that lead to a compulsive-addictive se pattern in most users. Cocaine may lie at either o these extremes, depending on the method of use.' For example, nasal inhalation of cocaine ("snorting") or chewing coca leaves is unlikely to lead to addiction while smoking ("freebasing") or injecting ("'shooting") the drug is. A switch in the pattern of cocaine use from snorting to freebasing could thus produce a big increase in the number of addicts without a change in the prevalence of cocaine use.

Some are talking now of a cocaine "epidemic" because use of the drug seems to be rising steadily." It would be more accurate to talk of a "long-term secular trend' because "epidemic" suggests a sudden imbalance between the forces that promote and retard a disease. However, a change in cocaine use in the Bahamas does meet the criteria for an epidemic of cocaine abuse.

Our study was initiated by physicians in the Bahamas who were concerned about an apparent rapid increase in cocaine abuse in clinical settings. Several sources were examined retrospectively to see if this clinical perception of a recent large increase in cocaine-related admissions to psychiatric facilities was accurate.

Methods

The only psychiatric hospital in the Bahamas is the government- run Sandilands Rehabilitation Hospital (SRH) on New Providence. Patients are referred there from the other islands. In 1980, almost two-thirds of the Bahamian population lived on New Providence, most of them in Nassau. The other three hospitals in the Bahamas (two on New Providence and one on Grand Bahama) seldom accept drug abuse patients and have few psychiatric patients.

The main community mental health clinic in the Bahamas is the Community Psychiatry Clinic (CPC) in Nassau. Most patients who do not go to private psychiatrists or other private physicians use the SRH outpatient services or the CPC. The two small government clinics in Freeport and Eight Mile Rock saw 47 cocaine addicts in 1984, only 14% of the total seen by Bahamian mental health clinics and only 9% of those seen at all government facilities. Drug abuse patients seen in emergency rooms are referred to SRH. Data from the CPC and the SRH on psychiatric cases provide a more complete picture than could be obtained in most areas of the world.

Unfortunately, age and sex specific population data from the 1980 census were not yet available so we could not calculate incidence rates. However, because the population was stable over the period of this study, data on trends of new cases are almost as interpretable as rates. An incident case of cocaine abuse was defined as the first admission to the CPC or the SRH for cocaine abuse, even if other diseases were present. If the predominant drug in a poly drug user was cocaine, the case was considered a cocaine abuse admission.

Data Sources

The CPC publishes a monthly summary of cases. We focused on new patients. Alcoholism, non-cocaine-related drug abuse, and cocaine-related drug abuse were studied from the beginning of adequate records in 1982 up to June 30, 1985. Monthly admissions to the SRH were available for 1980-84 and these data indicated the number admitted for alcoholism and/or drug dependence (and whether or not cocaine was the primary drug) and distinguished first from repeat admissions. Admissions to CPC and SRH for alcoholism showed a slow, steady increase and will not be discussed further. :

Drug abuse patients among the wealthy minority on the Bahamas will usually seek care outside the CPC or SRH (including the United States) and some cases from the family islands are treated by local physicians. However, there is no evidence of a change in the accessibility of care or the referral patterns in the Bahamas so changes in the pattern of few admissions reported here do reflect changes in the scale of cocaine abuse in the community. Some patients may have been admitted to both the CPC and the SRH, .there being no central data system to exclude such duplicate entries. However, doctors who work at both places feel that overlap will have been very small. During the study period, only 4 drug patients admitted to the SRH were referred from the CPC. Likewise, in discussion with most of'the few private psychiatrists on New Providence, it was clear that few of the Bahamian drug abusers they see are not referred to the CPC or the SRH. We conclude that the combined incidence data on new drug abusers from the CPC and the SRH cover most people in the Bahamas whose use of cocaine or other drugs caused problems severe enough for them to seek medical assistance.

Results

Community Psychiatry Clinic

The CRC opened in 1980 but new and returning patients were not distinguished in the clinic statistics until 1982. Fig 1 shows how quarterly numbers of new cocaine-related admissions have risen from none in 1982 to 299 in 1984, there being a probable decline in 1985. During the early phases of cocaine appearance in the CPC, some of the cocaine use may have been recorded only as "drug abuse" or "drug dependence", but the number of such cases would have been small. If the patient used several drugs (as most did), the drug that seemed to have precipitated the problems for which they sought help was recorded.

Drug abuse increased from 1% of the clinic's patients in 1982 to 9% in 1983 to 39% in 1984, and was 31% in the first 6 months of 1985. The big increase in 1984 was due almost entirely to cocaine dependence. Cocaine-related new admissions really began in the third quarter of 1983. New cases of depression and/or schizophrenia have been fairly stable over time, suggesting that the increase in drug patients was not primarily due to increased clinic awareness.

Sandilands Rehabilitation Hospital -
SRH has a long tradition of treating acutely ill alcoholics and drug addicts from the whole of the Bahamas. 86% of the 1984 drug admissions were from New Providence.

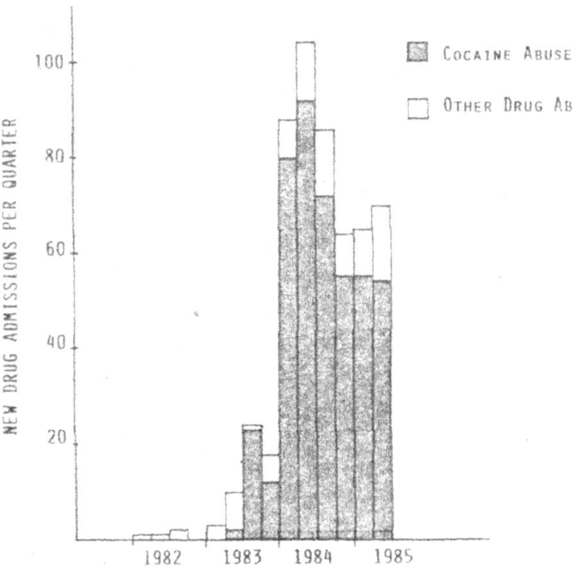

Fig 1—Incidence of new drug abuse admissions to the community psychiatry clinic, Nassau, Bahamas, 1982–85.

Although there were a few cocaine-related admissions during the first three quarters of 1983, a marked increase began in the last quarter of 1983. The number of first drug admissions for which cocaine was the primary cause increased sharply from 1 in 1980 to 224 in 1984 (fig 2). The number of first admissions due primarily to other drugs was more stable. So great was the increase in admissions for cocaine abuse that recording of admission numbers became less complete after November, 1984; numbers for the last quarter of 1984 are estimated from those for October and November.

Often a patient would be admitted with drug abuse and symptoms suggestive of underlying psychiatric disease. Usually the paranoia, hallucinations, and so on were due to the drug use, so whenever cocaine or other drug abuse was indicated as being important, the patient was considered a drug admission.

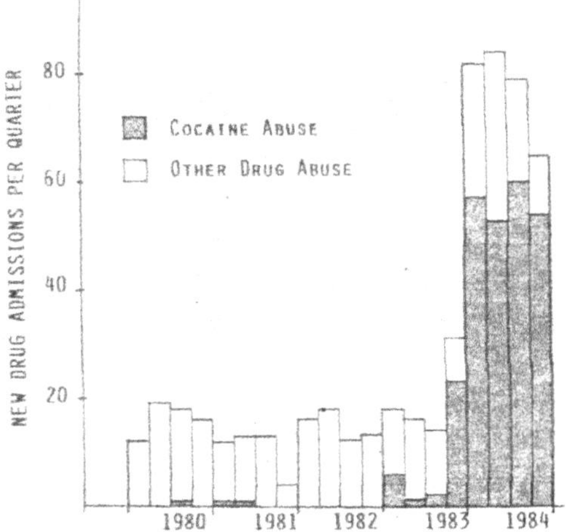

Fig 2—Incidence of first admissions for drug abuse, Sandilands Rehabilitation Hospital, Nassau, Bahamas, 1980–84.

Mode of Cocaine Use
Smoking (freebasing) accounted for 98% of cocaine-related referrals in 1984. Cocaine base (known in the Eastern USA as "crack") is produced when cocaine hydrochloride powder is' treated with. alkali. It is volatile with modest heating and is easily absorbed through the lungs and rapidly transmittéd to the brain. Some experienced addicts made their own freebase cocaine in the early 1980s but most did not know how to do it or did not bother, and the predominant form used to be snorting. By 1984 the pushers were selling only the freebase form, smoked using a home-made pipe ("camoke"). When cocaine is smoked up to 80% of it reaches the brain, and the "rush" can begin in 8-12 s, producing a short period of ecstasy. This fleeting sensation is most powerful on the first use of cocaine and though addicts seek to repeat it the same sensation is not experienced again.

The most common pattern of usage varies from a few hours, during which time the user may consume 4-5 g cocaine, to a few days of intermittent use, usually over a weekend, during which time up to 10 g may be consumed. Most patients report using the drug at freebasing parties or "base houses"'.

Clinical Spectrum
Cocaine-dependent individuals usually seek help during or after some crisis, financial, social, medical, or psychological. For example, an addict whose money had gone might seek help on his own initiative or under pressure from family, friends, or employers. Others, who had had total to support the habit or whose addiction had made them violent, were referred by the courts.

The most common physical problems were seizures, severe itching ("the cocaine bug"), loss of consciousness ("tripping out"), cardiac arrhythmia, vertigo, pneumonia, gastro-intestinal symptoms, and avitaminosis associated with severe malnutrition. Several addicts were referred from maternity wards.

The cocaine addicts often presented with severe depression, manifest by unkempt appearance, insomnia, anorexia, withdrawal, and suicidal ideation. There were at least 10 cocaine-associated deaths, 5 of which were suicides. Cocaine psychosis was common: the patient would present with severe agitation, impaired judgment, paranoid ideation, intense denial, violent behaviour, threats of suicide or. homicide, and hallucinations. In periods of lucidity they would try to mislead the physician, and a relative or friend was needed to confirm the psychotic state.

Demographic Characteristics
For 1984, 81% of cocaine admissions to SRH were males and male drug abusers in general were aged 11-56 years (mean 25). Cocaine users tended to be slightly older than other drug users (26 vs 22-5 years). Female drug addicts were aged 15-39 years (mean 24 years). Almost all patients were Bahamian.

Other Forms of Surveillance
Most patients seen at the Sandilands Hospital drug clinic were referred after discharge from the SRH so data from this clinic were not included. About 60% of the patients seen were using both cocaine and cannabis, although it had usually been cocaine that had precipitated the hospital admission. Neither suicide nor drug-related death is usually recorded on death certificates in the Bahamas so we decided not to use vital Statistics as a surveillance method. Police statistics showed some increase in street drug arrests in 1984, but not of the magnitude suggested by the clinic and hospital admission data. In 1980-83 drug arrests averaged 1094 a year with no clear trend over time. There were 1501 arrests for 1984, an increase of 37%.

Discussion
In the Bahamas, data from public psychiatric services demonstrate an epidemic of cocaine abuse requiring medical care. Cannabis and alcohol were often used to control adverse symptoms from cocaine use. In early 1983 something—a major change in the incidence of new drug users, especially cocaine users, or in the method of use—upset the previous drug-use equilibrium, suddenly forcing hundreds of people to seek treatment for complications of drug abuse.

The most obvious explanation is that cocaine was suddenly introduced to the islands or that its price fell. Former addicts, who were on cocaine in the 1970s, confirm that cocaine powder had been available, if expensive, for years, but that in late 1982 or early 1983 the drug suddenly became much more plentiful as production in South America increased. The street price of cocaine in Nassau fell to one-fifth of its former level.

Ex-addicts also told us that at about the time that cocaine became more plentiful and cheaper drug pushers switched from selling powdered cocaine ("snow") for nasal inhalation or injection to the pure alkaloid form ("rocks" or ""freebase") which is used exclusively for smoking. It suddenly became very difficult to obtain powder in Nassau. By making this change, the drug pushers were forcing all cocaine users to become addicts. Many pushers are themselves addicts and have to sell the drug to feed their own habits. Selling freebase guarantees an eager market for the increasingly available cocaine. *

Smith[10] claims that an important reason for the increase in cocaine deaths in the San Francisco area was higher potency cocaine. Siegel' reported that the recovery of cocaine free base from pure cocaine hydrochloride, using various street kits, ranged from 41% to 72% and, although the kits removed some of the adulterants, some lignocaine and ephedrine, for example, was often left with the cocaine. Ex-addicts indicated that the street cocaine powder in Nassau had usually been "cut" (diluted) about 50% before sale. Although we have no direct data about cocaine purity, the sources for the cocaine 'remained similar; nor is the extraction process perfect. Changes in levels of purity seem to be an inadequate explanation for our findings.

We conclude that the medical epidemic of cocaine-related physical and psychiatric problems in the Bahamas was related to the interaction of the availability of cheaper cocaine and a switch from powder to free base.

Monitoring the method of selling may be critical both for Western nations, the targets of the cocaine market, and for developing nations such as the Bahamas via which the drug is shipped and those South American countries that produce it. We found surveillance of medical services to be a quick and effective way of monitoring some aspects of the drug situation in the Bahamas, and it could be in the self-interest of target nations to assist producer and trans-shipment countries not only to control drug abuse but also to maintain an intensive surveillance system. As cocaine freebasing becomes more popular and particularly if the vending pattern switches to the freebase form (as is starting to happen in some US cities), emergency rooms, mental health clinics, and, psychiatric hospitals will need to prepare for an unprecedented influx of drug addicts.

Supported in part by grant from Council for International Exchange of Scholars, US Information Agency. J. F, J. is a Fulbright faculty research fellow. We thank Dr Norman Gay, Minister of Health, Commonwealth of the Bahamas; Ms Barbara McKinley Coleman, National Drug Council; and Mr Mozes Deveaux, Sandilands Rehabilitation Hospital for their support. And we pay tribute to the memory of Chrysostom Finlayson who, besides providing critical insight for this paper, gave his life in the war against drugs.

Correspondence to J. F.J., Department of Epidemiology and Public Health, School of Medicine, Yale University, PO Box 3333, 60 College Street, New Haven, Connecticut 06510, USA.

REFERENCES

1 Siegel RK. Cocaine smoking. *J Psychoactive Drugs* 1982; 14: 271-355.

2 Robins LN. The natural history of adolescent drug use. *Am J Publ Health* 1984; 74: 656-57.

3 O'Malley PM, Bachman JG, Johnston LD. Period, age, and cohort effects on substance abuse among American youth. *Am J Publ Health* 1984; 74: 682-88.

4 Forno JJ, Young RT, Levitt C. Cocaine abuse: the evolution from coca leaves to freebase. *J Drug Educ* 1981; 14: 311-15.

5 Spotts JV, Shontz FC. Drug-induced ego states I: Cocaine: phenomenology and implications. *Int J Addictions* 1984; 19: 119-51. :

6 Howard RE, Hueter DC, Davis GJ. Acute-myocardial infarction following cocaine abuse in a young woman with normal coronary arteries. *JAMA* 1985; 254: 95-96.

7 Kleber HD, Gawin FH. The spectrum of cocaine abuse and its treatment. *J Clin Psychiatry* 1984; 45: 18-23.

8 Bozarth MA, Wise RA. Toxicity associated with long-term intravenous heroin and cocaine self-administration in the rat. *JAMA* 1985; 254: 81-83.

9 Pollin W. The danger of cocaine. *JAMA* 1985; 254: 98.

10 Smith DE. Cited in *Med News* Dec 10, 1984: 6.

A Resocialization Intervention Model in the Prison - The Family: People Helping People Project

Nine Years of the Freebase Cocaine Epidemic The Bahamas

James F. Jekel, M.D., David F. Allen, M.B.B.S.,
Nelson Clarke, M.B.B.S., Henry Podlewski,.M.B.B.S.,
Hannah Gray, M.P.H., Carolyn Roberts, A.B. ,

Nine years after the beginning of the epidemic of freebase (crack) cocaine abuse in the Bahamas, this historical study was done to characterize the natural course of the epidemic and to estimate the effectiveness of control measures. The authors, data include the incidence of new cases-at the only psychiatric hospital in the Bahamas and at the primary community psychiatric clinic in the nation. The Bahamian response included 1) demand reduction, 2) supply reduction, and 3) reduction of money laundering. The annual number of new cases of crack abuse presenting for treatment declined from 1987 to mid-1991 in both facilities, but in 1992 it began rising again in the inpatient setting only. The changes in recent years have been accompanied by an increase in violent crimes against persons, especially robberies. (American Journal on Addictions 1994; 3:14–24)

In 1983 the first known nationwide epidemic of freebase ("crack") cocaine outside of a South American producer nation began in the Bahamas.[1] The crack epidemic soon spread to other nations, especially the United States.[2] The Bahamas were involved early in the crack problem because of location, geography, geology, and demography, which made the Bahamian islands an ideal trans-shipment location for cocaine being sent from Colombia, South America, to the eastern United States. Beginning in the early 1980s, huge quantities of cocaine began moving through the Bahamas, which made cocaine easily available and extremely inexpensive to Bahamians.

Two other factors contributed to the onset of the epidemic at that time and place: 1) a new, safe, and easy technique for making crack from the hydrochloride,[3, 4] and 2) a marketing decision by Bahamian drug pushers to sell only crack (i.e., not cocaine hydrochloride) in order to increase profits.[1] By 1983, these factors together had produced a rapid, massive increase in the number of cocaine abusers presenting for treatment in the two major substance abuse treatment facilities in the Bahamas.

The use of inhaled or swallowed substances is not new to the Bahamas, but prior to the mid-1970s, there was little known use of substances other than alcohol and cigarettes. And, despite the alcohol use, violence against individuals was rare in the Bahamas until the mid-1970s, when other substances, particularly marijuana, began to be used with increasing frequency. Marijuana was used by individuals from all parts of Bahamian society, but most intensively by the Rastafarians there. Rastifarianism is a religious movement that originated in Jamaica in 1930 and that considers Emperor Haile Selassie I of Ethiopia to be divine. "They have developed an elaborate ritual system using marijuana (ganja) as a sacrament...[5] The increasing use of marijuana, although creating only a modest social problem in itself, may have prepared the Bahamians for the idea that pleasurable experiences can be sought through smoked chemicals, and thus may have helped to pave the way for smoking freebase cocaine.

Purpose

This paper is a sequel to the first report of the epidemic in the Bahamas." It seeks to understand the natural history of the crack epidemic there and to

Received December 10, 1992; revised March 28, 1993; accepted June 18, 1993. From the Department of Epidemiology and Public Health, Yale University School of Medicine, New Haven, CT 06510. Address reprint requests to James F. Jekel, M.D., Dept. of Epidemiology and Public Health, 60 College St., New Haven, CT 06510.

evaluate the Bahamian response to it. The Bahamas provides a special environment in which to study the crack problem because it is a small island nation that lacks borders with other countries and because the Bahamian people have a strong aversion to needles, so that drugs are seldom injected. Moreover, because the epidemic hit there before other nonproducing nations, such a study may provide insights as to where the crack problem may be headed in other lands. The Bahamas provides a relatively circumscribed environment in which to study the long-term pattern of a crack epidemic that was largely uncomplicated by intravenous drug use.

Setting

The Commonwealth of the Bahamas consists of more than 700 islands and cays spread over an area of ocean approximately 750 miles long and 100,000 square miles in area. Fewer than 30 of the islands are inhabited. The 1990 population is estimated to be about 250,000 persons. The islands tend to be long and narrow, flat, and deserted, ideal for making landing strips near beaches for the transfer of drugs from incoming airplanes to pleasure boats and to outgoing aircraft.

BAHAMIAN RESPONSE TO THE EPIDEMIC

The Bahamian effort to control the crack epidemic was a multifaceted systems approach with three primary objectives: demand reduction, supply reduction, and reduction of money laundering.

Demand Reduction

Demand reduction consisted of educational efforts and the treatment of crack-abusing persons.

Educational Efforts. The national educational efforts were spearheaded by the National Drug Council, the Drug Action Service, and the public school system, with strong efforts also being contributed by many churches in the Bahamas. The National Drug Council sponsored public information through media, speakers, materials to assist others, and rallies. The Drug Action Service worked especially with teenagers and families, and it sponsored a drug hot-line. Operation Hope on Grand Bahama pioneered in training teen peer counselors and in teen prevention.

Both public and parochial schools developed drug and alcohol education efforts for children of all ages, and they cooperated extensively with other groups that brought educational efforts into the schools. Most denominations in the Bahamas developed anticocaine and substance abuse programs for their parishioners, and many voluntary, nonprofit groups did the same for their members. Messages about the negative, unglamorous side of crack abuse were reinforced, because most citizens soon came to know someone who was a crack abuser.

Treatment Programs. Treatment efforts were an important part of demand reduction. When users observed successful treatment in friends, they were more inclined to come for treatment themselves. Large crack abuse treatment programs were established at the Sandilands Rehabilitation Hospital (SRH) and the Community Psychiatry Clinic, (CPC), both in Nassau, which have been extremely active in cocaine abuse treatment since 1983. Other, smaller programs, such as Teen Challenge and Cocaine Anonymous, were started. These offered some aspects of a full treatment program, but the SRH and the CPC were the only medically based, full-treatment programs in the Bahamas.

Recovering addicts proved to be effective educators for teenagers and young adults, because it was clear that they knew their subject. Discussions with addicts in 1991 made clear that, beginning around 1987, crack began to lose its glamour for young people.

Supply Reduction

Supply reduction was attempted in two major areas: 1) local police efforts to remove and punish drug trafficking and possession, and 2) interdiction of the supply of cocaine.

Local police efforts resulted in the elimnation of major urban centers of drug vending. By 1990, although there still were many drug vendors in the Bahamas, they were dispersed rather than, as before, congregated into known drug, "bazaars" (including crack houses). The number of drug pushers declined because, increasingly, drug middlemen found it necessary to limit the number of street pushers with whom they dealt to a few trusted (usually. non-cocaine-using) individuals. Pushers who also were addicts tended to inform on the middlemen when they were arrested, so they lost favor with the major drug dealers.

Addicts in treatment reported that the actual supply of cocaine began dropping by some time in 1987, the year when a major increase in Bahamas—United States cooperation in drug interdiction began. The amounts of cocaine seized each year from 1981 to 1989 are shown in Figure 1. The total cocaine seized in the Bahamas rose to huge amounts, due to a marked augmentation of antidrug efforts by the Bahamian Defense Force. This increase resulted from a major increase in United States cash assistance to the Bahamas for drug traffic control, as well as to a large number of antidrug forces sent from the United States in 1987 and thereafter. In 1988, about 5.5 tons of cocaine, slightly more than half the total seized that year, was due to joint United States,ÄîBahamian activities. Both a Bahamian and a U.S. marshal are on all ships and helicopters, so that an arrest can be made wherever a suspect is apprehended (ie., whether in Bahamian or U.S. waters.)

Control of Money Laundering: Banking System Changes

The Bahamas first began to tighten control over their "offshore" banks in 1973, causing many so-called "shell banks" to leave at that time. Banking laws were tightened again in 1983 by requiring that a deposit of $5,000 or greater be reported, and careful identification of the individuals made. In 1985 the Bahamian banking system voluntarily developed the Bahamas Association of International Banks and Trust Companies Code of Conduct (on which the Basel Code of Conduct [1987] was patterned).[6] Nevertheless, because the controls were largely voluntary, and little reporting was required, an uncertain amount of drug money may have been laundered before 1987, although only one Bahamian bank was disciplined for infringement of the 1983 banking law.

In 1987 the Bahamas enacted a tough new law called the Tracing and Forfeiture of Proceeds of Drug Trafficking Act of 1987. In January 1989 the Bahamas became the first nation to ratify the 1988 United Nations Convention Against the Illicit Traffic in Narcotic Drugs and Psychotropic Substances.[7] Since then, the required surveillance and reporting in the Bahamas is thought to be among the most effective systems of control over money laundering in the international banking system. The cited report goes on to say:

> A 1988 study conducted by the U.S. Drug Enforcement Agency into international drug money laundering did not list The Bahamas among the leading 18 centers where drug money is laundered.

THE PATTERN OF THE CRACK EPIDEMIC

Our data come from 1) statistical reports from the Sandilands Rehabilitation Hospital (SRH), which is the only psychiatric/substance abuse hospital in the Bahamas; 2) statistical reports from the Community Psychiatry Clinic (CPC) in Nassau, the only full-service outpatient psychiatric clinic in the Bahamas (except for the follow-up clinic at SRH); 3) the annual statistical reports of the Royal Bahamian Police Force; 4) several studies funded by the United Nations Fund for Drug Abuse Control (UNFDAC); 5) discussions with persons currently being treated for cocaine abuse; and 6) interviews with selected Bahamian leaders in the areas of health, law enforcement, and banking.

Treatment Incidence

Here cocaine treatment incidence is defined as the number of cocaine abusers in a specified time interval who enter a cocaine treatment facility for the first time for cocaine abuse. Ideally, there should be no duplication of counts between facilities. The Bahamas is a good country in which to use this strategy because there are only two major cocaine treatment facilities in the country, the SRH and the CPC. With the exception of non-Bahamians and a few wealthy Bahamians who are usually treated in the United States, almost all Bahamians who seek medically based treatment for cocaine abuse are counted in the records of one of these two facilities. Very few cocaine abusers are only treated privately by Bahamian psychiatrists because of the cost and the patients' need for group therapy experiences.

Figure 2 shows the number of persons entering the CPC and the SRH for the first time at each institution for the treatment of cocaine (mostly crack) abuse; the data are shown by quarter from 1983 to mid-1992. To smooth out random quarterly variation so that the trends can be more easily seen, the lines shown are "moving" averages (i.e., each point is based on three quarters, with the middle quarter being the one charted). For example, in the moving average, the number of admissions to a facility for the first quarter in 1990 shown in the figure is the average of the number of admissions to that facility in the last quarter of 1989 and the first two quarters in 1990.

Following the initial peak in 1984, the new admissions were fairly steady at what might be called a high endemic (hyperendemic) level until early 1987, after -which a fairly steady decline in numbers began, which continued until mid-1991. Since the third quarter of 1991, there has been a steady rise for *inpatient* first admissions but not for Outpatient first admissions.

The possibility exists that someone reported to have been treated for the first time at one facility might have been treated earlier somewhere else. However, when the epidemic began, with rare exceptions, all of the cases reported were true treatment incidence. As the years progressed, there was a greater probability that a person entering one program for the first time had been treated previously at another. Therefore, Figure 2 undoubtedly underestimates the decline in new, first-time cocaine abuse treatment cases.

These data were supplemented by interviews with cocaine abusers in treatment at the CPC. There was complete agreement among the addicts that the incidence of new abusers has decreased markedly compared to the peak from 1984 to 1987. There was a similar decline in the number of cocaine abusers currently undergoing any phase of treatment at the CPC, as shown by the fact that one of their treatment groups, which initially had consisted entirely of crack abusers, had none in 1991. The other treatment groups at the CPC have some cocaine abusers and some patients with other kinds of problems.

IMPACT OF THE CONTROL EFFORTS

There appears to be little doubt that between 1987 and 1991 the number of new cocaine abusers in the Bahamas declined steadily. This conclusion is supported by the evidence from treatment incidence, treatment prevalence, police arrests for drug offenses, urine Screening, and the testimony of the addicts themselves. It is, however, difficult to establish exactly how much of this decline is due to the specific control efforts of the Bahamas, including increasing United States assistance and cooperation, and how much is due to a natural cycle of the development of aversion to and rejection of a new illicit drug, as pro-posed by Musto.[7]Actually, there probably is little contradiction between these hypotheses, because the specific control efforts in the Bahamas can be seen as part of the natural drug cycle that Musto postulates.

There was, however, a synergism between formal social efforts and the changes in knowledge, attitudes, and practices of individual Bahamians. For example, the growing abhorrence of the effects of crack in the Bahamian population was partly informed and validated by public messages. Also, successful treatment assisted police efforts by reducing the number of abusers. Interdiction made crack more costly and dangerous, reducing the numbers willing or able to use".

The formal, three-pronged attack by the Bahamas was closely associated in time with the reduction of crack incidence. The starting years for each of the major control efforts is shown in Table 1. Because in 1987 the Government of the Bahamas obtained some strong new assistance in the anti-cocaine fight, and in the same year the decline in treatment incidence began, these may be related.

We wondered whether the large number of new crack abusers since 1983 could have reduced the size of the at-risk population sufficiently to explain the recent decline in new cases. By use of the incidence data from Figure 2, even assuming that only half of new crack users ever came in for treatment, the total number of crack abusers over

TABLE 1. First years for each of the major control efforts

Effort	Year
Beginnings of joint Bahamian-U.S. cooperation	1982
Treatment of crack abusers	1983
Local police action against trafficking	1983
Organized educational efforts	1985
New joint drug interdiction bases opened	1985, 1986
Major increase in U.S. interdiction role: first radar balloon; new U.S. drug law	1987
New Bahamian law against money laundering	1987

These were striking to Bahamians, because of the contrast to prior decades, but were modest by today's standards.

Substance abuse education in the future must focus more on alcohol than it has in the recent past. Education focused on alcohol, however, must take a different approach than was taken with crack cocaine. Crack was a new drug, unfamiliar, acute, and illegal, whereas alcohol is an old drug, familiar, more chronically abused in nature, and legal.

Amphetamines. There is no evidence at the CPC or SRH of a significant problem with amphetamines, despite their fairly common use as diet pills. No significant numbers of patients using methamphetamine ("speed") or its smokable form ("ice") have been reported by the treatment facilities.

Marijuana. Marijuana seizures are down impressively in recent years. Because of its bulk and the inability to dispose of it easily when arrest is imminent, and because of its low profit margin, marijuana importation has been reduced to a fraction of what it was a decade ago. This is not surprising,given the major increase in drug interdiction efforts in the Bahamas. As expected, the number of marijuana abusers seeking treatment also has dropped to low levels.

DISCUSSION

There is evidence of a major decline in new crack users and in crack treatment incidence and prevalence in the Bahamas. This is important because it shows that, at least under certain circumstances, the crack epidemic in the Bahamas is going through the historical process mentioned by Musto, mediated by the conscious control efforts of the involved nation.[7] However, the situation in the Bahamas has not returned to pre-crack epidemic status for many reasons, including the continued availability of the drug and the existence of a reservoir of chronic cocaine abusers.

The number of violent crimes against persons and the number of longstanding users seeking treatment at SRH are increasing rather than decreasing. The possibility exists that this violence is due, in part, to the joint use of cocaine and alcohol. The continuing problems of the Bahamas are complicated both by the epidemic's residual damage to social attitudes and institutions, especially the family, and the persistence of a severe form of chronic crack addiction called "chronic cocainism" in the Bahamas.

Similarities and Differences With Prohibition in the United States.

The crack epidemic hit the Bahamas in 1983, when it was, in many ways, similar to the United States in the early part of the 20th century. The population mostly lived in extended families, with close social ties, even between New Providence and the "family islands" (the name itself is significant). The population also was largely conservative, Protestant Christian, and many of the churches took strong stands against substance use. As Aaron and Musto have pointed out, in the United States the temperance movement developed partly from the threat represented by alcoholism and resulting family conflicts to a close, family-based society in which mutual support was vital.[10]

In contrast to alcoholism in the United States, however, the crack epidemic hit the Bahamas suddenly, and there was no long tradition of a gradually developing temperance movement. In fact, early in the 1980s, neither the police nor the population at large were particularly concerned with cocaine in any form, because few problems had been seen with it. Therefore, before and during the early phases of the crack epidemic, the nation was fairly permissive about crack sales, and the prices for it were quite low.[1,2]

The first responses to the crack problem, therefore, tended to be from health professionals, as they began to see the devastating impact of crack on individuals and families; action by the health community was soon followed by police and then government action. |

Another link to Prohibition in the United States was the extensive Bahamian use of the Alcoholics Anonymous 12-step program for the treatment of crack abusers,[2, 11] although it was modified for crack and had 14 steps. The highly social nature of Bahamian life, and the lack of extensive treatment resources, combined with the realization that crack abusers were not able to solve their own problems, led to a heavy dependence on outpatient therapy using local modifications of the 12-step approach. The strongly religious nature of the population reinforced this strategy.

As with Prohibition in the United States,[10] in the Bahamas there were also rumors of government and police involvement with drug traffickers and, in both cases, there was a major change in the government not long afterward.

Implications of the Bahamas for the United States

The crack cocaine epidemic began in the Bahamas 2 to 3 years before it did in the United States, so it is possible that trends in the Bahamas might presage what will happen in the United States. The differences in the cocaine problems of the two nations, however, are sufficiently great that the Bahamian story is probably better considered unique. The large amount of intravenous drug use in the United States, for both heroin and its relatives, for cocaine, and for "speed-balls," makes the United States' drug problem considerably more complex.

The situation in the United States is also more complicated in terms of its application of the three treatment approaches used by the Bahamas: demand reduction (prevention and treatment), interdiction of drugs, and control of money laundering. The mixture of languages, cultures, and religions in the United States, along with the vast size of the country and even its big cities, makes the prevention message much more difficult to deliver compared with the Bahamas. The extensive coastline, borders, and international travel in the United States also exacerbates control problems.

The treatment approach in the United States has been complicated by the mixed patterns of medical care eligibility and delivery and by the inadequate medical care payment system in the United States, where even persons otherwise adequately covered by medical care insurance may not be covered for treatment for drug abuse. These and other factors have made it impossible to provide an adequate number of treatment services in the United States.[9]

Although it put much stress on the system, in the Bahamas, every drug abuser coming for help was seen rapidly in either outpatient or inpatient treatment. This was achieved in a nation with only modest resources by emphasizing an outpatient treatment approach (combined individual counseling and group therapy) that drew heavily upon the national religious belief systems and the many churches, 12-step programs, and other community resources. Despite the limited resources, this approach may have been more effective than our current drug treatment, which is heavily hospital-based.[10]

In the United States, drug interdiction and other legal solutions have proved inadequate as the primary national strategy against illegal drugs. The Bahamian interdiction also was proving inadequate until it began to receive massive assistance from the United States. However, the United States, unfortunately, has no such interested super-power nearby, with 1,000 times the population and wealth to assist in the interdiction process.

The United States has gradually tightened the net around money laundering, but the international banking system in the United States appears to be much larger and more difficult to control than the banking system in the Bahamas, as the BCCI investigation and others have disclosed.

Under the assumption that the Bahamian control efforts did make a difference, the lessons from the Bahamas would appear to be several. First, a national response needs to include all of the available strategies simultaneously. Second, the national commitment to prevention must be a total one and must involve the "mediating structures" of society, such as families, churches, clubs, and voluntary agencies. Third, a national commitment to drug treatment should be such that every person who needs help with drug abuse can get that help within a short time without worrying about payment.o

It is not clear whether the pattern of chronic cocainism is idiosyncratic to the Bahamian situation or can be found in the United States and elsewhere as part of the natural history of crack epidemics. It was not noted by Musto as a long-lasting residual effect of past cocaine epidemics.[7] The current developments in the United States, however, also include, as in the Bahamas, a recent increase in emergency room visits for cocaine abuse and increasing major drug activity, violence, and gang patterns in major cities, combined with decreasing student use, suggesting that the United States may be moving into a similar phase.

The multifaceted Bahamian response, as well as its relatively low-cost, highly available treatment approach, may be models for emulation by the United States and other countries where crack cocaine use is a major problem.

REFERENCES

1 Jekel JF, Allen DF, Podlewski H, et al: Epidemic-freebase cocaine abuse: a case study from the Bahamas. Lancet 1986; 1:459-462

2 Allen DF, Jekel JF: Crack: The Broken Promise. London, Macmillan Academic and Professional Ltd., 1991 (published in the United States by St. Martin's Press)

3 Witkin G: The men who created crack. U.S. News and World Report 1991; 19:111:44-53

4 Jekel JF, Allen DF: Trends in drug abuse in the-mid-1980s. Yale J Biol Med 1987; 60:45-52

5 Collier's Encyclopedia. Rastafarianism. New York, Macmillan Educational Company, 1985, pp 669-670

6 Ministry of Foreign Affairs, Commonwealth of the Bahamas. Bahamas Narcotics Control Report—1990. Nassau, Bahamas, 1991, p 10

7 Musto D: Opium, cocaine, and marijuana in American history. Sci Am July 1991; 265:40-47

8 Clarke N, Allen D. Chronic cocaine addiction: the Bahamian experience. Presented at the American Psychiatric Association Caribbean Conference, Barbados, May 1991

9 Randall T: Cocaine, alcohol mix in body to form even longer-lasting, more lethal drug. JAMA 1992; 267:1043-1044

10 Aaron P, Musto D: Temperance and prohibition in America: a historical overview, in Alcohol and Public Policy: Beyond the Shadow of Prohibition, edited by Moore MH, Gerstein DR. Washington, DC, National Academy Press, 1981

11 Alcoholic Anonymous: Alcoholics Anonymous Comes of Age. New York, Alcoholics Anonymous World Services, Inc., 1957

Cultivating Gratitude: Contemplative Discovery Pathway Theory Applied to Group Therapy in the Bahamas

David F Allen[1]*, Mallery Mayo[1], Marie Allen-Carroll[1], James A Manganello[2], Victoria S Allen[3] and Jay P Singh[4,5]

[1] Renascence Institute International, Nassau, Bahamas
[2] Private Practice, Lexington, MA, USA
[3] College of the Bahamas, Nassau, Bahamas
[4] Molde University College, Molde, Norway
[5] Global Institute of Forensic Research, Reston, VA, US

Abstract

The positive psychology movement has given us new ways to conceptualize behavior. However, little research has been conducted examining the benefits of promoting the development of positive characteristics such as gratitude and love as part of treatment. To address this gap, the present article describes the implementation of a group therapy program grounded in Contemplative Discovery Pathway Theory (CDPT). The innovative program, "The Family", focuses on the discovery process to resocialize a sample of community members from the Bahamas. We conclude with a case vignette and recommendations for future research directions.

Keywords: Gratitude; Contemplative discovery pathway theory; Group therapy; Forgiveness

Introduction

For generations, four positive emotional experiences have influenced the thoughts and writings of philosophers and theologians: gratitude, forgiveness, humility, and love. Research in the field of health psychology shows that these emotional experiences are key ingredients to healthy interpersonal relationships and can reduce an individual's risk of internalizing psychiatric disorders such as depression and externalizing disorders such as substance abuse [1-3].

Gratitude refers to a community-focused emotion that can be defined as an awareness of all that is good in the world coupled with a belief that this goodness comes from an external source [4]. Increasingly, descriptive research is establishing gratitude as being strongly associated with both physical as well as psychological wellbeing [5-7]. Although gratitude has been said to be "one of the few things that can measurably change people's lives" [4] the effect of promoting gratitude as part of psychosocial interventions has received comparatively little attention.

Also linked with well-being is forgiveness, which refers to the emotional and cognitive experience of restoring a social relationship following a transgression [8]. Related to forgiveness are the character strengths of humility, which is the placing one's needs second to those of another [9], and love, which is the ability to build strong attachments to others in which both parties feel understood and valued [10,11].

These three supplementary emotions have been found to relieve individuals from weighted feelings of shame [12]. Shame by its very nature is persistent and its effects insidious, lingering long after a hurtful thought or event has passed or been forgiven. Indeed, factor analytic research conducted as early as the 1970s has demonstrated that shame is among the strongest precipitants of adverse psychiatric outcomes [13]. And in the wake of the tragic school shooting in Newtown, Connecticut, in the United States, a more fervent call has been issued to identify treatment approaches that may assist "withdrawn and isolated" and "angry and alienated" individuals diagnosed with a mental illness who may be experi-

This article was published in *The Journal of Trauma & Treatment*, June 28, 2014 encing extreme feelings of shame [14].

It may be that therapeutic interventions focusing on overcoming shame and promoting the positive emotional experiences of gratitude, forgiveness, humility, and love represent a promising way forward. However, such interventions have not been described or tested in practice settings. Hence, the aim of the present paper is to put forth a comprehensive theory and therapeutic approach that may aid in the process of resocialization (i.e., the process of discovering an inner vision of the Self extending beyond one's limitations to experience one's potential) and diminish feelings of shame through the cultivation of gratitude, forgiveness, humility, and love.

Contemplative Discovery Pathway Theory

Contemplative Discovery Pathway Theory (CDPT) was developed as an alternative to cognitive-behavioral theory that motivates clients beyond recovery to a stage of discovery, which focuses on universal ethical principles involving justice, equality, and respect for all humans. A developmental model, CDPT postulates that the Self follows a stepwise path from the Natural Self at birth to the Shame Self and its antithesis, the Shame False Self, in early development to the healthier Authentic Gracious self in adulthood and potentially even the Contemplative Transcendent Self late in life. In the following sections, we describe each of these stages in greater detail.

The Natural Self at Birth

Following the Judeo-Christian tradition, an individual comes from love, is born to love, and upon death returns to love. According to the CDPT, an infant's instinctual need for unconditional love at birth may be conceptualized as being comprised of three dimensions: Survival/ Security, Affection/Esteem, and Power/Control. These dimensions represent powerful sources of energy that interact with one another as the child struggles to establish basic trust [15]. A child exposed to a meaningful environment of stability, consistency, and predictability will undergo a separation individuation from the primary caretaker (often the mother, though not necessarily so) to form his or her identity as one who trusts his- or herself [16]. The internalization of the primary caretaker (the nurturing object) provides for the development of self-object transference within the child. As described by Kohut [17], self-objects are relationships that maintain the cohesion, vitality, strength, and harmony of the Self. These relationships form the basis for the development of human community. They also open one to the experience of shame.

The shame self and false shame self

As an individual develops, he or she faces life challenges and inevitable failures as well as successes. Having experienced a lack of unconditional love from other humans, individuals experience hurt, woundedness, and deprivation in one or more of the instinctual needs. From the perspective of CDPT, when persistent trauma and pain occurs early in life, all domains of instinctual need are affected through the development of a Shame Self, characterized by a number of shame schemata (Table 1). The emotional experiences associated with this Shame Self are so painful to confront directly that the mind creates a Shame False Self as a defense mechanism. This Shame False Self is addictive in nature and characterized by self-absorption, selfgratification, and a need for control. In reality, however, the Shame False Self is an obstacle to personal development.

The Authentic Gracious Self

By becoming aware of the Shame False Self through selfdevelopment, therapy, and/or spiritual guidance opens the door to the creation of an Authentic Gracious Self. It is critical to develop insight to the Shame False Self in order to be able to consciously embrace oneself wholly. During CDPT therapy, the client becomes aware of and confronts his or her shame, opening his or her heart to the experience of unconditional love. Thus, the person is able to discover a vision of the Authentic Gracious Self characterized by the appreciation of solitude, community, compassion, humility, and gratitude. The Authentic Gracious Self is not a fixed goal, but rather an ideal that one must continually and consciously seek to continue benefiting from the accompanying senses of relaxation, creativity, proactivity, and openness to the challenge and joy of living.

The Contemplative Transcendent Self

Many who have experienced the Authentic Gracious Self are awestruck at the experience of transcendence, a sense of oneness with the universe. Such experiences may occur through therapy, religion, nature, or the unconditionally kind acts of other humans. Paradoxically, the experience may also occur in response to a tragedy or illness which can result in people seeking out a power greater than themselves. Within the context of CDPT, such transcendence is viewed as a gift resulting from deep commitment and faithfulness. In our experience, the Contemplative Transcendent Self requires spiritual discipline to develop, including practices such as mindful prayer, solitude, and sacred reading. The deeper love manifested in the Contemplative Transcendent Self represents the death of the Shame Self, resulting in a deep sense of joy that absorbs chaos, exudes calm, and instills hope.

Principles of Treatment

CDPT embraces seven fundamental principles of treatment which will be described below: (1) therapy as a whole person process, (2) the development of insight, (3) experiencing vulnerability and developing empathy, (4) addressing cognitive components of shame, (5) authenticity, (6) humor, and (7) contemplative prayer.

Therapy as a whole person process

Therapy is an ongoing process designed to address different aspects of a client's life including his or her shame. Working through shame creates space for the awareness and experience of love. By focusing on transforming the whole individual rather than simply reinforcing individual behaviors, a more comprehensive set of physical and social changes may result.

The development of insight

Therapy from the standpoint of the CDPT model is like physical therapy. Just as when a muscle has a knot it needs to be massaged over and over again until the knot or cramp disappears, so the healing of the mind requires repeated massage and working through for healing to be effective. Thus, insights from treatment need to be revisited and developed skills practiced to be useful in the long-term.

Experiencing vulnerability and developing empathy

Working through thoughts and feelings of shame both exposes and increases vulnerability. Vulnerability is not weakness but rather willingness to accept the uncertainty, risk, and emotional exposure of daily life. Such acceptance is a result of the client's courage, purpose, and commitment to face reality. The level of defensiveness that stands in the way of vulnerability reflects the client's fear, disconnection, and shame. Once vulnerability can be experienced by oneself, the vulnerabilities of others may be experienced through the development of empathy. Empathy combats shame and enables the client to feel valued and respected by being better able to value and respect others.

Addressing cognitive components of shame

One sees the world and others through the lens of his or her thoughts. Shameful thoughts are cynical, gloomy, and generally negative. The experience of the shame of failure may produce negative thoughts that create a vicious cycle of self-fulfilling prophecies, increasing the likelihood of failure, poor self-image, and alienation. Clients are instructed that shameful thoughts and labels encourage such self-sabotage and that focusing on the self is a hallmark of the Shame False Self reflected when an individual over-personalizes events and experiences. In addition, clients are warned of the negative consequences of blaming others, which can create a passive victim mentality that makes constructive change more difficult.

Authenticity

To let go of the expectations and consciously embrace oneself is important in the CDPT model. Operationally, such authenticity involves not only sharing one's life story but also owning that story no matter how painful the events therein. As a client becomes more authentic, shame decreases.

Humor

The ability to laugh at oneself is a powerful antidote to shame. It is a self-transcendent experience and provides the client with a sense of mastery. In its expression, one experiences a form of surrender. The client realizes that his or her essential being cannot be characterized only by shame.

Contemplative prayer

Spirituality reflects a relationship with a higher power grounded in compassionate love. True spirituality includes expressions of awe, reverence, peace, joy, meaning, value, purpose, hope, humility, and gratitude. Therapy associated with spiritual development incorporates contemplative practices (e.g., personal accountability, silence, prayer, mindfulness, sacred reading, community, and the doing of good deeds). This process leads to the formation of the Contemplative Transcendent Self and can help to move a client from recovery to a discovery mindset.

The Role of the Therapist

Shame is difficult to treat because it is ubiquitous, evasive, deeply internalized, and hidden. Compared to other emotions able to be released by catharsis and grief, shame is difficult to admit, express, and discharge. Shame can also be difficult to identify, as it has few associated verbal and non-verbal expressions with the exception of blushing, the turning away of the body, downcast eyes, and a muted voice [18]. Hence, the identification of shame can require a keen alertness on the part of the therapist to be able to pick up the subtle signs.

Developing a meaningful therapeutic alliance with a client in CDPT therapy requires patience, understanding and compassion. As the client re-experiences shameful thoughts and events, the therapist may become a disavowed object of hate, rejection, and disgust. In concordance with the psychoanalytic conceptualization of transference, the therapist must accept the negative introject in a loving manner with self-containment, respect, and a non-judgmental attitude. The therapist's work with transference takes special skill and assumes that he or she has already dealt with and accepted his or her own shame through a therapeutic intervention. If not, some therapist-client relationships may end up reinforcing the False Shame Self and impeding the development of the Authentic Gracious Self.

Shifting from Shame to Love

The concept of shifting from shame to love is introduced in therapy as a way to change a client's perception of the world by working through his or her shame. Focusing on love instead of fear is a counter-instinctual choice for the client, requiring conscious effort to overcome the illusion of the False Shame Self. As Sir John Templeton observed, "Unfortunately, too often people focus on the negatives and lose sight of the multitude of blessings that surround us and the limitless potential that exists for the future" [19]. Central to facilitating the shift from shame to love is teaching clients the 10 principles of "Conscious Shifting" (see Appendix).

Implementation of "THE FAMILY"

CDPT's developmental emphasis and goal of promoting selfdiscovery of the Contemplative Transcendent Self through empathy and contemplative prayer provided the foundation for a unique group therapy approach in the Bahamas: The Family. The Family was started in 2009 to improve socialization and confront the prevailing community adversity currently experienced in the Bahamas. The motto of The Family is "Jaw, jaw stops war, war." That is, if members of the community can dialogue, the resultant socialization creates a suitable environment for the teaching and cultivation of virtues such as gratitude, forgiveness, humility, and love. In theory, the group creates a therapeutic replica of a family, allowing clients to confront their issues in a safe and non-judgmental environment. Like other countries in the world, the Bahamas has suffered from a devastating cocaine epidemic starting in the 1980s and continuing to the present. The drug crisis along with recent so cio-economic troubles has led to a powerful dissocialization and erosion of socio-cultural values.

The Family provides support and advocacy for its members, m to discover themselves and grow as individuals. Albeit a faith-based intervention, clients are given the opportunity to practice the spiritual aspects of the approach in any way they choose. At any given point in time, clients in the group will include between 40 and 50 mostly Bahamian adults, including referrals from the community or courts due to delinquent behavior, domestic violence, substance abuse, grief, vengefulness, anger management, conflict resolution, and traumatization from crime [20].

Group process

Family groups meet for two hours weekly, moderated by a therapist with the assistance of a co-therapist. Sessions are open, and new participants are welcome to join at any time. No fee is charged and therapists volunteer all services. Each group meets in a room where the chairs are arranged in a large circle so that members can see one another. Sessions begin with each member of the group introducing himself or herself and sharing the reason for being there and what they expect. Participation is optional, with discussions being guided by the therapists. At the end of each session, a therapist provides a summary of the group and offers a psychological/spiritual teaching to foster education and character development.

A few basic rules are in place to govern and maintain the confidentiality of the group. First, each person admitted to the group is given an individual intake session to identify their issues and expectations from the group. Second, during group sessions, members are encouraged to offer insight and opinions to other members of the group without being judgmental. Third, participants are encouraged to be punctual, supportive and to share openly. Fourth, persons suffering from a mental illness must be in compliance with their medications, and their doctor or medical clinic must be informed that they are attending the program. Fifth, as everything shared in the group is confidential, members may only share information about themselves with non-group members. Sixth and finally, special attention is made when discussing painful topics such as rape, incest, sexual abuse, or catastrophic loss.

Illustrative Case

Anecdotal reports from group members frequently reflect positive outcomes after participating in The Family. The case described below serves as an exemplar, illustrating an average therapeutic process from the perspective of CDPT. Identifying information has been changed out of respect for client confidentiality.

A 40-year-old, separated mother of three children was referred for services by her attorney. The attorney felt she was in crisis and was at high risk of either suicide or homicide. She claimed her life between the ages of 9 and 17 years was traumatic, as she had been sexually abused by her father. She reported marrying her husband to get out of her home environment; however, her husband was unfaithful, frequently abusing her. When the client was first interviewed, she was depressed and spent much of her time in contact with police and the courts.

She was initially overwhelmed by a negative self-image, necessitating individual therapy to uncover feelings of shame associated with being abused by her father and husband. In these sessions the client expressed deep feelings of anger towards men, often expressed as negative transference with her male therapist. She was subsequently referred to The Family to continue working on uncovering her feelings of shame.

The first sessions as part of The Family were difficult for the client, though she did receive positive feedback from other group members. She demonstrated signs of her Shame Self through anger, selfabsorption, and overeating. Initially, the insight that her Shame False Self increased her pain and accentuated her low self-esteem resulted in more hopelessness and suicidal ideation. However, as she continued to attend The Family, she began to show more vulnerability and began to empathize with the pain of other group members. Her increased ability to connect with members of the group helped her to better visualize her Authentic Gracious Self and, in turn, she began expressing gratitude for her situation. The gratitude she felt also reflected alignment with her Contemplative Transcendent Self. At this point, she stated that she knew only God–a figure larger than herself–could have saved her. After attending the group for 3 years, she re-married and continues to actively work to maintain her Authentic Gracious Self. Given such positive anecdotal evidence, it is our intention to begin empirically studying the efficacy of The Family in promoting positive outcomes.

Future Directions

At the individual, group, and societal levels, applying CDPT can lead to a discovery of a Gracious Authentic Self as well as a Transcendent Self through the cultivation of gratitude, forgiveness, humility, and love. Combating shame in a manner that provides lasting, positive change for clients, the CDPT model emphasizes selfdiscovery from a cognitive-spiritual perspective. The next step will be to qualitatively and then quantitatively test the model in a longitudinal fashion using assessment and outcome data collected over the past five years. Preliminary qualitative analyses suggest that participation in The Family have shown an improvement in depressive symptomatology as well as a greater capacity for interpersonal intimacy and trust. As part of continued longitudinal study of the efficacy of this intervention, we plan on developing a statistically-reliable assessment instrument to effectively measure resocialization at the level of the individual. Baseline scores on this assessment instrument will be retrospectively derived for when they first entered treatment. Adjusting for the length of time spent in The Family, we plan on examining changes in gratitude, forgiveness, humility, and love using non-parametric statistical methods such as dependent samples t-tests. Finally, additional Family groups will be established in the coming year under the auspices of newly trained counsellors both in the Bahamas as well as in the United States, which we hope will provide insight on the impact of culture on the effectiveness of the therapeutic model.

REFERENCES

1. Kendler KS, Liu XQ, Gardner CO, McCullough ME, Larson D, et al. (2003) Dimensions of religiosity and their relationship to lifetime psychiatric and substance use disorders. Am J Psychiatry 160: 496-503.
2. Tsang J, McCullough M E, Fincham FD (2006) The longitudinal association between forgiveness and relationship closeness and commitment. Journal of Social and Clinical Psychology 25: 448-472.
3. Westberg G (2010) Good grief – 50th anniversary edition. Augsburg Fortress Publishers, Minneapolis.
4. Emmons R (2007) Thanks!: How practicing gratitude can make you happier. Houghton Mifflin, Boston.
5. Emmons R (2004) The psychology of gratitude: An introduction, The psychology of gratitude, Oxford University Press, New York.
6. Emmons RA, McCullough ME (2003) Counting blessings versus burdens: an experimental investigation of gratitude and subjective well-being in daily life. J PersSocPsychol 84: 377-389.
7. Gordon AM, Impett EA, Kogan A, Oveis C, Keltner D (2012) To have and to hold: gratitude promotes relationship maintenance in intimate bonds. J PersSocPsychol 103: 257-274.
8. Bono G, McCullough ME, Root LM (2008) Forgiveness, feeling connected to others, and well-being: two longitudinal studies. PersSocPsychol Bull 34: 182-195.
9. Powers C, Nam R, Rowatt WC, Hill P (2007) Associations between humility, spiritual transcendence, and forgiveness. Brill Academic Publishers, Herndon, VA.
10. Allport S (1997) A natural history of parenting. Harmony Books, New York.
11. Meyers DG (1999) Close relationships and quality of life. Well-being: The foundations of hedonic psychology. New York: Russell Sage Foundation.
12. Allen DF (2010) Shame: The human nemesis. Eleuthera Publications, Washington.
13. Izard CE (1972) Patterns of emotions: A new analysis of anxiety and depression. San Diego: Academic Press.
14. Walkup JT, Rubin DH (2013) Social withdrawal and violence--Newtown, Connecticut. N Engl J Med 368: 399-401.
15. Erikson EH (1993) Childhood and society. Norton and Co, New York.
16. Mahler M, Pine F, Bergman A (1974) The psychological birth of the human infant: Symbiosis and individuation. Basic Books, New York.
17. Kohut H (1984) How does analysis cure? Chicago: University of Chicago Press.
18. Vick SJ, Waller BM, Parr LA, Smith Pasqualini MC, Bard KA (2007) A Crossspecies Comparison of Facial Morphology and Movement in Humans and Chimpanzees Using the Facial Action Coding System (FACS). J Nonverbal Behav 31: 1-20.
19. Herrmann RL (2004) Sir John Templeton: Supporting scientific research for spiritual discoveries. West Conshohocken, Templeton Foundation Press, PA.
20. Westberg G (2010) Good grief – 50th anniversary edition. Augsburg Fortress Publishers, Minneapolis.

APPENDIX

1. **Awareness that we can shift from shame to love:** Although love is always present in the world, you can live without awareness of that love. It is a choice to live in shame, and doing so puts you in a victim mentality. Consciously acknowledging love is a first step in self-transformation, as the willingness to empty the heart of shame opens you to love.
2. **Stopping to take time out**: Shame, fear and anger speed us up by way of physiological arousal, resulting in emotional and physical fatigue. Alternatively, experiencing love slows us down, resulting in emotional and physical recovery. Hence, taking time out for a break, even a brief one, can result in clearer judgment and decision-making.
3. **Confronting shame directly:** An awareness and re-experiencing of the hurt experienced over time allows for the identification of shame triggers. Working through these triggers can reduce their negative effects. To confront shame directly, you can actively write down the experiences and emotions associated with past shameful experiences. It may also be helpful to develop a timeline of shame (pinpointing ages and events to discuss in the therapeutic context).
4. **Deep breathing with eyes closed:** Breathing is synonymous with life. When we were young and carefree we breathed deeply. Age and the worries of life lead us to shallow breathing, which can lead to anxiety and increased irritability. Closing your eyes while breathing deeply allows you to relax further, and taking time to focus on relaxing individual body parts can result in even deeper relaxation.
5. **Silence:** Remaining silent for a few minutes will allow your own heart rate to settle and make you more aware of your deeper self. Focus on the universal love in the greater world around you.
6. **Prayer:** With your mind relaxed, admit your problems and ask your God or the universe around you to open your heart to love. Whereas human love is temporal and temperamental, eternal love is unchanging and unconditional. However, we frequently lose sight of eternal love and focus on seeking the love of those around us. A simple prayer or meditation can help you to focus on anchoring yourself in eternal love. Your prayer might be, "God have mercy upon me and forgive my resistance to your love. I surrender my heart and shame to your healing and unfailing love."
7. **Identify streams of love:** Most of us can identify a person in our childhood who expressed unconditional love toward us. Perhaps it was a parent, relative, pastor, priest, rabbi, teacher, or even a stranger. Who provided a stream of love to you? Think of or write down the names of those persons and, as you do this, you will begin to relax and shift from focusing on shame to love.
8. **Identify a sacred space of love:** In a sacred space we feel free, loved, and inspired. For many of us from the Bahamas, the sea provides that place. Visiting a sacred space – either physically or mentally – is relaxing and provides another way to shift from focusing on shame to love. Although we may only physically visit a sacred place one time, the memory and sense of personal meaning it brought us can feed us for years to come. Try to reexperience all of the sensations associated with that space when you imagine yourself there.
9. **Gratitude:** Being thankful for what is often taken for granted is a doorway to love and enables us to move beyond shame to self-transcendence and new meaning. Practicing such gratitude allows you to experience your deepest self. To facilitate a shift to gratitude, write down three things for which you are grateful.
10. **Practicing love:** After shifting from shame to love, practice love by reaching out to others. Make a commitment to view the world through a lens of love. Practice seeing without thinking, naming, judging, or interpreting – just be present. Whether those around you are expressing love in return or appealing for love through anger or fear, respond lovingly. Seek not only recovery but also discovery of your Contemplative Transcendent Self.

Cocaine Addiction:
The Nemesis of Modern Culture

by David F. Allen, MD

Presented at the Jack W Provonsha Lectureship for the Alumni Postgraduate Convention on March 3,1997

Someone has said that the further we look into the past, the better we understand the future. This is certainly true of cocaine. Cocaine is derived from the coca plant grown in South America, particularly Columbia, Peru, and Bolivia. Coca leaves have been chewed by the Indians of South America for centuries. In the Inca empire, coca leaves were used for ceremonial and sacred purposes. It was believed that the god Inti sent the Indians the coca plant to reduce the burden of life. Another myth is that a woman, executed for adultery, sent the coca plant to seduce and punish her persecutors. Notice the association of the coca plant with spiritual and sexual connotations. This continues today when addicts talk about the spirit of cocaine and how it is associated with a galloping sexuality in some people.

In the 15th century King Philip of Spain forbade the chewing of coca leaves by the Indians. However, he changed his edict when he was informed that chewing coca leaves reduced the appetite and increased the motivation and stamina of Indians working in high altitudes. Notice the powerful precedence of economic interest over moral concerns in cocaine addiction.[1]

Cocaine hydrochloride was first synthesized in Europe in 1859 by Albert Niemann, professor at the University of Gottinghen. In 1859, Pablo Mantegazza wrote his prize-winning essay heralding cocaine hydrochloride's ability to remove fatigue, increase strength, raise spirits, and cure impotency. In 1865, the Corsican Andrew Mariani introduced the popular wine-cocaine mixture, "vin Mariani," as a cure for everything. Enjoying immense popularity in Europe and America, it ıade him wealthy and drew testimonials from such luminaries as Thomas Edison, the Czar of Russia, Jules Verne, Emile Zola, Henrik Ibsen, the Prince of Wales, and Sarah Bernhardt. Pope Leo XIII, a frequent imbiber, gave Mariani a gold medal for his service to mankind. In 1880, the Russian nobleman Professor Vassili Von Anrep discovered the local anesthetic properties of cocaine, and in 1884, Sigmund Freud, a student of Von Anrep, published his "uber coca," the first of his enthusiastic papers about the experience of using cocaine. According to Freud, cocaine hydrochloride lifts the spirit, decreases fatigue, relieves impotence, and cures depression. Freud turned away from the therapeutic use of cocaine when a friend, Von Fleisel, who was taking cocaine as treatment for morphine addiction, developed a toxic psychosis in which he became delirious and saw snakes crawling over his body. In 1885, Albrecht Erlenmeyer accused Freud of unleashing cocaine as the third scourge of mankind, after alcohol and opiates.[2]

In 1886, John Styth Pemberton of Atlanta, Georgia, combined cocaine and caffeine into a brown syrup which became the popular soft drink, Coca Cola. This spawned a dozen cola competitors, and cocaine became a favorite ingredient in both patent medicines and pharmaceutical products.

This article was published in UPDATE Volume 13, Number 3 (September 1997).
Loma Linda University Center For Christian Bioethics

In 1891, 200 cases of cocaine intoxication were reported. In 1898, the medical community turned against the wonder drug. Southern politicians launched a racist campaign suggesting that cocaine not only gave black men superhuman strength but made them want to rape white women. As a result, in 1903 cocaine was taken out of Coca Cola. In 1907, cocaine use peaked with over 1.5 million pounds entering the country. The problem of addiction was particularly serious in New York City. Like today, there was a sense of hopelessness about the efficacy of treatment, and one New York Times editorial is purported to have stated, "Let the cocaine fiends die." The problem of escalating addiction led to the passage of the Harrison Act in 1914, the first federal anti-drug law providing severer penalties for cocaine than opium. But illicit drug use continued. In 1922, the narcotic drug import and export act misclassified cocaine as a "narcotic," so cocaine use went underground for about five decades, mainly being used by the wealthy and some jazz musicians. The new openness to drugs in the 1960s gave rise to a cocaine renaissance, and in 1972, led by the entertainment industry, cocaine reemerged as the "in" drug of the so-called "beautiful people," and began its spread down scale.[2]

My clinical ,experience with cocaine began in psychiatric training when my first patient suffered from a cocaine psychosis in which she saw multicolored rabbits jumping around my office. Returning to my island nation in 1980, I was exposed to a new phenomenon involving young men and women destroying themselves by smoking a drug they called Bahamian rock. They said that, by heating cocaine hydrochloride with baking soda and water, they obtained a volatile rock-like substance. After snorting cocaine hydrochloride powder for five years or more, they claimed that when they smoked the rock cocaine the high was more intense. They described the high as giving a thousand orgasms, or as a never-ending Christmas party. In 1983, there were 32 cases and in 1984 the total number of cases jumped to 564 cases entering into treatment. The sudden increase in addiction occurring in a vulnerable population was defined as an epidemic.

This form of cocaine, now called "crack," spread like wildfire. It appeared to be a no-barrier drug, affecting persons in all levels of society. I recall a letter from a 15- year-old girl. She said that her pusher asked for her mother's jewelry, and she gave it to him. He asked for her mother's money, and she gave it to him. And now he wanted her body. It was her letter that encouraged a nation-wide campaign against this debilitating drug experience which was corrupting our young men, destroying our young women, and wreaking havoc on families, neighborhoods, and communities. To compound matters, the National Broadcasting Company (NBC) made allegations accusing the Bahamian government of corruption, and harboring members of the Columbian cocaine cartel, as for example, when Carlos Lehder bought beautiful Norman's Cay in the Exumas. This eventually led to a Bahamian Commission of Enquiry[3] confirming complicity in the drug trade. As matters worsened, I was appointed head of the National Task Force on Drugs[4] which developed a report outlining the causes, scope, and other aspects of the crack cocaine epidemic. This resulted in an official study and publicizing of the first country-wide crack cocaine epidemic.[5] In 1984, Carleton Turner from the Reagan White House visited the Bahamas to examine the extent and damage of the epidemic.

Subsequently, the crack cocaine epidemic entered the United States circa 1985-1986. It is extremely amazing to see the damage the drug has done in ten years, especially in the inner city, where men's and women's lives have been destroyed through drugs, crime, and violence. It is terrifying to think what could happen in the next ten years the situation is not brought under control. Although the epidemic has subsided, cocaine addiction is now endemic, continuing to devastate individuals and the infrastructure of communities. According to *The National Drug Control Strategy* report (1966):

the insidious nature of addiction has been realized as many of these formerly occasional users have progressed to chronic, hardcore drug use. Families and neighborhoods are being torn apart by the crime and health consequences that so often accompany addiction. While one in four users is a hard-core drug abuser, this minority consumes the majority of the illegal drugs and commits a disproportionate number of drug-related crimes. About two thirds of these hard-core users come in contact with the criminal justice system each year. [6]

Recognizing the seriousness of the situation, what is our socioethical responsibility in dealing with this devastating phenomenon? According to Potter, socioethical analysis involves empirical definition of the situation (the facts), quasi theological assumptions, that is, concerns about the range of human freedom and the extent of human power to predict and control historical events and human destiny, modes of moral reasoning, and affirmations of loyalty. And, of course, no socioethical analysis is complete without implementation)

I. The Facts

Good ethics demand good data. Perhaps the most pervasive impediment to dealing with the drug problem in general, and cocaine addiction in particular, is a strong sense of denial. Manifested in every hue and color, denial involves misinformation about the danger involved, misplaced idealism, simplistic solutions, and strong projective tendencies to blame. Projection may make us feel better with a sense of false pride, but healing is only possible when we take responsibility. Denial is also expressed in such statements as: "The war on drugs has failed;" "Treatment does not work;" "Addiction is an inner-city problem," and "Legalization is the only solution." Matching the public sense of denial is the addict's denial- "I can handle it," or the pusher's rationalization, "I will do one more cocaine trip, make some money, and then stop." Most dangerous is the parent's denial, "It could never happen to my family," or "Only derelicts and losers go on drugs."

Denial has produced a state of confusion, lack of information, hopeless innuendo, and inaction. It mitigates against uniting community support to produce a symphonic togetherness in dealing with the problem. Facing the facts of cocaine addiction in general, and crack cocaine in particular, requires a deep sense of humility and unflinching commitment to the truth. Firth's "Ideal Observer" theory offers a good model to deal with facts. According to Firth, the ideal observer aims to be omniscient (informed), omnipercipient (perceptive), disinterested and dispassionate (objective), consistent, and otherwise normal (recognize limitations).[8]

When cocaine hydrochloride is snorted, 25 percent pure cocaine crosses the blood-brain barrier in 15 to 20 minutes, giving a high that lasts from 15 to 25 minutes. But when crack cocaine is smoked, 80 percent pure cocaine crosses the barrier in eight seconds, providing a high which lasts for about one minute. Using up the pleasure neurotransmitter, dopamine, the subsequent highs are less intense, of shorter duration, and the fall more precipitous. Acting as a positive reinforcement, the memory of the first high lures addicts into binge use with diminishing highs and more devastating lows. Post-cocaine crashes then act as negative reinforcement to seek more crack. The crack binge may go on for days, with the addict taking minimal food and water. In order to ease the crash, addicts use strong alcohol (rum, whiskey, etc.), or marijuana and heroin. As a result, crack cocaine addiction increases the use of other addictive substances. The chronic addict who suffers neurotransmitter depletion has decreasing highs and increasing lows. Thus, the drug promises euphoria but gives dysphoria.

Cocaine addiction in general, and crack cocaine smoking in particular, affects all body systems, producing diminished respiratory function, irregular heart rate, headache, stroke, etc. Psychologically, cocaine leads to depression, and variants of cocaine psychoses with paranoia. Socially, cocaine produces ethical fragmentation and decreased social inhibition, leading to stealing, prostitution, murder, etc. Producing community fragmentation at all levels, the drug destroys families, corrupts governing authority, and leads to "bombed-out" neighborhoods.

Of particular importance are the chronic heavy users who make up one quarter of the addicts, use two-thirds of the total cocaine, and account for two-thirds of those involved in the criminal justice system annually.[9] They also act as vectors and reservoirs for infectious diseases, such as AIDS and tuberculosis. As cocaine use becomes endemic in an area, the resulting fragmentation leads to increased crime rates and the proliferation of youth gangs which provide protection, a sense of community, and control of drug supplies. In crack cocaine addiction, cue reinforcement occurs in which persons, money, or gold associated with the use of cocaine produces a pseudo-high in non-using addicts, propelling them to seek the drug. This has particular relevance to understanding the connection between hard-core chronic cocaine addiction and crime. For example, a chronic addict is stimulated by seeing someone wearing a Rolex watch. They attack the person to steal the watch, but find that when they pawn the watch and buy cocaine, the high from the cocaine is less than the high they experienced from the cue stimulation.

In my experience, whether by causation or association, cocaine is a viologenic drug. Crack associated violence has increased in urban areas; for instance, in Atlanta, the DEA reports increased hand gun violence and in Lubock, Texas, young Hispanic gang members distributing crack have led to turf wars and increased drive-by shootings. Manchrek, et al, showed that 55 percent of cocaine psychosis is associated with violence. [10]

Cocaine arrests show a mixed picture. Declines have occurred in Boston, Miami, and New Orleans, with increases in New York City and Honolulu.[11] A number of drug indicators in the past year indicated increased cocaine use among youth. For example, past-month use of cocaine increased for 10th graders primarily due to crack cocaine use.[12]

Although vast sums of money have been spent on the interdiction process, there has been only marginal success in curbing the supply of cocaine. The late Dr. Sidney Cohen, a well-known expert in the field of drug abuse treatment, put it this way:

There have been massive seizures of cocaine and coca [in the] past, laboratories were destroyed in Columbia, and thousands of coca bushes uprooted and burned in Peru and other countries. But in spite of this, the coca plantations have spread over the immense land areas of northwestern South America.[13]

This depressing reality does not imply that enforcement activities should be curtailed, but that enforcement alone is not enough. Demand-reduction strategies such as education and rehabilitation should match our commitment to law enforcement.

Cocaine addiction has invaded the work place, and along with existing high rates of alcoholism, leads to poor attitudes, decreased productivity, stealing, and violence. Although the subject of much debate concerning the civil liberties of employees versus the protection of society, urine screening has been widely implemented in the work place. Mandatory random urine testing has been recommended for employees whose alertness on the job may affect public safety, such as pilots, train captains, nuclear industry workers, etc.

The invasion of cocaine into professional sports has had a dethroning effect on this powerful alternative to drug abuse which is held in such high esteem by young people. Seeing the drug scourge take hold of sports heroes-the ones who have made it against so many odds-is especially tragic not only for the ones whose lives are destroyed, but for young people desperately looking for role models.

These and other issues provide a bird's eye view of the urgency and complexity of the cocaine problem. Good ethics demand good data. There can be no proper resolution without a commitment to examine all the issues involved.

Being Perceptive

The solution to the drug problem depends not only on our being informed, but also on our ability to empathize or identify with the pain of those who suffer. This requires the ability to place ourselves in the position of others, to feel what they feel, and then move to treat them as we would like to be treated. Such empathic projection requires patience, tolerance, and understanding. It means moving beyond the narcissistic calculus to be touched by another. According to Alfred North Whitehead, this sensitivity transforms ' a fact from being a mere fact to being invested with all its possibilities, thus becoming "the architect of our purposes, and the poet of our dreams."[14]

The fearsome spectacle of widespread drug abuse is more than a red line on a statistical chart-it is destroying our families, prostituting our daughters, and robbing the manhood of our sons. Hear the mother detail the death of her child. They told her to do the best for her kid, and she tried. They told her to send her child to school, and she did. They told her she lived in a green and pleasant land an idyllic paradise-and she believed them. But the high went higher than high, the crash even deeper, and the bullet rang;

the rope tightened, and her son-her child was dead. As a psychiatrist, I have mourned with many such grieving mothers. What a terrifying experience!

Is cocaine addiction the new slavery? Hear a pusher call an addict "my slave." Running out of money, addicts sell themselves to pushers to obtain more cocaine. Is this not the classic character defense of the repetition compulsion? Upon being freed, the slave chooses to return to the bondage of a new slavery. Consider the effects on the addict's children. Listen to the poetry of an 8-year-old girl whose mother is a cocaine addict and leaves home for a week at a time:

Life is nothing to me,
Life don't mean a thing to me.
With my life, it is terrible;
People pulling me apart.
The things I go through are horrible,
And some are breaking my heart.

Can we feel the violence destroying her life? Is her personalized pain universalized in our hearts?

Being Objective

Recognizing the complexity and emotional nature of the cocaine problem, a sense of objectivity is necessary in working towards meaningful solutions. Using the model of the legal jury system, this might best be achieved by multidisciplinary formats to prevent particular interests or biases from dominating the process. A microcosm of society itself, the cocaine crisis requires input from all segments of the community. Noting the difficulties in achieving this type of cooperation, Archibald says,

Researchers can't communicate with treatment workers, physicians can't communicate with educators, and so on. At the /same time, people in research, treatment, and prevention tend to look down on the police. And vice versa.[15]

Although there were growing pains, the multidisciplinary composition of the National Drug Council of the Bahamas provided a mutual educational experience, broadly based analysis of the local cocaine situation, and a cooperative approach in working toward its solution. This led to a symphonic response with the community, calling for action against drug abuse.

Being Consistent

Consistency dictates that, even as we press to eliminate illegal drug use, whether it be cocaine, designer drugs, or marijuana, we simultaneously seek to affect healing related to the abuse of prescription drugs, alcohol, and cigarettes. Abuse of any substance is often related to abuse in other areas. Cocaine addicts admit increased alcohol and marijuana use to control the "crash" after the cocaine high.

Early marijuana use in school-age children is now seen as a precursor to subsequent cocaine use in the mid-teen years-for example, many high school students undergoing treatment for cocaine addiction began smoking marijuana in pre- or early adolescence. If the cocaine epidemic provides the stimulus for the development of a consistent and effective approach to all drug abuse, the community would benefit enormously.

Recognizing Limitations

It is magical thinking to believe that a short, simple solution exists. Healing must start with the development of an effective infrastructure which slowly brings about the desired changes. This process, fraught with ambivalence and frustration, confronts our limitations, taxes our patience, and often produces burnout. Confrontation with our limitations and helplessness is painful. As professionals, we are so enmeshed in our "perceived" role-as the great doctor or psychologist-that it is hard to relate to our actual role, that of a frail human being who is limited and vulnerable. To be effective in the field of cocaine addiction treatment requires a meaningful balance between the perceived and the actual role, manifested by a sense of competency with a realistic awareness of limitations. We must have the personal integrity to say, "I don't know;" the ability to tolerate frustration and failure, and still find the strength to persist, to give hope in spite of despair.

II. Value Beliefs

Impacting the cocaine problem requires not only accurate knowledge and technical expertise, but also an unflinching commitment to a humane value system and moral center. According to Arieti:

Values always accompany and give special psy-

chological significance to facts.... When we deprive facts of their value, we fabricate artifacts which have no reality in human psychology. An individual may suspend his value judgment when he wants to examine a fact from a specific point of view, but then the ethical content has to be re-established if the fact is to have human significance. If we remove the ethical dimension, we reduce man to subhuman animal.[16]

Emphasizing the importance of a moral center, Eisenberg argues that what one believes about the nature of human beings exerts a subtle but controlling influence on the attitudes, behaviors, and treatment of individuals.[17]

Western ethics are based on the Judeo-Christian tradition which, at its core, views all human beings as having been made in the image of God (Gen. 1:27). Providing the basis for personhood, dignity, and human rights, this age old concept is the operative force enhancing personal meaning, interpersonal relationships, and human community. Elaborating on this concept, Niebuhr says this "reverence" for all human beings is the quintessential element for meaningful social reform.[18] Thus all individuals, regardless of race, class, handicap, illness, sex, or age, are persons with meaning and dignity, deserving the utmost respect and concern.

The principle of autonomy inherent in this respect for the uniqueness of human personhood carries with it responsibilities and duties as well. The person with a cocaine problem should not be seen as a "junkie," but as a person who has the right to be respected, a right which may involve receiving proper treatment. Similarly, he/she has a responsibility as a person in society to other persons in that society to work on the drug problem by taking advantage of treatment opportunities offered. The basis of our relationship in caring for or working with addicted persons is our mutual personhood, with mutual respective rights and responsibilities. By recognizing in each other the shared human qualities which transcend individual differences or problems, we actualize the principle of reciprocity in a practical way so that we treat others as we would want to be treated.

The moral responsibility inherent in this reciprocal, empathic, interpersonal relationship requires allegiance to other vital principles such as trust, forgiveness, truth telling, love, promise-keeping, justice, liberty, and non-injury. Being absolutely germane to the human community, these principles may be called constitutive imperatives-the underlying principles upon which all laws governing society are made.

Johnson and Butler emphasize the importance of this concept:

Respect for individuals requires that every individual be treated in consideration of his uniqueness, equal to every other, and that special Justification is required for interference with their purposes, their privacy, or their behavior. It implies sets of liberties, rights, duties, and obligations especially of promise-keeping and truth-telling.[19]

The cocaine problem may be described as a crisis in values, as they relate to the community in general and the individual in particular. How could the cocaine epidemic spread so rapidly? The sad truth is that persons in the producer countries of South America, the transshipment areas of the Caribbean, and massive consumer centers like the United States; are willing to sacrifice basic human values for sordid gain through blood money. The words of a crack-addicted person ring true: "Money is more important than people and principle does not count."[20]

III. Moral Reasoning

The moral reasoning inherent in any process profoundly influences the way persons are treated. Forms of moral reasoning range from the ethical egoism of Kohlberg's Stage I to the more sophisticated formalism of Stage VI.[21] Western ethics are mainly influenced by two ethical systems: formalism and utilitarianism.

Formalism is deontological and requires commitment to basic principles such as justice, promise-keeping, honesty, and non-injury. The major thrust is being faithful to principles in spite of consequences or outcome. Utilitarianism, on the other hand, is teleological and has as its basic tenet the facilitation of the best balance of pleasure over pain and the greatest good for the greatest number.

Connected to utilitarianism is the prevailing value of instant gratification or success, as opposed to the formalistic approach which emphasizes the need to struggle for longterm, more enduring results.

In the areas of education, enforcement, or rehabilitation, the utilitarian perspective would emphasize immediate results. When and if such results are not forthcoming, frustration, anger, and burnout follow. There are no magical solutions to the cocaine problem, and even if the short-term results are not what we wish, it is our duty to persist in working toward a society where persons may choose a drug-free lifestyle and, if addicted, may receive treatment with dignity and respect.

Another major ethical issue is the utilitarian argument that drug addicts are the losers of society who choose to destroy themselves by their personal choice of addiction. As a result, they should not receive attention and resources at the expense of the majority. Firstly, this is a misunderstanding of the addictive process. The bane of addiction is that the user continues to use compulsively despite devastating adverse consequences. With cocaine addiction, a biological hunger drive is created, which puts the brain on automatic pilot for cocaine, though this may be contrary to the desire of the addict. Secondly, this form of social utilitarianism ignores the pathos of the vicious world of the addicted person. Though appealing to the majority of the most powerful, this philosophy offers little for those who are in the minority and/or without power. When unchecked, this motivation has led to atrocities inflicted on such disadvantaged groups as the mentally ill, the mentally retarded, and racially despised groups considered expendable for the greater good.

Underlying the social utility concept is the assumption that only life of a certain quality has worth. There is a tendency to define personhood on the basis of relative social utility. Whenever one's utility/disutility ratio is affected, worth as a person is diminished. Being a cocaine addict reduces utility and basic worth in society. Thus the utilitarian view of justice denies positive presumption and equality under the euphemism "for the public good." This strains the moral fiber of society itself and undermines the meaning of such principles as promise-keeping, justice, and liberty for all its members.

IV. Loyalties

Loyalties dictate the ultimate ends we serve. The war against drugs requires a clear understanding of loyalties in terms of ends and means. The ultimate goal is to create an environment in which individuals would freely choose a drug-free lifestyle, or, if addicted, would receive treatment in programs which respect the meaning and dignity of human personhood. Yet so often, whether in areas of enforcement, education, research, or rehabilitation, we become frozen in our own ideas and fused to our personal projects. Refusing to be flexible and open to the overall perspective, we are subject to petty jealousies, destructive competition, and defensive communication. As a result, efficiency and creativity are compromised, and the program becomes an end in itself rather than the means to serve the best interests of those being treated.

V. Implementation

The cocaine crisis, with its horror stories of threat to individuals, families, and countries, evokes panic and a tendency to impulsive action. On the other hand, as we learn more about the severity and complexity of the situation, there is a parallel tendency to feel overwhelmed, to despair, and to withdraw. Recognizing that both of these options are counterproductive, clarification of goals and effective implementation are best served by thoroughly analyzing the data base (facts), value beliefs, moral reasoning, and loyalties inherent in one's plan of action. In light of the complexity of the situation, the war against cocaine requires a multiplicity of well-coordinated approaches as represented in the following initiatives:

- **The Need for a Symphonic Approach.** In light of the complexity of the situation, the war against drugs in general, and cocaine in particular, requires a symphonic approach. Archibald stresses that, without coordination, success will be at best isolated and temporary:

Drug traffickers are multinational corporations with highly developed systems including marketing specialists, promotion specialists, and training for couriers. They have it in their power to change the political map of the world. In contrast, the addictions field is rife with territorialism and mutual disdain, specialty for specialty, group for group.[22]

In the Bahamas, it was not until each sector of

society realized it was under attack by the drug problem that a community groundswell resulted in an effective symphonic response. This meant the coming together of the police, educators, politicians, business persons, media, the religious community, and ordinary consumers in fighting against drugs .

• **The Development of Innovative Treatment Approaches.** Traditionally, the drug war has had an overemphasis on interdiction and reduction of supply. In my view, this is important, but must be balanced by an aggressive, continuous, and creative approach to demand reduction. Life is wounded, and we all experience a hole in our souls. As a result, we look for means of comfort, solace, and pain-relief by wrapping ourselves in numerous addictions, such as, drugs, money, sexual issues, workaholism, etc. My argument is that regardless of supply, unless we seek to find positive ways to heal the hurting hearts, especially of our children, the search will continue for substances to fix the holes in our souls. Beyond this, we need innovative approaches to treatment. Treatment should be simple, cost-effective, accessible, and built around a critical but limited number of professionals, supplemented by trained volunteers or retired person," According to the Rand Corporation Study, $34 million invested in treatment resources for cocaine use equals as much as an expenditure of $783 million for source-country programs, or $366 million for interdiction.[23]

Treatment services should follow a cone shaped model with few inpatient or residential centers at the apex and the majority of outpatient services at the base. In the Bahamas, the government took the lead in establishing an array of inpatient and outpatient services. This was supplemented by treatment outreach programs developed by each major religious denomination. Coordinated by the rehabilitation committee of the National Drug Council, the comprehensive array of services afforded each addict the opportunity for free, accessible, and effective treatment.

• **The Development of Treatment Programs in Prison.** As stated earlier, even though the number of new users of cocaine is down, by far the most troubling problem is the increasing number of hardcore chronic users. Going in and out of prison, these addicts are hardened and powerfully disruptive to society. The development of creative programs in prison can be extremely effective in their rehabilitation. However, from my experience, the treatment is more effective if the program in prison is interphased with a community treatment program upon discharge.

• **The Development of Treatment Programs in Homeless Shelters.** The crack crisis has lowered the average age of homelessness to about 22 to 27 years old. Sadly, giving a person a bed to sleep on and a -meal to eat may enable his or her addiction. As a result, some homeless shelters have become crack dens. In the past three years we have developed a pilot program at a homeless center at the Gospel Mission in Washington, D.C. The program consists of spiritual direction, prayer, scripture reading, 12-step approaches, development of values and community, remedial education (basic education including GED, computer literacy, and grooming), psychological support (anger management and impulse control), and vocational training, (training at fast food chains, etc.). The results are promising, because when addicts become homeless they hit rock bottom. As a result, they are humbled because their denial and projective defenses are broken, and they are more willing to seek help.

• **Relate Education, Training, and Work to the Treatment Program.** Thousands of addicts in treatment spend time in individual and group therapy with little exposure to educational training and work. This is counterproductive because an addict, even off drugs, is vulnerable to the vicious cycle of re-addiction if he or she has no future as far as education, training, or work is concerned. Why can't addicts in treatment clean parks, paint the homes of elderly persons, or volunteer to work with mentally retarded or physically handicapped persons? The hallmark of Haven programs in the Bahamas and Washington is that the addict is put to work immediately upon entering treatment.

• **Development of Drug Courts.** Drugs and crime are intimately related. Drug courts could delay sentencing to prison by placing the addict in a treatment program. The court then monitors the program of the individual by specific markers, such as behavior, urine screening, or drug use. Thus, if addicts do not follow through in treatment, /they are sentenced to prison. Recognizing that this is a form of mandatory treatment, I have seen it work in the Bahamas.

• **Save the Children.** We must put a ring around our children. The seeds of addiction are planted early in childhood through the breakdown of family, church, and school connections. Children need love in a structured environment. Being a transgenerational bonding community with its mandate to love and care, the church can be creative in reestablishing the connection between family and community. Volunteers, big brother programs, and foster grandparent programs are extremely helpful in creating a sense of caring in a community. In the Haven programs, the church has been a powerful bond between the community and the treatment program. In the Bahamas, crack addicts who have been sober for ten years or more have been integrated into caring religious fellowships. Chronic crack addiction tends to be trans generational, particularly affecting young males of crack-addicted fathers. One of the most beautiful experiences of my life was to be on a retreat for male crack addicts and their sons whom they had not seen for months or years. These retreats, held four times a year, allow father and children to be together in a caring environment.

Conclusion

Last, but not least, the spiritual perspective is extremely helpful in providing motivation, encouragement, and accountability in dealing with the many facets of drug addiction. Spirituality is that dimension of life which involves ultimate concerns or beliefs (God, higher power, Jesus Christ, etc.), as it relates to the evolution of personal meaning, the development of community, and an informed caring for the environment. Writing from the perspective of my own faith tradition, which is Judeo-Christian, I'd like to discuss some universal principles of spirituality as presented in the last supper.[24]

Love. Telling His disciples He loved them to the uttermost, Christ emphasized love as the building block and healing force of life. In a study of ten severe crack addicts with histories of violence and criminality, the one concern shared by all of them was that "they all wished they had a father who said he loved them!"[25] Regardless of the sophistication of the program, if love, expressed by such factors as acceptance, community, caring, honesty, and forgiveness is lacking, the program is less effective. I'll never forget the evening when one of the men in my program shared that he was a murderer who had served time in prison. He then asked me, "Dr. Allen, do you still love me?"

The psychiatrist may listen, the surgeon operate, and the physician prescribe, but only God's love heals! Communion. Enjoying a meal together, the disciples experienced a deep sense of communion and togetherness. The major goal of initiatives in the war against drugs is to encourage the development of a healing, drug-free community. This, however, requires a spiritual base for communion- for example, the desire to do the good in spite of the outcome. In other words, fighting drugs is the good, and even if we fail, it is the right thing to do. In the early days of the crack epidemic in the Bahamas when I headed the Task Force on Drugs, my office was in the Sisters of Charity Convent. Love, prayers, and support from the nuns gave me courage to face the multiple problems, painful experiences, and possible choices in fighting against crack.

Resistance. The last supper was punctuated by the discordant notes of Judas' resistant and destructive attitude. But the supper continued in spite of the resistance. The war against drugs is fraught with so much negativism, learned helplessness, and frustration. With our faith in God, our higher power, we are challenged to move on in spite of resistance. The spiritual allows us to move beyond our frustration, to light a candle in the darkness to radiate hope and courage.

Humility. Divesting Himself of His outer garments, Christ humbled Himself and became a servant. Healing is only possible by moving from a willful attitude of pride to a willing spirit of openness and humility. Humility is the antidote to despair in the war against drugs, because it allows us to see reality as it is, and therefore establish meaningful goals and appropriate agendas. Facing our responsibility, humility means breaking through the projective defense of blaming others to serve in our respective roles in the war against drugs.

Simplicity. Using the simple articles of a basin and water, our Lord prepares to show love to His disciples. Life at its heart is very simple. I am always humbled by the success of the simple approach in dealing with addiction problems. As head of the Bahamas Task Force on Drugs, I was appalled to walk into an area called Black Village, where twenty young men were hitting crack cocaine in broad daylight. They rejected any hint of psychiatric help or rehabilitation approaches. The situation was dismal and appeared hopeless. After much deliberation, we hired a young pastor, Brother Zeke, from the same area, to be a street worker. Each morning he would sing and pray with the men and feed them McDonald's Egg McMuffins. To my surprise, within nine months many of the men sought help and the area was totally cleaned up.[26]

Service. As our Lord washed His disciples' feet, so we too are called upon to serve each other. Drug addiction has touched almost every family, leaving many of us hurt, discouraged, and frustrated. We need to listen, help, and do our best through education, prevention, and treatment to heal those in our midst. It is difficult enough to wash the feet of those who agree with us, but maybe the test of caring is seen in Jesus washing the feet of Judas, the one planning to betray Him. Fighting against drugs is a dangerous enterprise, with small victories and terrible frustrations. Often the test of our commitment to care is serving even when it hurts.

Transcendence. The spiritual has its essence in God's transcendent love. This means seeing the spark of God in each person, whether an addict, pusher, or abused person. Calling us to look beyond our faults, limitations, and hopelessness, the reminder of God's transcendent love makes possible a thousand new beginnings and allows us to be surprised by joy in seeing victory snatched from the jaws of defeat.

After hiring Brother Zeke to do street work in Black Village, I went to check on the program about two months later. As I entered the area, I was accosted by six tough addicts. One of them whose name was Neal, had a bullet in his arm and lived in an old abandoned car. They accused me of injecting the Egg McMuffins with a drug. They complained that after singing, praying, and eating the Egg McMuffins, they were unable to get high on crack cocaine, so they had to hit as much cocaine as possible before visiting Brother Zeke. I don't understand this. But could it be that when they saw Brother Zeke, one of their own doing good, it awakened repressed memories of the spiritual teachings of their mothers, which neutralized the high from the cocaine?

Eight years later, I finally received permission for my drug programs to be accepted in Her Majesty's prison in Nassau. Going to the first session, I felt alone and nervous because other members of my team were not able to attend. As the guards closed the huge iron doors behind me, seeing about fifteen tough guys walking toward me, I felt scared and apprehensive. But then a guard, dressed in a khaki uniform with a prisoner carrying his coat, approached me. Putting his arm around me he said, "Don't worry, Doc, my name is Neal. I'm in charge here. Eight years ago, when I was a hopeless crack addict in Black Village, you sent Brother Zeke to feed me. I went to Teen Challenge in Florida to get off crack and then went on to finish school and return to work at the prison."

Shocked, I found it difficult to make the connection between the Neal I'd known living in the old abandoned car and this person standing beside me. It was an epiphany-the experience of the miraculous.

REFERENCES

1 D. F. Allen, F. Jekel, Crack: *The Broken Promise* (London, UK: McMillian Academic and Professional Ltd., 1991).

2 D.F. Allen, "The History of Cocaine" in *The Cocaine Crisis*, ed by D.F. Allen, (Plenum Press, New York) 7-13.

3 Report of the Commission of Enquiry 1987, Bahamas Government Publication.

4 *Report of the Task Force on Drugs 1985*, Bahamas Government Publication.

5 Jekel, D. F. Allen, et al "Epidemic Cocaine Abuse: A Case Study From the Bahamas" (*The Lancet I, 1986*), 459-62.

6 National Drug Control Strategy, 1996, p. 11.

7 R. Potter, *War and Moral Discourse* (John Knox Press, 1969), 23.

8 R. Firth, "Ethical Absolutism and The Ideal Ob-

server" (*Philosophy and Phenomenological Research*, 12 March, 1952).

9 National Drug Control Strategy, 1996, p. 11.

10 T. Manschrek, D.F. Allen, M. Neville, "Freebase Psychosis Cases From A Bahamian Epidemic of Cocaine Abuse," (*Comprehensive Psychiatry* Vol. 28, No. 6, Nov-Dec 1987), 555-644.

11 *Crack, Facts and Figures*, (Office of National Drug Control Policy, Feb. 1996), p. 19, P.O. Box 6000, Rockville, MD 20849-6000.

12 National Drug Control Strategy

13 S. Cohen, *Drug Abuse and Alcoholism Newsletter*, Vol. XIV, No.2, April 1985.

14 A. N. Whitehead, *The Aim of Education and Other Essays*, (London: Earnest Henn, London, 1962).

15 D. Archibald, "Coordinated Anti-Drug Action Is Imperative" (*The Journal* 15(2)-1, Feb. 1, 1986).

16 S. Arietti, "Psychiatric Controversy: Man's Ethical Dimension" (*Am. J. Psychiatry*, Jan. 1975), 132-1.

17 L. Eisenberg, "The Human Nature of Human Nature" (*Science* Vol. 176, April 14, 1972).

18 R. Niebuhr, *Moral Man and Immoral Society*, (New York: Scribners, 1932, 1960).

19 A.R. Johnson, L.H. Butler, "Public Ethics and Policy Making" (*Hastings Center Report*, Vol. 5, August 1975).

20 Remark made by cocaine addicted patient in a community psychiatry clinic, Nassau, Bahamas.

21 L. Kohlberg, "The Claim of Moral Adequacy of a Highest Stage of Moral Judgement" (*Journal of Philosophy*, Vol. 70 October 25, 1973), 603-46.

22 D. Archibald, 1980, op.cit.

23 P.C. Rydell, S. Everingham, *Controlling Cocaine: Supply Versus Demand Program* by Rand 1994.

24 John 13:1-21.

25 D.F. Allen, D. Matthews, Unpublished Study of a Review of the Characteristics of a Sample of Bahamian Crack Addicts .

26 This occurred in 1984. The Reverend Zeke Munnings now works full time at the Bahamas' National Drug Council.

Adapting Group Therapy to Address Real World Problems: Insights from Groups Offered in the Bahamas

ALEXIS D. ABERNETHY, Ph.D., CGP, FAGPA
DAVID F. ALLEN, M.D., MPH
MARIE ALLEN CARROLL, Ph.D.

ABSTRACT

This article presents a cultural adaptation of a group therapeutic approach that is being offered in the Bahamas. "The Family: People Helping People" project was designed as an intervention to improve socialization in New Providence, the Bahamian capital and its most heavily populated city. "The Family" group model offers support and training to improve communication in relationships and to encourage constructive emotional expression. This article will provide an overview of "The Family," address key elements of this approach that are culturally tailored, and offer clinical examples and note implications for group therapy training. This cultural adaptation offers helpful insights for addressing community problems, such as violence and societal fragmentation, and may inform the development of community-based group interventions in other settings.

Most therapeutic groups are offered in clinical settings on an outpatient or inpatient basis. Community-based groups provide the opportunity for community members to benefit from a therapeutic group experience. A special issue in the International Journal of Group Psychotherapy (2015, Issue 4) provided an overview of group therapy around the world and included select European countries, as well as Canada, Egypt, Israel, Australia, and Brazil. As expected, the history of group therapy, access to group therapy training, prevailing theoretical approaches, and the cultural context varied among these countries. In some international settings, such as the Bahamas, where there are few trained group therapists but challenging societal problems that have interpersonal dimensions, it may be even more important to develop group intervention models that maximize the ability of professional and lay persons to provide assistance to community members. Lay counseling models have a longstanding tradition in some religious contexts of professionals providing training to lay persons, and this partnership provides enhanced services to communities (Garzon, Worthington, Tan, & Worthington, 2009; Tan, 1991). Critical considerations in developing community-based interventions would be how the unique features of this specialized group might require a modification of traditional group techniques (Yalom & Leszcz, 2005) and how training and interventions might need to be culturally tailored for this population (Pasick, D'Onofrio, & Otero-Sabogal, 1996).

Bahamian Cultural Context

The Bahamas is an archipelagic nation situated between Florida in the southern United States and Cuba. The population comprises a majority of persons of African descent and a minority of Caucasians originating from the United Kingdom and the United States. Traditionally, the country has been a deeply community-bonded, family-based society held together by strong Judeo-Christian values. However, the countrywide cocaine epidemic of the 1980s and

Alexis D. Abernethy is a Professor of Psychology at Fuller Theological Seminary Graduate School of Psychology, Pasadena, California. David F. Allen is a Psychiatrist and Director of the Allen Institute of Training and Research, Nassau, Bahamas. Marie Allen Carroll is a Psychologist and Assistant Director of the Allen Institute of Training and Research, Nassau, Bahamas.
To cite this article: Alexis D. Abernethy, David F. Allen & Marie Allen Carroll (2017): Adapting Group Therapy to Address Real World Problems: Insights from Groups Offered in the Bahamas, International Journal of Group Psychotherapy, DOI: 10.1080/00207284.2017.1335582

its continuing sequelae, the international economic downturn, post-colonial development issues, and vastly diminished educational standards have led to social fragmentation. This crisis, manifested by widespread family and community disintegration, has resulted in burgeoning murder and violent crime rates, domestic violence disputes, and the formation of violent youth gangs.

In response to the social crisis in the Bahamian community, "The Family" is a group-based resocialization intervention designed to confront the prevailing community chaos. "The Family" is based on a group process model. In theory, the group creates a therapeutic replica of a homebased family, allowing members to confront their issues in a safe and nonjudgmental environment. "The Family" provides support and advocacy for its members, allowing them to discover themselves and grow as individuals. More important, "The Family" offers a sanctuary from the normal Bahamian culture, and encourages the expression of emotions that are normally taboo (such as grief, empathy, love, and hope). The primary goal is to improve socialization despite high rates of crime, family disintegration, and economic impoverishment. (Allen, Carroll, Allen, Bethell, & Manganello, 2015, p. 290) Reduced feelings of anger and decreased desire for revenge have been associated with participation in "The Family" (Allen et al., 2015).

Cultural Tailoring

"The Family" was culturally tailored to be consistent with Bahamian values. The American Psychological Association Ethics Code (American Psychological Association, 2002) outlines the importance of cultural sensitivity as stated in Principle E: Respect for People's Rights and Dignity.

> Psychologists are aware of and respect cultural, individual and role differences, including those based on age, gender, gender identity, race, ethnicity, culture, national origin, religion, sexual orientation, disability, language and socioeconomic status and consider these factors when working with members of such groups.

Pasick, D'Onofrio, and Otero-Sabogal (1996) define cultural tailoring as "the development of interventions, training practices and materials to conform to specific characteristics" (p. 145).

In making cultural adaptations of psychotherapy, Hwang (2006) identified six domains: dynamic issues and cultural complexities, orientation, cultural beliefs,client-therapist relationship, cultural differences in expression and communication, and cultural issues of salience. While all of these domains are relevant, three were particularly central to the development of "The Family": cultural beliefs, cultural issues of salience, and the client therapist relationship. The predominant religion in the Bahamas is Christianity, with over 90% of the population identifying as Christian. The integration of spiritual beliefs in these groups—and incorporating spiritual interventions—was an important cultural adaptation (Thompson, 2016). Other dimensions of a culturally responsive approach for Bahamians include integrating traditional healing practices, beliefs, ways of thinking, and political and social realities into individual and group practice (Thompson, 2016).

Despite the centrality of spiritual beliefs, there is recognition that religion may be a source of comfort and/or strain (Exline, Yali, & Sanderson, 2000), and members may use religion in maladaptive ways or use negative religious coping. Group leader interventions need to be respectful of this complexity and address maladaptive religious coping (Abernethy, 2012). In "The Family," these maladaptive responses are addressed. In addition, culturally consistent spiritual interventions, such as corporate songs, spirituals, and prayers, are incorporated in the work to foster bonding, group cohesion, and catharsis.

Second, key cultural issues of salience include societal fragmentation, violence, trauma, and shame related to mental health. Members frequently share their emotional, cognitive, behavioral, physical, and spiritual responses to these experiences. Stigma still exists regarding mental illness and therapy. Despite the acute need for supportive services, feelings of shame are associated with mental health challenges and help-seeking. In recognition of this shame, the groups are designed as community offerings to improve Bahamian society rather than an over emphasis on an individual's problems. Individual problems are recognized, but placed in a larger communal framework. This reduces stigma for the individual. In addition, the interactions among societal and individual responses are noted, so that individual responses such as violence are seen in the context of traumatic exposure. The name of the groups reflects a sensitivity to this stigma. Instead of calling the group a therapeutic group, it was intentionally named "The Family" to reflect Bahamian values related to family. Although there are many different groups with subtitled names that distinguish them, such as East Street, the groups are known and referred to as "The Family." So even in their diversity, they have a common name: it's "The Family" on East Street, rather than the East Street group.

Third, the member-leader relationship is different. While leaders are clearly leaders and facilitators in the group, they are also community members exposed to similar trauma, violence, and community fragmentation. Given a small country such as the Bahamas, members may know the leaders and/or their family members. Members who are mourning a family member may be well known to a leader. This familiarity between member and leader may also be present for community-based groups in rural communities, small towns, and urban community mental health centers. As in all groups, leader disclosure needs to be in service of the group rather than the leader, and a leader's empathy may not only be related to feeling with members, but also to their own mourning. Their ability to disclose their own grief can be a powerful tool for facilitating growth for both members and leaders. There remains a clear frame for the group, but the boundary between leader and member is not as thick as it might be in most groups.

This more porous leader-member boundary also influences training, as members who are potential leaders participate in training. The monthly training that is provided for the leaders and prospective leaders who may be current members of "The Family" seems to provide not only important instruction in group leadership, but also a community of support where leaders have the opportunity to hear didactic presentations and join smaller groups where they are able to share their concerns and obtain support. Leaders are more likely to experience vicarious traumatization, the cumulative effects that occur for therapists related to their empathic engagement with patients who are traumatized (McCann & Pearlman, 1990). In a qualitative study of peer-nominated master therapists, several protective factors were identified as key for mitigating the effects of traumatic exposure: countering isolation (in professional, personal, and spiritual realms); developing mindful self-awareness; consciously expanding perspective to embrace complexity; active optimism; holistic self-care; maintaining clear boundaries; exquisite empathy; professional satisfaction; and creating meaning (Harrison & Westwood, 2009). Several recommendations were made to combat the challenges of isolation, including ongoing involvement in consultation and supervision as well as being connected relationally in communities of support. Small group consultation and supervision that is offered only to leaders also provide important support and an opportunity for reflection and addressing countertransferential concerns.

DEVELOPMENT OF "THE FAMILY"

"The Family" is a supportive process-oriented community-based group intervention. The approach is an integration of interpersonally oriented, role-playing, and supportive techniques based on the Contemplative Discovery Pathway Theory (CDPT; Allen et al., 2014). The CDPT describes the process where shame ("Self Hatred Aimed at ME") impedes the development of a true self. It is proposed that early experiences block the child from adequate unconditional love and as a result lead to the shattering of their dreams of safety, meaningful relationships, and a sense of empowerment. The related pain from this and other trauma contributes to cultivation of a Shame Self involving abandonment, rejection, and humiliation. Shame is such a powerful, ubiquitous master emotion that it challenges the individual's psyche. An individual compensates by developing a defensive Shame False Self involving self-absorption, self-gratification, and control. The Shame False Self, a pervasive rescuer, hijacks lives into the wilderness of fear and leads individuals away from authenticity. A process of desocialization occurs in which individuals become victims of the negativity of shame, where they think less of themselves, others, and their community, and they may engage in destructive behavior. In contrast, resocialization may be defined as the process of becoming liberated from the negativity of shame to move beyond one's limitations, and to experience one's potential, characterized by the positive emotions of love, humility, forgiveness, and gratitude. In "The Family," the loving support of the group allows members to share their stories. As they surrender the grief and shame of their pain, they release their negativity and destructiveness and embrace the positive healing emotions of love and support. As a result, the Shame False Self melts away, giving rise to discovery of the Authentic Gracious Self characterized by love, community, compassion, humility, and gratitude.

Sharing painful experiences in a contemplative atmosphere of love, mindfulness, and non-judgmental listening develops a powerful healing bond. Referring to Daniel Siegel's work, Kurt Thompson explains that recent studies in neuroscience have demonstrated that empathic listening can "re-wire" our thinking.

> An important part of how people change—not just their experiences, but also their brains—is through the process of telling their stories to an her story and is truly heard and understood, both they and the listener undergo actual changes in their brain circuitry. They feel a greater sense of emotional and relational connection, decreased anxiety and greater awareness of and compassion for others' suffering. Using the language of neuroscience, Dr. Siege labelled the change as "increased integration." (Thompson, 2010, p. ix)

"The Family" started with one group in 2009, but has now grown to 30 groups offered to over 500 members. Some of the groups are smaller, with 8–10 members, but a few are larger groups of 25–40 members. The groups meet for two hours and are open-ended. There is no fee for the groups. New members are expected weekly and attend the groups following an initial assignment based on either a phone intake and/or screening if they are referred by a mental health or law enforcement professional, are on medication, or have a history of domestic violence. Prospective members are screened by the mental health staff from "The Family." If members have significant mental illness, they are referred for psychiatric treatment. Similar to an inpatient group with fluid membership, leaders manage the arrival of new members and also seek to foster group cohesion. Members typically stay for over a year. Participation is optional, with interaction being guided by the leaders. The facilitator provides a summary at the end of each session and offers a psychological/spiritual teaching to foster education and character development.

DEVELOPING A SPECIALIZED GROUP

"The Family" project has developed a group approach that fosters the inclusion of some of Yalom's traditional therapeutic factors: interpersonal learning, imitative behavior, universality, self-understanding, and the instillation of hope. Yalom and Leszcz (2005) highlight three considerations in developing a specialized group: assessment of the clinical situation, formulation of goals, and modification of the technique.

Assessment of the Clinical Situation

Key factors in assessing the clinical situation include the number of patients, availability of co-leadership, type and severity of pathology, and duration of therapy. The frame for these groups, including decisions related to the number of members and the duration of groups, is more flexible. Haim Weinberg (2016) in the 2016 Annual Foulkes Lecture, "Impossible Groups That Thrive in Leaking Containers," describes the importance of greater flexibility in frame related dimensions of certain groups, such as trauma-focused, demonstration, and community-based groups. Given that these groups are offered in a community-based versus treatment context and the urgent need for support, "The Family" was designed to reach more members than most treatment groups, and the groups are typically larger in size and may range from 8 to 40 members. Most of the groups have between 12–20 members. In the groups that have more than 12 members, there are typically two primary co-leaders and one to three additional leaders in the group. In addition, the leaders of these groups include professional and trained community members. Some of the leaders are former group members who have been trained in group leadership.

It was recognized that these groups would not be for patients, but for community members in various settings and locations including church sites, juvenile delinquent settings, prisons, and homeless outreach settings. While the severity of problems and pathology facing these group members varies greatly, they share common difficulties related to shame, loss, exposure to violence, and societal fragmentation.

Formulation of Goals

Despite the diverse backgrounds, unique problems, and pathology of its members, common goals are identified. The theoretical lens of listening for the development of the Shame Self and its associated challenging affects, including hurt, pain, and anger, and moving toward a process of resocialization, provide a common context for articulating goals for members. Members may identify early or current experiences where they did not feel valued and express a sense of shame or sadness related to them. Others may present with anger and a desire for revenge in response to the violence directed toward them or a family member. Their shame may be associated with the recognition that this retaliation is not appropriate even if they believe it is justified. There is a focus across groups on shame as a response to deep hurt and rejection and related feelings of worthlessness, hopelessness, and helplessness. Members expect group members to respond in a similar unloving and rejecting way. The group offers a corrective emotional experience. Common goals in these groups include the development of interpersonal skills, self-esteem enhancement, anger management and conflict resolution, revenge elimination, community bonding, affective learning, and mature spirituality.

Modification of Technique

In addition to the clinical situation and goal articulation, these groups required a modification of technique. First, the common presence of more than two co-leaders with varied levels of professional training complicates the process. As noted earlier, the role of the group leader is different in these groups due to the leader's level of group training as well as the size of the group. All groups are led by a trained therapist who may be partnered with one to three lay facilitators who have received training in group facilitation provided by psychologist Dr. Marie Allen. Dr. David Allen is centrally involved in the training of the core professional leaders as well as the lay group leaders. Typically, leaders receive monthly day-long training over the period of a year before they lead a group. Ongoing consultation and supervision frequently address the challenges associated with group size, varied pathology in the groups, and co-leadership. While the two primary leaders are identified and the most active, the additional leaders may intervene, especially either in response to an invitation by the co-leader or in response to affective expressions, such as crying, that might be occurring in their physical proximity. At other times, members may move to different chairs in order to be closer to the primary co-leaders and continue their work there. While a leader's secure presence is important in all groups, Weinberg (2016) argues that more flexible boundaries are possible in these "impossible groups" in the presence of a leader with a secure presence. This security and stability is a critical counterbalance to the volatile and traumatizing context of members' lives. The secure presence of the leader helps to contain the group: often the senior professional leader embodies this presence.

Although certain groups may incorporate the arts in the work, a unique feature of "The Family" is the spontaneous use of song during the process. The use of song in "The Family" is consistent with the salience of music in Bahamian culture. In addition to a closing song, music is typically introduced by the leader at unpredictable moments; these songs, often spirituals or hymns, foster cohesion, express the unexpressed, or deepen emotional connections. A common spiritual sung frequently in group is, "Sometimes I Feel Like a Motherless Child;" this song has a key phrase, "a long, long way from home." In "The Family," home represents the place of safety, peace, and rest, a place where one experiences the positive emotions of love, humility, forgiveness, and gratitude. This particular song captures universal themes of abandonment, loneliness, and sorrow, and more recently has helped to express the increasingly unrecognizable landscape of a violent, disintegrating

Bahamian society. In some ways, these spontaneous songs serve as a musical metaphor. Abernethy (2002) noted that, "to engage with others' metaphors provides an opportunity to connect with their creativity and their individual and cultural selves" (p. 220). Metaphors may catalyze group process and promote understanding.

Flow of a Typical Group

While the integration of meditation is more common in some groups, a typical "Family" group begins with a period of guided meditation and silence that is culturally tailored to the natural beauty of the Bahamas. Participants are encouraged to relax, breathe deeply, and focus on the color blue, which characterizes the Bahamian sea and sky. The technique seems particularly effective in allowing members to come home to themselves. Members of the prison groups, for example, have reported that the exercise is deeply liberating, as they can see the sky and imagine themselves afloat in the clear Bahamian ocean. Through deep breathing, clients move into a deeper sense of consciousness by blocking the incessant flow of thoughts, preparing them to allow their authentic stories to emerge. Depending on the situation, the silent meditation ends with a brief prayer asking God (or a higher power) for guidance and healing in the group. At this juncture, new members are welcomed, and individuals who are willing to share their stories, disclose. "The Family" facilitators are trained to demonstrate and encourage member sharing within group sessions. If there is resistance, a facilitator may share some aspect of his/her personal story from the week, or ask the group about community incidents, perhaps a shooting death, violent crime, or other tragic event.

The posture that is cultivated during "Family" sessions is one of listening, allowing participants to open up, not only to the content of what is shared, but also to the sense of connection and bonding that may occur among group members during a given session. When something deeply painful is shared, such as childhood sexual abuse or the murder of a relative, facilitators are trained to call for a period of silence to allow members to feel what is occurring and to digest their thoughts. These points are labeled "holy moments" because they represent the "still point" or the "now" (Eliot, 1944). The still point occurs where chronological pain is intersected by the feeling of love or the "kairos" of God's presence. In "The Family," the still point often occurs in deep silence as a sense of oneness develops in the group. Often, the still point seems to invite members to share at an even deeper level. For example, a person might share how he had watched his wife being murdered. The facilitator responds by calling for a still point. Following group silence, the facilitator asks whether the person wants to share anything else. The group is then asked how this story affects the "Family." When members genuinely share, there is a ripple effect that tends to open and deepen the moment for the entire group.

At one session, a woman—one of six sisters molested by their father—expressed a desire to share. She had been in the group for three months, saying very little, often with tears streaming down her cheeks. On this day, she was finally able to express the pain of having been threatened by her father to keep the incest a secret. Over time, most of her sisters had died. Suddenly, she erupted into a loud, cathartic scream that continued for almost two minutes. The moment was deeply touching. It so resonated with members that others who had experienced abuse in their lives joined her in the scream. Others remained silent, some crying, some meditating, others praying. Later in that session, the group processed this experience.

Such group sessions frequently unleash "hot points," moments when someone says something that jolts the group: "I was abused," "My grandson was shot and killed," "Someone was murdered in front of me on Wednesday afternoon," "Somebody shot me," or "Someone raped me." Facilitators are trained to recognize hot points and process them.

Unaddressed hot points can lead participants to rationalization and intellectualization, and they can create an "elephant in the room" that overwhelms the group session and might eventually threaten the group itself. One of first principles of "The Family" therapeutic groups is to help its members become healthy through authentic self-expression. Hence the mantra, "Jaw-jaw stops war-war," that highlights the importance of talking versus engaging in violence, resonates deeply within the group. A related principle involves helping group members move from alexithymia to discernment between thoughts, feelings, and behaviors. Many members are able to recognize thoughts but repress feelings and go directly to behavior (violence). "The Family" works to make sure the process of the group identifies thoughts and remains open to feelings. Over time, individual and group behaviors tend to become more responsive and less reactive.

As sessions near their end, facilitators may call for another "rest period" of silence. Then the facilitator may call for a song, or a group member may "raise a chorus" like "Be Still and Know That I am God" or "We Shall Overcome." Negro spirituals and gospel songs have powerful resonance in the Bahamas, which has strong kinship affiliation with African-American communities in the Southeastern United States. In the two most marginalized "Family" groups, one hymn closes almost every session: "Blessed Be the Tie That Binds." This hymn provides comfort, strengthens community, and inspires members to face life with new determination and drive.

Yalom and Leszcz (2005) have identified imitation, identification, and internalization as key mechanisms of change that occur in typical groups. In "The Family," at least two of these mechanisms are operating as members engage in imitation and identification. The leaders assist members in working through feelings of shame, sadness, anger, and revenge. Allen and colleagues (2014) note that, "developing a meaningful therapeutic alliance with a client in therapy requires patience, understanding, and compassion. As the client re-experiences shameful thoughts and events, the therapist may become a disavowed object of hate, rejection and disgust" (p. 3). In "The Family," the leader may not only become a negative repository for these affects, but also have the potential to become a positive transferential object. This use of positive and negative transferential feelings is consistent with psychodynamic approaches.

In addition to the leaders, members learn from more seasoned members and imitate healthier responding. Role-playing is sometimes in dyads with a leader, but also may involve two members. Members have the opportunity to shift roles and gain more insight into and empathy for other members' perspectives, including the perpetrator and the survivor.

Abernethy (2009) noted that when a person has been offended, he/she has an opportunity to follow models that encourage scapegoating and sacrifice (pursuing justified blame, including revenge-seeking and retaliation) or to imitate the desire of God, who demands mercy and not sacrifice (transcending blame). "The Family" provides individuals with models of an orientation toward transcending blame in response to relational offense. These include peer, group leader, and spiritual models. If individuals seek to follow this example, this destructive cycle is reversed, relationships are healthier, and more positive health outcomes may emerge. A transcending blame (non-sacrificial) perspective moves away from a focus on justified anger, penalty for disobedience, and violence and moves toward forgiveness, transformation, healthier individuals, relationships, and communities.

CLINICAL ILLUSTRATIONS

Poverty and Social Deprivation

Rejected by his family, John left home at 13 years of age to fend for himself on the streets. Living on the beach and in abandoned buildings, John hustled daily to make ends meet. He was severely abused—physically and sexually. Later on, John was shot in his face and side and admitted to the hospital. On the third day of his hospitalization, the person who shot him was also shot, admitted to the same hospital, and placed two beds away. Angry and filled with thoughts of revenge, John wanted him dead. The next day, John's gang came to the hospital, seeking to kill the person who shot him. They begged John to point the shooter out to them, but he refused. Instead, John surrendered his feelings of revenge and prayed for a better life.

After being released from the hospital, John experienced further challenges. He wound up living in a tomb in one of the cemeteries before eventually being referred to "The Family." Facing a loss of confidence in himself, John was shy, ashamed, and unable to speak. The group was very receptive and showered him with love, giving him odd jobs, clothes, food, and money. After a number of sessions, John began to speak freely and socialize with the participants in the group. A few months later, he shared that when he first came to "The Family," he felt his life was hopeless. He said he is now determined to live again because of the love he found in our sessions. John is still in "The Family," has a job, and volunteers in "The Family" basketball outreach program to marginalized youth.

Discussion. John's early life experiences were characterized by neglect and abusive violence directed toward him. These experiences resulted in his feelings of shame, low self-worth, and anger. "The Family" provided him with a corrective emotional experience, where instead of being violated, he was supported and affirmed. The leaders and members demonstrated genuine care for him and continued to work toward reducing his desire for revenge. They provided feedback and support, which encouraged him to learn how to effectively relate to others and to share his emotions in a constructive way. Consistent with the collectivistic cultural context of these groups, not only was emotional and informational support provided, but also tangible support, including financial and other resources. While this might pose a challenge in traditional therapy groups—and the meaning of these exchanges would need to be weighed—this was an important part of the socialization and supportive process. For some, this mutuality might be considered confusing or a potential frame or boundary crossing, but it also might be a way of understanding the power of "The Family" in this communally oriented country. A more porous boundary does not mean that there is no boundary.

Revenge and Its Destructive Effects

Many people in "The Family" have experienced either murder, violent attack, or abuse of a loved one. As a result, revenge is a major issue in "The Family" and may include wanting the perpetrator killed or his family injured.

A young woman visited "The Family," and after sitting quietly for a while, she shared that her only sister had been murdered by her husband. As the group listened attentively, she said, "I am angry, and I want revenge. My sister is dead, and I have the responsibility of now caring for all of her children." Suddenly, she stopped and said, "This is too painful. I can't talk about it." As the group waited in silence, the facilitator asked her if she would join him in a roleplay in which he would act as her sister's husband. After much reluctance, she finally agreed. The woman and facilitator moved into the center of the group. As the facilitator looked at her, she screamed, "I hate you! I hate you! You killed my sister! You are an animal and I hope you suffer the rest of your life! Do you know that you destroyed our whole family? We knew that you were no good for her. You always tried to keep her from us. You would never let her come to our family gatherings. Now she is gone. I wish you were dead!" Then, she suddenly stopped. Looking intently at the facilitator, she said, "If you are bad enough, come out on bail and you'll see what happens!"

Shocked and confused, the group again became silent as she wept profusely, shaking her head in disbelief and pain. The group ended, and people slowly and reverently left. Saying goodbye to her, the woman expressed to the facilitator that she felt relieved at being able to release her pent-up feelings. She was visibly shaken. Thanking her for coming, the facilitator responded, "Letting go of painful, revenge feelings takes time, patience, and is a long, long journey."

Discussion. This interaction allowed the facilitator to become a repository for this woman's anger and frustration. She was able to express both her anger and her desire for revenge in a safe, supportive place. The leader modeled a secure presence for her to express her anger and her sadness. While the intensity of these feelings may have scared her and other members, the group was able to bear the intensity of this pain. The facilitator did not resolve these feelings, but offered compassion, hope, and perspective that the process of healing is a journey. This modeling was important, as other members had similar feelings and were encouraged that the group, particularly the leader, could handle the intensity of their affect. The collective, reverent response of the members also conveyed a sense of solidarity in this pain so the member was able to experience universality as she became aware that she was not alone in her feelings.

CONCLUSION

This innovative community-based group approach for responding to societal fragmentation builds on standard group therapeutic principles, but it also extends and adapts these approaches to tailor them to the cultural and psychological needs of the community. This adaptation can serve as a model for community contexts where there are few mental health professionals, where there is a need to serve a large number of people, and where there are significant challenges related to community violence and societal fragmentation. While there are potential challenges associated with this adaptation, including boundary crossings, leader disclosure, and vicarious trauma, these groups also seem to possess a potential for change and transformation. Members who might otherwise follow a destructive spiral toward violence have the opportunity to engage in a group experience that offers an opportunity to work through these associated feelings and to imitate member, leader, and spiritual models that transcend blame and eschew violence. "The Family" illustrates how community-based (or embedded) groups may be designed to accommodate the cultural context and how classic group therapy may be adapted to be responsive to real world problems. Principles from this adaptation could inform work in other settings where community members are exposed to violence and trauma. Responsivity to the unique cultural values of these settings would be a critical component of this adaptation and increase the likelihood of fostering change for individuals and communities.

FUNDING

This work was supported by the Templeton World Charity Foundation (TWCF 0073).

REFERENCES

Abernethy, A. D. (2002). The power of metaphors for exploring cultural differences in groups. Group, 26(3), 219–231.doi:10.1023/A:1021061110951

Abernethy, A. D. (2009). *Relational conflict, worship, and transformation.* Professorial lecture, Pasadena, CA.

Abernethy, A. D. (2012). A spiritually informed approach to group psychotherapy. In J. L. Kleinberg (Ed.), *The Wiley-Blackwell handbook of group psychotherapy* (pp. 681–705). Chichester, West Sussex, UK: Wiley.

Allen, D. F., Carroll, M. A., Allen, V. S., Bethell, K. Y., & Manganello, J. A. (2015). Community resocialization via instillation of family values through a novel group therapy approach: A pilot study. Journal of *Psychotherapy Integration*, 25(4), 289–298. doi:10.1037/a0039563

Allen, D. F., Mayo, M., Allen-Carroll, M., Manganello, J. A., Allen, V. S., & Singh, J. P. (2014). Cultivating gratitude: Contemplative discovery pathway theory applied to group therapy in the Bahamas. Journal of Trauma & Treatment, 3, 197. Retrieved from http:// omicsgroup.org/journals/ trauma-treatment.php.

American Psychological Association. (2002). *American Psychological Association ethical principles of psychologists and code of conduct.* Retrieved from http:// www.apa.org/ethics/code2002.html.

Eliot, T. S. (1944). *Four quartets.* London, UK: Faber and Faber.

Exline, J. J., Yali, A. M., & Sanderson, W. C. (2000). Guilt, discord, and alienation: The role of religious strain in depression and suicidality. *Journal of Clinical Psychology*, 56(12), 1481–1496. doi:10.1002/1097-4679 (200012)56:12<1481::AID-1>3.0.CO;2-A

Garzon, F., Worthington, E. J., Tan, S., & Worthington, R. K. (2009). Lay Christian counseling and client expectations for integration in therapy. *Journal of Psychology and Christianity*, 28(2), 113–120.

Harrison, R. L., & Westwood, M. J. (2009). Preventing vicarious traumatization of mental health therapists: Identifying protective practices. *Psychotherapy: Theory, Research, Practice, Training*, 46(2), 203–219. doi:10.1037/a0016081

Hwang, W. (2006). The Psychotherapy Adaptation and Modification Framework (PAMF): Application to Asian Americans. *American Psychologist*, 61, 702–715. doi:10.1037/0003-066X.61.7.702

McCann, I. L., & Pearlman, L. A. (1990). Vicarious traumatization: A contextual model for understanding the effects of trauma on helpers. *Journal of Traumatic Stress*, 3, 131–149.

Pasick, R. J., D'Onofrio, C. N., & Otero-Sabogal, R. (1996). Similarities and differences across cultures: Questions to inform a third generation for health promotion research. *Health Education Quarterly*, 23, S142–S161.

Tan, S. (1991). *Lay counseling: Equipping Christians for a helping ministry*. Grand Rapids, MI: Zondervan.

Thompson, A. D. (2016). Toward a Caribbean psychology: Context, imperatives, and future directions. In J. L. Roopnarine, D. Chadee, J. L. Roopnarine, & D. Chadee (Eds.), *Caribbean psychology: Indigenous contributions to a global discipline* (pp. 15–44). Washington, DC: American Psychological Association. doi:10.1037/14753-002

Thompson, C. (2010). *Anatomy of the soul: Surprising connections between neuroscience and spiritual practices that can transform your life and relationships*. Carol Stream, IL: Tyndale House.

Weinberg, H. (2016). *Impossible groups with leaking containers*. 2016 Annual Foulkes Lecture. London, UK.

Yalom, I., & Leszcz, M. (2005). *The theory and practice of group psychotherapy* (5th ed.). New York, NY: Basic Books.

Alexis D. Abernethy, Ph.D., CGP, FAGPA
Graduate School of Psychology
Fuller Theological Seminary
180 North Oakland Avenue
Pasadena, CA 91101
E-mail: aabernet@fuller.edu

A Resocialization Intervention Model in the Prison - The Family: People Helping People Project

Abstract

The Bahamas is suffering from a serious social fragmentation process, due to the cocaine crisis of the 1980's and its continuing sequelae. Burgeoning murder and violent crime rates associated with family and community disintegration have led to the incarceration of many young persons. The Family: People Helping People Project is a community based intervention designed to confront social fragmentation and promote re-socialization among the inmates at the Bahamas Department of Corrections. The method used is a dynamic supportive group process, involving storytelling, personal reflection and transformation based on the psychotherapeutic principles of the Contemplative Discovery Pathway Theory (CDPT). Since the program's inception, there have been 109 group sessions. A thematic analysis of these sessions indicates the four most common themes were violence, anger, revenge and addiction. The thematic analysis of the Prison group, described in this paper indicates the depths of negativity of shame but also provides hope for Resocialization and preparation for the inmates to live a meaningful and crime-free community life upon their release. This paper discusses the Resocialization process of a group of inmates who attended the program for three (3) years.

Keywords: Social fragmentation; Incarceration; Resocialization; Freedom; Anger; Prison

Introduction

The Bahamas, like many other countries in the Caribbean and South America is facing a serious social fragmentation process related to the widespread cocaine epidemic of the 1980s and its continuing sequelae of drug trafficking and violence due to an excessive supply of guns and the high unemployment rate relating to the recent international financial downturn [1]. Involving family and community disintegration, the social fragmentation has spurned a culture of violence with burgeoning murder and violent crime rates, domestic violence, violent youth gangs and different types of abuse [2].

The family: People Helping People Project was initiated by Dr. David Allen to provide a space for mothers who had lost their sons to murder to help them work through their grief. These meetings were eventually forged into support groups and later developed into the Family: People Helping People Project. This project is a community based intervention designed to confront social fragmentation and promote re-socialization. American Sociologist Erving Goffman coined the phrase 'community resocialization' and described it as the deconstruction and reconstruction of one's values, abilities and beliefs [3]. The program is offered in 24 marginalized Bahamian communities and select populations, including a group for inmates at the Bahamas Department of Corrections (Her Majesty's Prison). In the context of 'The Family Prison group' the resocialization intervention is offered in two stages involving an 18 month pre-release group during incarceration and an after release group when ex-inmates are strongly encouraged to be part of the community Family program.

Persons are encouraged to share their stories in a contemplative environment of love, silence and non-judgmental listening creating a powerful healing bond which we define as "Family". In both the community populations and the program at the pris-

David F Allen[1]*, Maria Flavia D'Alessandro1 and Keva Bethell[2]
1 Allen Institute of Research and Training, Bahamas
2 Department of Public Health, Allen Institute of Research and Training, Bahamas
*Corresponding author: David F Allen, Director, Allen Institute of Research and Training, Bahamas, Email:
Received: August 15, 2017 | Published: October 16, 2017

on, resocialization is developed through a dynamic supportive group process, involving storytelling, personal reflection and transformation based on the psychotherapeutic principles of the Contemplative Discovery Pathway Theory (CDPT) [4]. The Family project attempts to redefine the complex concept of resocialization through the collaboration between both societal group settings involving closed institution groups and open community groups. The Family has hosted 109 group sessions at the Prison since its inception in April 2014.

The incarceration conditions at The Bahamas Department of Corrections (also known as Her Majesty's Prison) are challenging with an overcrowding rate of 72.7%. Built to house a maximum capacity of 1000 prisoners, the Prison's population in October 2016 was 1727 prisoners. According to World Prison Brief of the University of London, the Bahamian prison population rate is 439 per 100,000 persons. The Bahamian rate is more than three times the world average and higher than the Caribbean rate of 347 per 100,000 [5].

The Family Prison Group

The purpose of this article is to describe the challenges of establishing a Family group in the Prison and to discuss the qualitative analysis of the various themes presented by the inmates. Our hope is that the qualitative analysis along with the testimonial data will provide a clearer understanding of the challenges of resocialization in the prison population. The Family offers a weekly group meeting at the prison lasting90 minutes and is attended by 20 to 25 inmates. Initially, there were about three female inmates in the group. However, they were withdrawn by the authorities and we eventually became an all-male group. Most of the inmates are part of a pre-release program and are expected to leave the prison in 18 months. However, a few of the inmates in the group are facing life sentences. We are allowed to set the guidelines, but the inmates are selected by the prison officers. In the development of the group, we stress the importance of three (3) major principles:

i. Confidentiality: inmates are encouraged to leave what is discussed at the group meeting and only express how they were affected after the group. This encourages trust and helps the inmate to face their problems and work toward their solutions.
ii. Non-judgmental approach: We encourage a strong non-judgmental approach to enhance respect for persons sharing their personal and painful stories.
iii. Free expression: each person is given the time and space to share their story.

The group is conducted by three (3) facilitators. After each session, a praxis report is written by one of the facilitators. This praxis includes a description of the interactions, a list of the themes and a short reflection about the session. The themes are then analyzed by a researcher and the incidence of the most prominent themes is coded in a thematic analysis.

The Allen Resocialization Scale

The Family Project is research-based. Participants are required to undergo psychological testing every six months to document their progress in the program. The participants were tested in two cohorts. Participants who were a part of cohort one were required to fill out a background questionnaire and a test battery that included nine psychological test scales, namely the Beck Depression Inventory, Buss-Durkee Hostility-Guilt Inventory, Gratitude Questionnaire-Six-Item Form (GQ-6), The Hope Scale, Self-Deception Questionnaire, Internalized Shame Scale (ISS), the Spiritual Well-Being Scale (SWBS), Satisfaction with Life Scale (SWLS) and the Transgression-Related Interpersonal Motivations Inventory-18-Item Version (TRIM-18). Participants who were part of cohort 2 were required to fill out a background questionnaire and the Allen Resocialization Scale.

The Allen Resocialization Scale was created by conducting a thorough literature review of current accepted scales of rehabilitation and wellness. Forty-one (41) evaluation questions were selected from established questionnaires that have been used to measure different aspects of well-being as it relates to Resocialization. These include items assessing the management of emotions, alexithymia (feeling awareness), resilience and outlook on life. Other elements measured include shame, suicidal ideation, satisfaction with life and depression. Responses were standardized to a Likert-type scale, ranging from 1='Strongly disagree,' 2='Disagree,' 3='Neither agree nor disagree,' 4='Agree,' and 5='Strongly agree'. Participant responses were tallied at the end to form a comprehensive score. The inmates were part of cohort 2. Results from the Allen Scale indicate increases in positive emotions such as well-being, spirituality, awareness, forgiveness and stress management. Decreases in family bonds were reported, however, additional testing is required to prove significance in this area.[6] The inmates' responses to their changes in anger and revenge since participating in the Family program indicate the program's success in re-socializing its participants. It is interesting that even though there has been a decrease in thoughts of violent revenge, there seems to be an increase in non-violent revengeful thoughts (Figure 1). We believe this is because the inmates need more time to work through their deep hurt and shame.

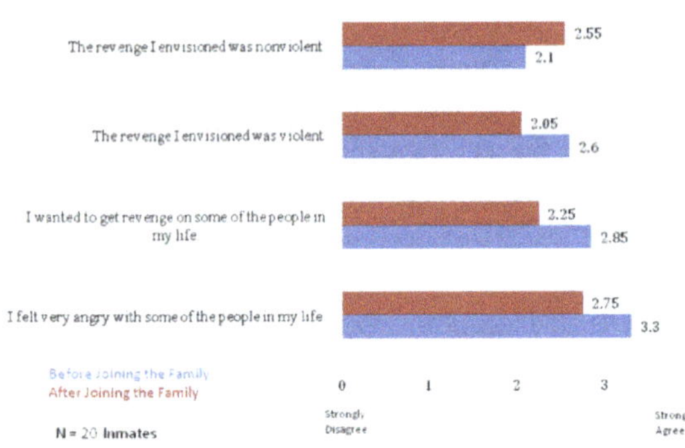

Figure 1 Self-Reported Differences in Anger and Revenge.

Development of group cohesion

As the group members shared their stories, a sense of belonging and empowerment developed. Endeavoring to have ownership of the group, the inmates named the group the 'Free Your Mind Group' because this was the only space where they had a chance to express their feelings freely. The group members wanted to punish those who disobeyed the requirements but we agreed to a compromise that persons not complying would be suspended for a period and reinstated. Eventually, when the men became aware that they were angry and agitated, they excused themselves and returned when they felt ready to do so.

Anger was the most prominent theme in the group and we chose to work through it by exploring the underlying fears and hurts involved. We found that using the metaphor of seeing anger as a siren on an ambulance was very helpful. Thus, when anger occurred in the group, it alerted us that the person was hurting deeply and he needed our support. Another initiative which was helpful in making the group their own was the institution of a "graduation ceremony". We agreed to this and every June, they receive a certificate of participation with their names on it. This ceremony is appreciated deeply and they show their gratitude through songs, poetry, speeches and small gifts. For some, this was the first certificate they ever received and it meant a lot to them.

We also found that stories and myths were an excellent way of connecting with them. For example, they particularly liked the Slave Myth. In this ancient myth, a slave was captured and chained to a stake. He walked around the stake, looking out at the distant mountains and dreaming of being free to start a new life. Then looking at his chain, he realized that he was trapped and freedom was impossible. The myth continues that one night an angel broke the chain. When the slave awoke the next morning, he was shocked to find his chain broken. Getting up, he ran toward the mountains hoping to take advantage of his new found freedom. But then he started to fear the unknown. Looking back at his broken chain, his pain, he was caught in the dilemma of running to his freedom or returning to the prison of the familiar. After much hesitation, he returned, picked up his broken chain and walked around the stake the rest of his life. Although the external chains were broken, the internal chains around his heart were still intact. This story had a powerful effect on the group and initiated a discussion about physical and mental freedom. They realized that one can be physically free but still mentally imprisoned or vice versa. True freedom is not only breaking the external chains, but more importantly, breaking the chains around our heart. They cited lyrics from Bob Marley's "Redemption Song", 'emancipate yourselves from mental slavery, none but ourselves can free our minds' Throughout our group sessions "The Slave Myth" has been discussed repeatedly. We stressed that although we were aware that they were living in a real prison "made of concrete", the Family's mission was to liberate them from their "internal chains", and help them to realize the potential of their inner life. Victor Frankl, who lived in a concentration camp, describes this when he says, "Everything can be taken from a man but one thing: the last of the human freedoms to choose one's attitude in any given set of circumstances, to choose one's own way".[7] The inmates claim they share the information gained from their group with their families and friends. This is important because this expands the resocialization work beyond the prison walls.

The development of trust is central to the group. Initially, they were curious and were not sure what to expect. In the first months of our group meetings, group members tested our commitment by "pushing the boundaries" (e.g. accusations, provocation, fighting, shaming), trying to use us for personal gain (money, gifts or sending messages to friends and family) or rebelling against the rules. However, our commitment to stability, consistency and predictability engendered trust. But they were still skeptical (e.g. they accused us of working for an American Intelligence Agency and spying on them). To counteract this distrust, we were fortunate to have on our team Mr. André Chappelle, a recovered drug addict who had been imprisoned five times. The inmates made it very clear that they knew him and trusted him. But it would take time for them to trust us. Mr. Chappelle was a catalyst for hope and change. In fact, the miracle of his transformation from a homeless drug addict and criminal to a knowledgeable co-facilitator in the group was a powerful statement. Many of the men recognized him from the streets and became emotional when they realized the transformation of his life. They told him, 'you give us hope. If you can change your life, we can also'. Mr. Chappelle initiated the first "Prison Arts and Crafts Show" which was a great success. The public was very impressed, particularly with how well the inmates conducted themselves.

Sadly, Mr. Chappelle was diagnosed with cancer and died within six months. This had a major impact on the group forcing them to face their feelings of grief. Painful as it was, this introduced a deeper dimension to the group. The men were very moved and expressed their sadness openly by crying and reflecting on their own lives. In a strange way, Mr. Chappelle's life, illness and death enhanced the resocialization process of the group.

The Role of Shame

Shame is a powerful multi-faceted emotion which results from the shattering or loss of cherished expectations, wishes or dreams, creating in us the sense of abandonment, rejection and humiliation.[8] Though hidden and attached to our deepest, personal secrets, the faces of shame are seen in society as anger, violence, revenge and abuse. As a result, the person becomes at war with themselves so that shame may be defined as Self Hatred Aimed at ME. Social fragmentation results when a person becomes a victim of the negativity of shame, giving them a diminished view of themselves, others and the world. Conversely, re-socialization is the liberation from the negativity of shame to experience the positive emotions of love, forgiveness and gratitude, resulting in increased self-esteem and the development of meaningful community. Our hope is that by analyzing the overt themes of 'The Family Prison Group', we would have a better understanding of the predominant issues of shame in the inmates and have the opportunity to confront and work through them.

The Family group process is based on the Contemplative Discovery Pathway Theory (CDPT). This is a psychodynamic theory that integrates psychopathology, positive emotions and contemplative spirituality. It is a developmental model that postulates that the Self follows a stepwise path from the Natural Self at birth to The Shame False Self, to the healthier Authentic Gracious Self in adulthood and potentially even the Contemplative Transcendent Self later in life.[9] As described earlier, the term 'Family' is defined as the bond created by the sharing of our authentic stories in an environment of love, acceptance and non-judgmental listening. As the group shares their stories of shame and pain, they destroy their defensive Shame False Self, based in fear and anger and move towards their Authentic Selves based in love and gratitude. Thus, the group experience is the healing agent and the role of the facilitators is to remove or reduce the obstacles to the healing process. This is done by:

i. Positively reinforcing healing behaviors and insights (offering conditions for safety, connection and empowerment).
ii. Kindly but firmly redirecting behaviors that are considered obstacles to healing (abandonment, rejection and humiliation).
iii. Role-modeling behavior: resocialization through an experience of love, forgiveness, humility and gratitude.

The Family group process is open and dynamic. New inmates are welcomed to join once approved by the officers. Each group session involves the following components:

The stillness meditation exercise

All our sessions begin with a stillness meditation exercise based on breathing techniques and visualization exercises using the color blue. This exercise is very meaningful to the inmates. Many of the men were raised on the ocean and were used to seeing the deep blue sea. In prison, this is not possible, so they replace the sea by observing the blue sky. The exercise is also appreciated because the inmates claim it helps them to relax. Even though their accommodations are limited and crowded, they practice the stillness exercise in their cells, which brings peace and relaxation to them. The stillness exercise ends with a prayer of gratitude. The goal of this exercise is explained to the group every session. We explain that the exercise is used to prepare our mind to be more aware and attentive. According to David Foster Wallace: "Learning how to think really means learning how to exercise some control over how and what you think. It means being conscious and aware enough to choose what you pay attention to and to choose how you construct meaning from experience think of the old cliché about 'the mind being an excellent servant but a terrible master'".[9]

Open group discussion

The stillness exercise is followed by 60-minute open group discussion where the inmates share stories of their lives and relate to national and international events. Often, handouts are given to enhance the discussion using quotes from persons like Nelson Mandela, Viktor Frankl and Maya Angelou. The group found that using the metaphor of our heart being like a sponge was very helpful. Like a sponge, the heart absorbs the love as well as the hurt and shame. Sadly, as the sponge becomes full of hurt and shame, it makes it difficult to receive or give love. The goal of the Family group in Prison is to squeeze the sponge to release the hurt and shame from our heart and allow love to increase self-esteem and create caring community. Group members alternate in sharing their stories and the facilitators' role is to assure the flow of the group process. Role-playing and centering techniques enhance sharing and healing. As persons get in contact and release their shame, a powerful catharsis results. This is a time for silence, understanding and non-judgmental listening.

Ending a session

The last 15 minutes are used to summarize the main issues of a session. Usually, an inspiring story is told to illustrate principles expressed during the meeting. Closure is established when the session ends with a song, poetry and a closing prayer.

Discussion

In The Family Prison Group, the four most common themes are violence, anger, revenge and addiction. In 109 group sessions those themes appeared 80 times (Figure 2). Group participants indicate that anger is perceived by them as the fuel for violence. Revenge is the most common justification for violence and addiction is used as their coping mechanism. Violence has been at the center of their lives from childhood to present. It was at home (e.g. beating of children, fights between siblings, gender based violence), in the communities (e.g. killings for gang rivalry, punishment for stealing, revenge motivated violence) and now in the prison (e.g. poor conditions and fighting). Although constantly describing violence in the group, the group participants never use the term 'violence'. They do not see it as a problem, but as a normal component of their lives.

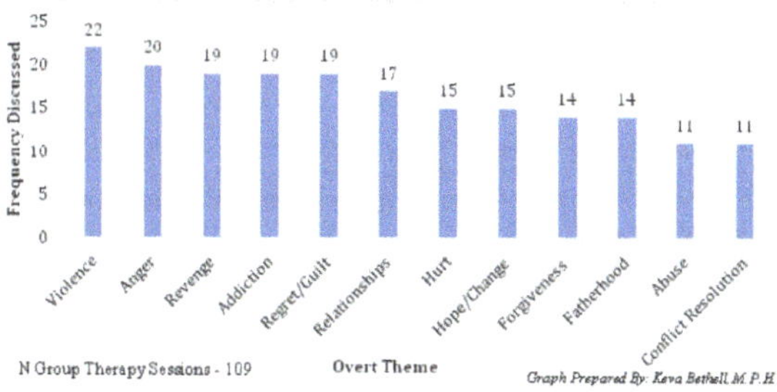

Figure 2 Thematic Analysis of Family Sessions at Her Majesty's Prison.

Anger is perceived as a natural response to an attack but it may be toxic, uncontrollable and destructive. According to one of the inmates, 'when you kill for the first time you feel sick and can't stop thinking about it. You feel like you're going crazy. After a while you get used to it, get drunk and high, and you feel numb'. Anger and revenge are intimately linked. A knowledgeable inmate said his impression was that 'at least 45% of murders involve revenge'. Sadly, revenge is perceived as 'an act of love'. In a society with minimal trust in social justice, revenge abounds. According to the inmates, there are only two counter arguments to the idea of revenge as love:

i If caught and punished by society for a revengeful act, it will make your loved ones suffer and

ii If one is religious, God is responsible for vengeance and not us. But they admit that revenge is natural or instinctive. Forgiveness is difficult and requires a lot of growth and development to think that way.

Case vignettes

Here are some excerpts from the group process dealing with the four most prevalent themes of volatility (violence), anger, revenge and addiction:

An example of emotional volatility (violence) in the group

A group member confronted another member saying, "I am waiting for you to apologize to me!" Responding, the accused person jumped up, ready to fight the accuser. Suddenly, the other inmates jumped up and stood between them to prevent a fight. The officer on duty immediately intervened, taking both men out of the room to cool down. The facilitators told the officers that they wanted the men to return to the group as soon as they were willing to continue talking and not fight. While they were gone, the inmates expressed their annoyance with the accuser who they claimed was explosive and destructive. Other members were shocked at the escalation of the altercation. The facilitators encouraged the group to work it through by sharing their feelings. Many shared and agreed that even though the accuser was a trouble maker, the accused did not have to react so aggressively. Eventually, they started to plan how to help both men overcome the situation. They shared such ideas like, "let them cool down for a couple of days and then we will talk with them".

The accuser came back smiling. The officer explained to the group that the accused was still very angry and would return to the group the following week. The accuser explained in detail the problem he had with the accused. The group's annoyance was palpable and tensions started to rise again. The facilitators reminded the group that we just had an amazing opportunity to learn about anger. They asked each member of the group to share how the experience affected them. Sharing their feelings, the members calmed down and some even became humorous to diffuse the atmosphere. The men shared that growth is difficult and requires patience and understanding. One person said he has to grow and soon leave prison because his two daughters, whom he loves deeply, are waiting for him.

An example of how anger manifests in group process

Another example of how the group process diverts anger is the following group interaction: 'A participant tells the group he is not sure if he can practice meditation by himself because he fears "going crazy". Explaining, he said "my mind is in deep struggle. I want to walk away from conflict but it is hard not to keep thinking of revenge". He shared with the group how other inmates are constantly provoking him, e.g. stealing his property, not respecting his personal space and making jeers at him. He said this last Sunday, he was very provoked and could have reacted violently. He said if this had happened on the outside, he would have killed in a heartbeat. But taking time to think it over, he said he kept imagining the facilitators asking about him. He could hear the group members saying "He can no longer come. He is in maximum security prison now because he got in trouble". Continuing, he said, "I remember you (facilitators) asking about two other participants who were no longer in the group. I can't disappoint the group. I am here to ask for help because I find it hard to let go of revenge from my mind!"

Mocking him, two group members reacted sarcastically, "You don't want to let go of revenge because you really want to kill. You are not ready to change". Realizing the developing conflict, the facilitators intervened immediately, reframing the discussion by reminding the group that everyone has the right to express themselves freely.

Another participant shared: "I understand you. I feel the same, but after coming to this group and learning about revenge, I have been out of trouble for one year now. I know it is hard but you must walk away. We don't want to stay in this place forever".

An example of how revenge manifests in group process

A member of the group said he disagreed with the statement 'you should destroy evil by destroying the evildoer'. He said "I have done evil and they have destroyed me by putting me in prison. I want everyone to be treated like me. I want all evildoers killed'. The group challenged him that evil could happen to anyone. Destroying all evildoers would mean no one would be left.

Recognizing that the group members disagreed with him in a respectful and accepting manner, he continued to talk about his hurt and anger. Describing the depth of his anger, he said, 'I hate people. I can't trust them because they hurt me badly. My mother abandoned me at eight years old, went to the U.S. and had another family. My father also abandoned me and my grandmother raised me, but the rest of the family members and neighbors scorned me. My daughter is my only love but sadly I've abandoned her and I hate myself because I've done to her what was done to me.'. Obviously, the gentleman was becoming aware of his hate for himself, that is, his shame (Self Hatred Aimed at M.E.). He recognized the repetition compulsion where he abandoned his daughter like everybody else abandoned him. Sharing this had a powerful effect on him. He confessed to the group that sharing like this is unusual for him and he was surprised that he was able to do it.

An example of how addiction manifests in group process

By far, the preferred drug of choice is cannabis. Group members often describe their 'love for weed'. They use it to calm down and avoid violent outbursts. They said that when they are rewarded with cigarettes for performing chores, they find it easy to obtain cannabis and put it in their cigarettes.

Alcohol is synonymous with celebration, e.g. a birthday party with friends and getting drunk together. But some of the men shared that they were deeply hurt by alcoholic parents. One gentleman said, 'I got tired of seeing my parents drink and fight. I became curious about the bottle they liked so much. I was eight years old when I got drunk for the first time. I wanted to feel what my parents were feeling'. The inmates agreed that the time spent in prison was an excellent opportunity to work on themselves and become sober. The men not only discussed addiction to drugs and alcohol, but also described being addicted to guns, sex, power and money. One inmate admitted 'I am using this time to think about my life. Greed brought me here. I had a job, but it was never good enough. I was mesmerized by making fast money and went into drug trafficking. As a result, it landed me in prison'.

The evil violence tunnel

The Evil Violence Tunnel Syndrome is characterized by intense and murderous rage directed to oneself or other. The introduction and discussion of this phenomenon in the group was received with enthusiasm. Group members recognize all symptoms of the syndrome and even admitted that: 'we live in this tunnel' (Figure 3). Inmates then engaged in an exercise to use their own words to describe the steps that lead someone to participate in impulsive violent acts. Discussing preventive measures for avoiding the tunnel also became a priority, once they realized that 'once you are deep in the tunnel, it is difficult to get out'.

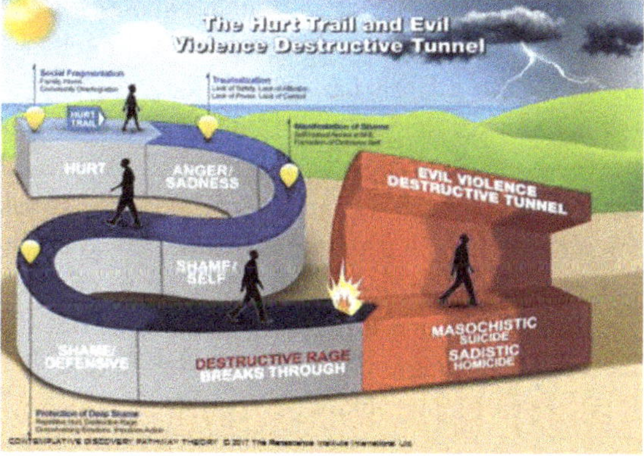

Figure 3 The Evil Violence Tunnel.

The stages of the Evil Violence Tunnel are: cognitive restriction, physiological arousal, emotional numbness, intense negative energy, ethical fragmentation and repetitive destructive behavior. After being taught the stages of the tunnel, the inmates decided to describe the stages in their own language. According to the inmates, the stages of the Evil Violence Tunnel are:

1. Fixation on the person who they wish to harm.
2. Physical and chemical reactions in their body destroy any kind of rational thinking.
3. The loss of feeling, especially fear.
4. They become overwhelmed by negativity and destruction and lose all sense of positive or compassionate feelings.
5. The breakdown of their value system where they do not consider or care about right and wrong regarding harming the person.
6. A continual path (pressure) to stab, shoot or strike the person without any awareness of the consequences.[10]

There are a staggering number of examples of group members sharing about committing acts of violence, but one of them stands out. For a brief period of time we had a few female inmates in our group. During one of these sessions, a lady shared her experience of being 'in the tunnel': 'I was raised by my grandmother and I knew all kinds of abuse growing up. When I was in my late 20's I was a single mother with a good enough job at a hotel. I started dating this policeman because I wanted to 'play him'. I wanted to make him believe I was carrying his child so he could take care of me and my children. As time went by, he started to become more and more violent and I started to hate him deeply. I even told him the child was not his. One day I was back from work and I was combing my hair while he was screaming at me, calling me names and threatening to rape me one more time. Suddenly I attacked him with the comb in my hand. To my horror the metal comb went all the way into his skull. The blood came pouring out and he died instantly. I still remember seeing my son cleaning the blood on the floor with the mop. I was in the newspaper and felt ashamed. I attempted suicide by setting the prison cell on fire. I am happy I survived because I realize now that my children and my mother are waiting for me to get out, so I have people I love and this keeps me going'.

Resocialization-based themes

Following violence, anger, revenge and addiction, the next most common themes were regret/guilt, relationships, hurt, hope/change and forgiveness. These themes appeared later in the group process, once group cohesion was established. Our facilitator, Mr. André Chappelle, initiated the discussion of these themes when he spoke freely about his painful experiences with family disputes, severe substance abuse, several incarcerations and homelessness. We laughed and cried with him as he told his authentic story. He stated: 'There were deep scars of abandonment, humiliation, and rejection that I had run from my whole life and would never have admitted to anyone. But in The Family, I began to open up by telling my story and sharing my fears. The beautiful thing was, this was met by love and it produced peace within my heart. I came to realize that our heart is like a sponge. It becomes filled with the hurt, fear and shame of a lifetime, often blocking love and hope, pushing our life towards despair. When we can squeeze the sponge to empty the hurt and shame by sharing our story in a caring environment like The Family, we make space for love to enter our hearts and peace soon follows. This peace I treasure and value and it acts like a barometer, for whenever I sense my inner stillness being ruffled, I check myself. I check myself because it's not what's happening on the outside that determines the state of my inner world, but rather it's the peace of God within me that allows me to determine how to respond. This is a choice: the choice to respond either from a heart of fear or a heart of love. You can either be a thermostat or a thermometer!'.[11]

Group members shared their reaction to seeing Mr. Chappelle homeless in contrast to seeing him fully rehabilitated. They congratulated and hugged him, saying, "if you can do it, anyone can!"As the men shared their stories, the bond uniting the group became stronger. They said they were taking a risk in being emotionally vulnerable and warned us, 'if our family comes to visit and starts crying, we will tell them not to come back'. Most group members agreed and admitted that, 'Prison is no place for grieving. If we start thinking about our families, our wrongdoing and how we left them stranded without protection we will lose our minds'.

Below are excerpts from group sessions that centered on the themes of regret/guilt, relationships, hurt, hope/change and forgiveness:

An example of regret/guilt and forgiveness

An inmate said: 'I have been here for 31 years of life. I missed it all: my children growing up, my grandchildren being born, my parents' funerals and all graduations and weddings. I have survived all this anger and sorrow through Faith'. The group was respectfully silent as he spoke. Continuing, he said: 'I was bad since childhood. My father wasn't there, my mother had to work all the time and I was raised by my grandmother and other relatives. They never had a kind word of love or encouragement for me. I had to be out of their sight and do whatever they commanded. I was beaten often. I looked to my mother for comfort, but she beat me saying I should respect my relatives. At 7 years old after another bad beating, I decided to give up on love and my heart became cold. I enjoyed being bad, ran away and spent most of my time "on the blocks" where I was more appreciated. My criminal life started young'. The group asked him 'how his heart turned cold'. He said 'that is what happens when you believe you will never be loved'. He explained 'I always loved my mom and now I know she loved me. When I was sent to jail and given a long sentence she cried. I denied my wrongdoing and lied to her again. But after thinking about it–that's all we have to do in this place –I decided to change because I am a Christian. It took me two years to tell my mother the truth. If I could tell my mother the truth, maybe I could admit the truth to myself. I tried to reach out to the families of the victims to ask forgiveness. It took a long time before I could finally talk to them. Even though some did not forgive me, I had to ask because it made me feel better. But the most difficult thing was to forgive myself for the time I have lost with my children.'

An example of hope/change

Another inmate has been in prison for 25 years and is running a "toast master" program to help inmates learn to speak publicly. He is planning to create an association to provide guidance and support for discharged inmates.

An example of hurt

Group members admitted that having a loved one die while incarcerated is one of the most painful experiences. Feelings of regret and guilt are overwhelming. Crying is a sign of vulnerability and there is no private space to cry while incarcerated. We have heard stories of multiple losses in a short period of time. One inmate stated "I have lost eight people in the last two years. I now feel numb'.

An example of relationships

A participant who has not been in prison for a long time has a powerful influence on the group because he is a good listener. The men respect him very much and they are very grateful to him.

Another participant did not say very much, but when he shared his story, he spoke non-stop in describing his life. He admitted being a drug addict who had spent many years being zoned out. Because of this, he was an absent father for his two daughters. He described being stabbed and nearly died. But he nurse caring for him was an angel and motivated him to recover. He was inspired by Maya Angelou's poem

'Why the Caged Bird Sings' and said 'we now have a bird that visits us in the cell. We feed him and call him Freedom. 'Recently, he has shown definite signs of resocialization. He described a situation where he was physically challenged and wanted to seek revenge. He said he held back because he did not want to disappoint the Family group.

Signs of resocialization in group process

The following are some examples of the emerging Resocialization process occurring in the group.

1 The increased ability to delay gratification and have better impulse control:
   a. The men ask to leave the group when they are angry so they can cool down and return to continue the discussion. This means they are moving from a purely instinctive reaction to a thought out response to the situation;
   b. We notice now that the men wait to talk to each other and often ask a week in advance to speak at the next meeting;
   c. They can now have a discussion without getting angry and threatening because they have learned to communicate with each other. For example, they say "I am just talking about myself" or they admit "we can agree to disagree".
2 The men make less generalizations in the group, e.g. originally they would make broad statements such as "all men cheat". Now they take personal responsibility and are willing to say "I admit that I cheat, but it does not mean that all men do as I do".
3 The men have developed better conflict resolution skills and are able to have more harmonious conversations and effective communication. They speak slower and have less threatening outbursts when the group does not agree with them. They are more respectful to us the facilitators and to each other. For example, because they are interested in participating, they would ask beforehand if they could lead the meditation.
4 As the group has developed, the men are able to express vulnerability by sharing intimate, personal and emotional stories. As a result, they are more open to being emotionally labile or even crying.
5 The group has expressed a deep gratitude to us for starting the Family group in the prison. For example, at Christmas, they planned a special ceremony to thank us for our interest and work. We have also noticed that at the end of each group, many of the men come up to us and say "thank you" before returning to their cells.
6 As the group has developed, the men are more open in describing their artistic expression, particularly as it relates to music, prayer, poetry etc.
7 The men have become more self-reflective and are able to share their inner feelings more openly, e.g. they can express painful feelings such as depression, sadness or anger.
8 Developing better impulse control, the men are less reactive and revengeful, creating more harmonious relationships among themselves.
9 The men have a deep emotional investment in the group and have taken ownership and personal responsibility by naming the group the "free your mind group". They also invite others to the group and share the information they learn with family and friends. They are very excited about attending the group and claim they can't wait for the time to come for the group to take place. They also say they make special preparation to come to the group, e.g. shaving and appearing neat. This illustrates the development of a deeper sense of self-care and increased self-esteem.
10 As the group developed, the concept of forgiveness instead of revenge has emerged as a major theme. They are beginning to understand that forgiveness is the only process that can heal a wound of the past that cannot be changed.
11 Most exciting is that the men have become more hopeful about their life. According to them, they can't wait to return to the community and live a more simple life by helping others.

Conclusion

The Family Prison Group was developed to create a safe space for traumatized, incarcerated persons to work through their shame and pain. The participants have accepted the mantra of The Family 'jaw, jaw stops war, war'. They are learning that in sharing their personal stories and accepting responsibility for their actions, they experience a deeper sense of freedom. The Family Program aims to enhance Resocialization by helping persons to become familiar with their inner life. As they become more self-reflective and share their personal stories, they develop powerful bonds of connection, enhancing the development of caring community.

The thematic analysis of the Prison group, described in this paper indicates the depths of negativity of shame but also provides hope for Resocialization and preparation for the inmates to live a meaningful and crime-free life upon their release. Our hope is that this group process intervention could increase its positive effect for marginalized populations inside and outside the prison walls. We realize this is just a start, but we are encouraged by the results of the group and are planning to start a group for the female inmates in the future. Hopefully, this will lead us to develop a group for discharged inmates giving us a full spectrum of services for the inmates in prison and also when they are released into the community. It is important for all of us to realize that the inmates in prison will someday return to live in the community. Thus, the better we prepare them for successful reentry into society, the more effective our law-enforcement program.

Acknowledgement

None.

Conflict of Interest

The author declares no conflict of interest.

References

1 Allen. Report on Crime. 2013.

2 Jekel JF, Allen DF, Podlewski H, et al. Epidemic, free-base cocaine abuse: Case study from The Bahamas. *Lancet*. 1986;1(8479):459–462.

3 Goffman E. *Characteristics of total institutions*. USA: Holt, Rinehart and Winston; 1961. p. 312–338.

4 Allen DF, Mayo M, Allen Carroll M, et al. Cultivating Gratitude Contemplative Discovery Pathway Theory Applied to Group Theory in The Bahamas. *Journal of Trauma & Treatment*. 2014:7.

5 Institute for Criminal Policy Research. *World Prison Brief*. UK: Birkbeck University of London; 2016.

6 Allen DF, Allen Carroll M, Bethell KY, et al. An Instrument for Assessment of Longitudinal Community Resocialization Through a Group Process Intervention. *J Trauma and Treat*. 2017;6:355.

7 Frankl VE. *Man's Search for Meaning*. USA: Beacon Press; 1946.

8 Allen DF. *Shame: The Human Nemesis*. USA: Eleuthera Publications; 2010.

9 David Foster Wallace's. Commencement address at Kenyon College published in The Economist Magazine in September 19th 2008. USA; 2005.

10 Allen D, Bethell K, Allen Carroll M. Anger and Social Fragmentation: Evil Violence Tunnel. *Journal of Psychotherapy Integration*. 2017;27(1):79–92.

11 Allen DF. The war for Peace Within Ourselves: By André Chappelle. *EC Psychology and Psychiatry*. 2017;1.6(2017):226–232.

Spirituality and transformation in a community-based group in the Bahamas

Alexis D. Abernethy[a], Gillian D. Grannum[b] and David F. Allen[c]
[a]Graduate School of Psychology, Fuller Theological Seminary, Pasadena, CA, USA; [b]Wellspan Philhaven Behavioral Health, Lancaster, PA, USA; [c]Allen Institute of Training and Research, Nassau, Bahamas

Abstract
Understanding the specific contexts where spirituality may or may not be helpful has been identified as a priority in spirituality and health research. The study aims were to clarify the helpfulness of spirituality and the interrelationships among transformation, spirituality, and forgiveness in this community-based group offered in a societal context of violence. Sixteen group participants from the Bahamas were selected and interviewed. Nine participants were female (56%); 75% identified as Black and 25% identified as White/ Caucasian. NVivo 11 software was used. Transformation and spirituality themes were prevalent: themes related to prayer, group connection, and compassion were prominent. Selected spirituality themes were proximal to transformation themes, particularly forgiving others. The group process themes were closely linked to transformation themes. Participants noted that modelling by the group provided support for them to forgive and change. These findings may inform future efforts to intervene in communities experiencing violence and societal fragmentation.

Overview of "The Family" program

The Family: People Helping People" program is a culturally tailored community-based approach that was designed to improve socialisation in New Providence, the capital of the Bahamas. The majority of the population of the Bahamas is comprised of persons of African descent. Traditionally, Bahamians have been a family-based society held together by strong Judeo-Christian values. However, the cocaine epidemic of the 1980s and its sequelae, including financial crises, post-colonial issues, and educational challenges, led to social fragmentation. These crises caused widespread family and community disintegration, and resulted in burgeoning murder and violent crime rates, increased domestic violence, and the formation of violent youth gangs. "The Family" is a group-based resocialisation intervention designed to improve socialisation (Allen, Allen-Carroll, Allen, Bethell, & Manganello, 2015, p. 290).

Cultural tailoring

Pasick, D'Onofrio, and Otero-Sabogal (1996) define cultural tailoring as "the development of interventions, training practices and materials to conform to specific characteristics" (p. 145). Cultural tailoring includes a consideration of key domains or principles around which cultures may differ. "The Family: People Helping People" project was developed by Dr. Allen in the Bahamas. "The Family" group model offers support and training to community members to improve communication in relationships and to encourage constructive emotional expression. Dr. Allen has included interpersonal group techniques, role playing, and supportive interventions in this community-based group (Abernethy, Allen, & Allen, 2017). He has tailored these interventions to the Bahamian population.

Hwang (2006) identified six domains for culturally adapting psychotherapy: dynamic issues, and cultural complexities, orientation, cultural beliefs,

MENTAL HEALTH, RELIGION & CULTURE
https://doi.org/10.1080/13674676.2019.1579177
ARTICLE HISTORY: Received 26 July 2018. Accepted 3 February 2019
KEYWORDS cultural tailoring; group; spirituality; community; transformation

client–therapist relationship, cultural differences in expression and communication, and cultural issues of salience. Three domains were particularly relevant to the development of "The Family": cultural beliefs, cultural issues of salience, and the client–therapist relationship (Abernethy et al., 2017). Over 90% of the Bahamian population identify as Christians. In contrast to most group offerings that do not include music or spiritual elements, incorporating spiritual beliefs and spiritual interventions was an important dimension of cultural tailoring for this population (Thompson, 2016): religious hymns, spirituals, and prayers were integrated into the work to foster group cohesion and catharsis. Salient cultural issues include stigma and shame related to mental illness, societal fragmentation, and violence. In recognition of this stigma, the groups were framed as community offerings to improve Bahamian society rather than an individual solution. The connection between societal fragmentation and violence was made so that individual responses such as revenge seeking were seen in the context of traumatic exposure. The group was purposely named "The Family" to reflect Bahamian values related to family. The groups were located within the community in church settings and other more accessible community-based settings rather than in clinical settings (Abernethy et al., 2017). Third, the member–leader relationship differs and the leader is more transparent than in many groups. Although the leader had a clear leadership role in the group, these leaders were also community members and had been exposed to similar trauma and violence and might be mourning as well. The leader's ability to disclose heir own grief can be a powerful tool for facilitating the work of the group. Research supported by Templeton World Charities Foundation has been conducted on "The Family". Reduced feelings of anger and decreased desire for revenge have been associated with participation in "The Family" (Allen et al., 2015).

Spiritual transformation

Although there are varied definitions for religion and spirituality, religion generally connotes specific behavioural, doctrinal, and institutional features, whereas spirituality represents one's subjective experiences in attempting to understand life's ultimate questions and find meaning/purpose (Pargament, Mahoney, Exline, Jones, & Shafranske, 2013). Spiritual transformation has become an increasing focus in studies of spirituality. Sandage and Shults (2007) define spiritual transformation as "profound, qualitative, or second-order changes in the ways in which a person relates to the sacred" (p. 264). Although limited research has been conducted on spiritual transformation (Schultz, Altmaier, Ali, & Tallman, 2014), spiritual growth has been positively and spiritual decline has been negatively associated with religiousness (Cole, Hopkins, Tisak, Steel, & Carr, 2008).

> Stressful changes (whether positive or negative) require interpretations and coping strategies. Transformation is a developmental process of relating differently to stressors through new interpretations and coping strategies. Spiritual transformation is a reconceptualization of one's spiritual worldview. (Worthington & Sandage, 2016, p. 50)

Sandage and Shults (2007) identify advantages of their relational model of spiritual transformation. Two dimensions will be highlighted here. The first is the emphasis onthe reciprocal influence of spirituality and interpersonal relationships. Applying this dimension to an understanding of the group process means focusing on the leaders' spirituality in relationship to the members, God, and their mutual influence. The second contribution of this relational framework is that it draws on models of human personhood and appreciates not only the emotional but also the embodied and social dimensions of spirituality. The stressful societal context that Bahamians are facing may deeply challenge not only their interpersonal relationships but also their sense of God's presence in their lives. An approach that includes an opportunity for members to reconsider and reflect on their spiritual lives as they adjust to stressful experiences is an invaluable resource that has become an increasing priority in culturally competent care (Nelson, 2009). In proposing a broader framework for exploring spiritual experience following stressful events, Bray (2010) argues for helping professionals' increased role in fostering this exploration. This supportive and open posture toward spiritual concerns is consistent with the emphasis of "The Family". Understanding the relationships among spirituality, transformation, and group themes may offer some insight for critical aspects of spiritually focused groups.

Spirituality in group therapy

In Pargament's (2007) delineation of the orientation of spiritually integrated therapy, he argues that patients bring a larger cultural context to therapy which may make spiritual concerns a salient dimension of their problem and may inform how they relate to others. Pargament's perspective is consistent with Yalom's description of the therapeutic factors that contribute to healing in groups (Yalom & Leszcz, 2005). Yalom identified11 therapeutic factors as mechanisms of change, including group cohesion, interpersonal learning, imitative behaviour, existential factors, and instillation of hope. Group cohesion refers to the connections among the members and the leader. Interpersonal learning highlights the importance of members learning from one another and gaining interpersonal skills. Imitation is one way that this learning occurs. Existential factors and hope may be particularly significant in a spiritually informed group (Abernethy, 2012). Others have examined the spiritual themes that emerge in group (Jacques, 1998).

Forgiveness is an example of a spiritual theme that may emerge in groups. Paris (1995) noted that a communal spirituality prevalent in communities of African descent helps to inform African and African American approaches to forgiveness. Forgiveness has been associated with positive health outcomes including well-being and has been found to have a mediational role in the relationship between religiosity and health (Lawler-Row, Hyatt-Edwards, Wuensch, & Karremans, 2011; Strelan, Acton, & Patrick, 2009). Other work on forgiveness has considered the social context and the potential deleterious effects of interpersonal forgiveness in some neighbourhoods (McCullough, 2008).

> Forgiveness of others in most social environments will reduce interpersonal conflict and anger and allow for an individual to create and maintain social support networks that are essential for health and well-being. In more noxious environments, however, there is reason to expect that forgiveness will be harmful for health. (McFarland, Smith, Toussaint, & Thomas, 2012, p. 68)

Forgiveness may have negative consequences and expose individuals to retaliation. In a study that examined forgiveness, health, and neighbourhood context in older Blacks and Whites (McFarland et al., 2012), researchers noted that the positive relationship between spirituality and health for Blacks may be related to extensive family and social ties as well as church involvement. Groups offered in these environments may instill not only hope but also forgiveness. Forgiveness that may be linked to a changed spiritual outlook and that emerges out of the context of a supportive group where forgiveness is modelled may be quite distinct from a more isolated decision to forgive.

Focus of the present study

There is increasing understanding of the importance of incorporating spiritual perspectives in culturally competent care, but Pargament's question remains unanswered.

> How helpful or harmful are particular religious (and spiritual) expressions for particular people dealing with particular situations in particular social contexts according to particular criteria of helpfulness and harmfulness? (Pargament, 2002, p. 178)

This study offers an opportunity to examine some aspects of these questions for Bahamian Christians who are facing a violent societal context. For example, how helpful or harmful is forgiveness in this specific social context? This study is part of a broader research project on spirituality, emotions, and group processes that included five major categories of themes for a total of 54 individual themes. The five major categories of themes for the larger study were experiences such as violence, spiritual practices, feelings, impact of "The Family", and spirituality. In order to more fully understand the relationship between spirituality and transformation in the group process, this study focused on two categories, spirituality and the impact of "The Family". The impact category included transformation as well as group process themes. Specific research questions included:

1. In comparison to other themes, how prominent were group process-related, spirituality, and transformation themes in interview responses?
2. Were themes focused on group process related to transformation?
3. Were themes focused on spirituality related to transformation?
4. To what extent did descriptions of forgiveness and transformation highlight the power of their connectedness in group and their sense of God's presence?
5. In describing how "The Family" affected them, what experiences had the greatest impact?

Materials and methods

Community-based intervention

"The Family: People Helping People" is a Bahamas-based group resocialisation program founded by Dr. Allen. "The Family" started with one group in 2009, but now offers 30 free weekly groups for over 500 members. Some of the groups are smaller with 8–10 members, but a few are larger groups of 25–40 members. The groups meet for two hours and are open-ended, but members typically stay for over a year. New members attend the groups following an initial evaluation based on a screening and/or intake by the mental health staff from "The Family" if they are referred by a mental health or law enforcement professional, on psychotropic medication, or have a history of domestic violence. If members have significant mental illness, they are referred for psychiatric treatment. During group sessions, participation is optional, with interaction being guided by the leaders.

"The Family" is grounded in the Contemplative Discovery Pathway Theory Model (Allen, Mayo, Carroll, Manganello, & Allen, 2014) and uses the tools of dialogue and spiritual practice (e.g., contemplative prayer) to build empathy and cultivate virtues such as love, forgiveness, and gratitude (Allen, Mayo, Carroll, Manganello, & Allen, 2014). The hope of the program is that participation in the group sessions will help members to become increasingly vulnerable, authentic, and empathetic toward themselves and others. The facilitator provides a summary at the end of each session and offers a psychological/spiritual teaching to foster education and character development (see Abernethy et al., 2017 for a fuller description).

Participants

This study employed a qualitative research methodology. The relatively small sample size of 15–20 was chosen based on guidelines for ideographically oriented research; smaller sample sizes allow for intensive analysis of individual cases and the emergence of the particular voices of subjects (Robinson, 2013). A more homogenous sample can be helpful in illuminating specific dimensions of experience for certain types of qualitative analysis, including Interpretative Phenomenological Analysis (Robinson, 2013; Smith, Flowers, & Larkin, 2009). The recommended smaller sample size for Interpretive Phenomenological Analysis (Smith & Osborn, 2003) allows for some balance between competing goals of cross-case generalisability, ease of analysis, and individuality of response (Robinson, 2013; Smith et al., 2009).

A purposive sampling approach to participant selection was taken as the goal was to interview participants who had had some experience with "The Family". Sixteen participants for the present study were recruited from the current attendees of "The Family" and selected from two groups that are co-led by Dr. Allen. These two groups were selected in order to include more mature participants and participants from a challenging geographical area given the importance of examining the interrelationships of these variables in a particularly challenging societal context. One group included 30–40 members and 5–6 facilitators; the other included 15–20 members and two facilitators. From these two groups, members who were comfortable speaking about their group experiences and related topics were recommended by Dr. Allen and invited to participate in the study.

Participants ranged in age from 35–44 (six participants), 45–54 (five participants), 55–64 (three participants), to 65+ (two participants): 69% of the participants were between ages 35 and 54. Nine were female (56%) and seven were male (44%); 75% identified as Black and 25% identified as White/Caucasian. Eleven participants (69%) reported completing some post-secondary education; five participants completed four years of college. Ten participants were employed, and the remainder were unemployed, retired, or homemakers. Most participants described themselves as moderately or very religious/spiritual (75%), and all but one participant reported weekly church attendance. All reported religious affiliations were Christian Protestant, with a variety of denominations represented, including Baptist (three), Anglican (two), Methodist (one), Assemblies of God (one), Pentecostal (one), and non-denominational (two).

Procedure

Selected group members who had been members of "The Family" for at least a year were invited to participate in the research project. Fuller's Graduate School of Psychology's Institutional Review Board approved this project. Participants consented to participate in recorded interviews via a signed consent form. They completed a brief demographic questionnaire and were interviewed by a clinical psychology graduate student researcher in an office setting in Nassau, Bahamas. Interviews were recorded via audio capture software and transcribed to text for analysis.

Interview protocol

The researchers generated 17 open-ended interview questions based on preliminary themes derived from the literature reviewed above for the larger study (Grannum, 2017). The questions addressed key areas exploring the participant's experience of shame, group participation, spirituality, and worship. The interviews ranged from 30 to 60 min. For this study, responses to questions related to spirituality and group participation were the primary focus. Interview questions explored the extent that "The Family" provided support and was meaningful, offered connection and an experience with God, and fostered forgiveness and hope.

Thematic analysis

This study employed a qualitative research methodology, which is particularly useful for exploring experiences and acknowledges the role of the researcher as integral to the process of research (Biggerstaff & Thompson, 2008). De-identified interview transcripts were reviewed for themes using Interpretive Phenomenological Analysis which focuses on how participants understand and make meaning of their experiences (Smith & Osborn, 2003). The two stages of this process include the participant's interpretation of his/her experience and the researcher's interpretation of the participant's comments. Researchers reviewed interview transcripts and identified themes articulated in the interviews from several interviews. Themes were defined and organised into clusters based on their conceptual connections. Additional themes were added as articulated by participants in subsequent interviews. A final list of themes was generated and finalised.

A pair of raters using NVivo 11 software coded compiled transcript data for identified themes. The following coding process was adopted in order to ensure adequate agreement between raters. First, each rater coded the same transcript independently, and the level of agreement between their analyses was calculated via a Kappa coefficient. If the average Kappa coefficient of the themes was at least .70, each rater proceeded to code three separate transcripts individually. However, if the average Kappa coefficient was less than .70, the raters reviewed their coding and clarified unclear or disputed themes, consulting with the research team if necessary. Independent coding continued after achieving a Kappa of .70. The average Kappa reliability was .72.

Using NVivo 11, word similarity for coded themes was compared using cluster analysis. Complete linkage cluster analysis compares themes in qualitative data and identifies the closest pairings based on similarities. The product is then displayed via a dendrogram, a two-dimensional representation of thematic relationships in qualitative data (Kurian, 2015).

Results

Frequency of theme occurrence was measured in several ways, including number of interviews in which the theme was present (pervasiveness) and number of coding references for a particular theme (prevalence). Of the 54 themes, the following 10 top themes were present in at least 50% of the interviews and had at least 24 coding references: Prayer (36 references), Connectedness to group (32), Compassion for others (32), Learning from/teaching other group members (28), Dr. Allen and Family leadership (27), Violence (27), Support (26), Shame (24), Transformation (24), and Forgiving others (24). The top rated themes related to group, spirituality, and transformational outcomes were identified for this study. Five group-related themes with more than 14 references were identified as specific research variables for this study: Connectedness to group, Learning from/Teaching other group members, Support, Opening up/Sharing one's story, Family leadership. Five transformational outcomes with more than nine references were identified: Acceptance, Compassion for others, Self-compassion, Transformation, and Enhancement. Three Spirituality themes with more than 16 references were identified: Forgiving others, Sense of God's presence, and Hope. Table 1 depicts the frequency occurrences for these research variables.

For research question 1a, group-related themes were most prominent as Connectedness to group, Learning from/Teaching other group members, Dr. Allen and Family leadership, and Support were four of the most frequent 10 themes. For research question 1b, one spirituality theme (Forgiving others) was present among the 10 most prominent themes. For research question 1c, two transformational themes (Compassion for others and Transformation) were among the 10 most prominent themes.

Cluster analyses

In order to examine research questions 2 and 3, cluster analyses based on word similarities were conducted in order to identify the relationships among themes; these analyses are depicted as dendrograms. Three different cluster analyses depict the more proximal and distal themes. Figure 1 illustrates the interrelationships among all of the themes that were a focus of this study. The themes that include similar words that are more proximal on the right side of the page represent those that were most closely associated when all 13 themes were entered into the analysis. The most closely associated themes were Compassion for others and Learning from/Teaching other group members. This pair was linked closely to Connectedness to group and Support. Opening up and Sharing one's story was more closely linked to Transformation. Interestingly, Dr. Allen and Family leadership was closely linked to a Sense of God's presence.

Figure 2 depicts only the group and spirituality themes. As in Figure 1, the Group connection and Learning themes were most proximal, followed by Support and Opening up. Dr. Allen's leadership and Forgiving others were more proximal to the other

Table 1. Themes related to Present Study, ordered by number of coding references.

Theme (Category)	Coding references	Interviews
Connectedness to group (Group)	32	16
Compassion for others (Transformation)	32	15
Learning from/teaching other group members (Group)	28	15
Dr. Allen & Family leadership (Group)	27	9
Support (Group)	26	11
Transformation	24	14
Forgiving others (Spirituality)	24	15
Sense of God's presence (Spirituality)	18	10
Hope (Spirituality)	16	9
Opening up, Sharing one's story (Group)	14	10
Self-compassion (Transformation)	10	5
Acceptance (Transformation)	9	6
Enhancement (Transformation)	5	4

group experiences. Hope and Sense of God's presence were linked but more distal. Some support was found for research question 2 as Figure 3 depicts the group process and transformation themes. Partial support was found for research question 3 as Figure 4 depicts the spirituality and transformation themes. Compassion for others and Transformation were most closely linked, followed by Acceptance and Forgiving others. Enhancement and Self-compassion were more distal. Hope and Sense of God's presence were linked again, but distinct from other spirituality and transformational outcome themes.

Figure 1. Clustering of Study Themes.

Connectedness to Group (32 coding references, 16/16 participants). Connectedness to Group was both the top most pervasive theme and the second most prevalent theme. Responses from several participants included the following:

> As a result of the interaction, and the empathizing...you get to feel as one.
>
> When I hear a very similar story that is connected to mine, then automatically, there is that connection...a bond that's created. And that bond...is what we call Family.
>
> We have a song that we sing, like: Bind Us Together. It impacts you in that you're not only binding with God but with each other...you take that with you?
>
> These people really act like they's [sic] your family...could be a God thing...For people to come together and just be your sisters and brothers.

These responses describe the sense of connection that members felt through interacting,

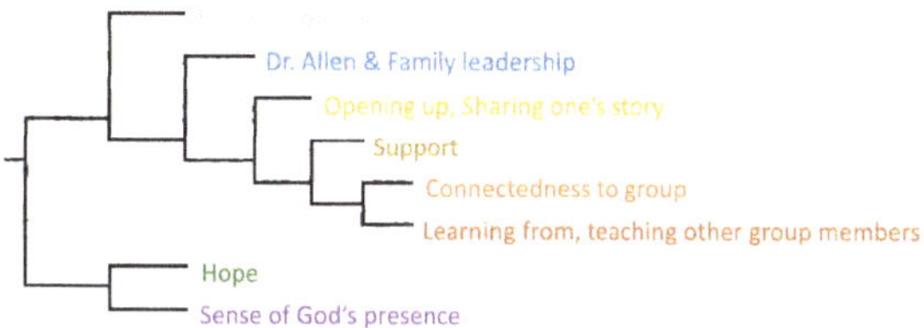

Figure 2. Spirituality and Group Themes.

Figure 3. Group and Transformation Themes.

Support (26 coding references, 11/16 participants). Members described their experience of support.

> The Family provides support for me mentally and spiritually. They support me by making sure that...I take responsibility for myself and my actions...Making sure that I see a different perspective...
>
> They give me comfort to know that everything is gonna be alright. They generally support me with love, with encouragement, with spiritual guidance.
>
> It's been a great emotional support...When I feel a certain burden...the support I get in the group...when the two hours is up, that burden is like released so I'm able to face another week...to deal with circumstances in my own life.
>
> The group setting...when I come to tell my story, they are sympathetic, they are empathetic, and they are nonjudgmental. So I feel comfortable enough to share what I would not share with other people.

Members described different types of support, including emotional, cognitive, relational, and spiritual support that translated into practical assistance. This included a changed perspective on a situation that included deeper personal insight and self-examination, and also a more informed perspective on the larger reality. Members described the burdens and challenges that they often bring to the group and they experienced relief and help that propelled them to address their life circumstances more effectively. The importance of non-judgmental support was identified as a critical aspect of receiving support.

Transformation themes

Five transformational themes were identified: Compassion for others, Self-compassion, Transformation, Acceptance, and Enhancement.

Transformation (24 coding references, 14/16 participants). Participants shared their journey toward transformation and change.

> At one point...I was a gang leader...That's why I can thank the Lord now that...through the Bible and...groups like the Family, I can stand firm and encourage others.

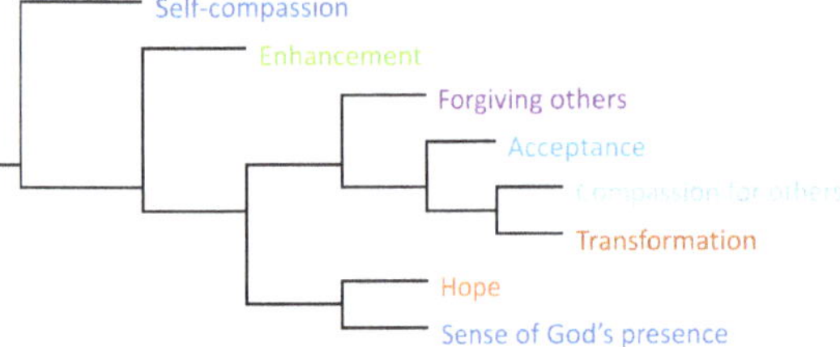

Figure 4. Spirituality and Transformation Themes.

I've seen one women...they had killed her brother, and the guy was out on bail. And she knew where he hung out and everything...no justice...She was going to chop him up herself. But after we talked to her and somebody counseled with her, she was released from it, you know...it really changed her life. God has used this program, um, to stop a lot of murders, to stop a lot of broken homes, to bridge a lot of marriages and relationships, and bring families together.

When you see them months later, their whole demeanor's changed. They're calm and they're smiling; they're laughing. Some come back, some don't. But those that come back, you see it working...This the best medicine. In The Family, we get to see the process...of healing after the traumatic event. Yes, so that's for me, that's one of the most rewarding... and being able to be a part of that. The members described the dramatic process of transformation from being a gang leader to a helper and a grieved sister intent on revenge to a sister who was mourning, but released from the cycle of vengeance. The raw starkness of the murders comes through their stories, but they also described a shift from retaliation to an awakening that occurred that included a sense of God's divine action and healing. These responses support research hypothesis 4 that descriptions of transformation would highlight the power of their connectedness in group and their sense of God's presence.

Spirituality themes

The top three spirituality themes were Forgiving others, Sense of God's presence, and Hope.

Forgiving others (24 coding references, 15/16 participants). Participants described an increased ability to forgive.

> I asked her to forgive me, and I told her I forgive her...I went by the grave and like tell her that. But Dr. Allen likes to do role play... You relive something when you role play with someone else because you getting to say what you wanted to say to that person but didn't get to say it...And it helps you to help others.

> Yeah, forgiveness...because you are tempted at all times...And when those times come upon you, it may be within the same week...but just by going to The Family meeting and expressing that...you can leave there knowing that...I'll let that one go. I forgive that one...As opposed to, if you didn't have that group, who knows what decisions you would have made?

> The guy who killed my daughter...I had to forgive him...I choose to just forgive.

> Knowing that I could turn around and look at my shooter in the face and say: I forgive you.

Members described forgiving others and requesting forgiveness. Sometimes this forgiveness was expressed powerfully even when the person was not present at the cemetery or through role play, but the process of granting forgiveness remained critical. The role of group intervention, role play, in promoting this forgiveness was noted. The ability to forgive a daughter's murderer was a profound statement. The sense that granting forgiveness was quite vital for the grantor in way that almost eclipsed the recipient. The final response is such a direct expression of granting forgiveness not against a shooter who shot a relative, but granting forgiveness to the person who shot the grantor and communicating that face to face. The incredible power and depth of such forgiveness is immense.

These responses make some reference to the power of the group, but little explicit reference to God. Only one of the coded references links being forgiven by God to granting forgiveness. These responses provided partial support for the research question 4 that descriptions of forgiveness would highlight the power of their connectedness in group and their sense of God's presence.

Sense of God's presence (18 coding references, 10/16 participants). Descriptions of God's presence were striking. A member offered a vivid sense of God's presence.

> Sometimes you can actually sense His presence?...You can see this person delivering a message for the person in need. You can actually tell that the hand of God is on this person.
>
> Member X and I experienced how her and Member Y was ready to give up. But that's when... the moment when Dr. Allen prayed... that's when I experienced God...I experienced God through her...I experience God through compassion, through humility, through faith, through love. I experience God through healing, because I've seen people being healed.
>
> Members described sensing God's presence in one another, in Dr. Allen, and in the room.

Certain virtues were linked to God's presence such as humility, faith, and love. So when members experienced these virtues, they felt a deeper sense of God's presence. They also noted God's presence in the midst of healing as members were being transformed and even a sense of His pervasiveness and being one with Him.

> **Hope** (16 coding references, 9/16 participants). A sense of hope was expressed by several participants. Because sometimes it's more uplifting when you can hear about somebody that has been through the same thing you have been through. Much more hopeful. Because I see, not only I see hope in my own life, but...I see people's lives changing also...God is able, God can change anything. There's always hope, but when I sat and listened to others` stories and the trials and the tribulations that other people have been through worst off than you, and they have the strength and courage to sit and share that with you makes you realize that, yeah, there's hope for her, there's hope for me.

Members conveyed a sense of hope that arises from hearing others' stories. Similar stories encouraged members as a fellow traveller, but more difficult stories modelled profiles in courage. If those members were able to survive even worse circumstances, hope in one's current circumstances was increased. This hope was not only in the relational bond, the survival story, and the encouragement, but also in a sense of God's ability or action.

Meaningfulness question

In order to understand what was most meaningful about "The Family", selected responses to this question are presented below.

> We all nurture one another. We all hold hands together. We all are one with each other. That's the most meaningful part - the nurturing, and the love.
>
> Meeting myself and other people at their lowest point. So like, we could find strength in the Most High...when I am able to share my deepest darkest fears and shames, it's like then I could sense a sense of strength, spiritual strength coming inside.
>
> The way they care for you, the way they take time out to, you know, deal with a situation

> you would be going through. Like when my daughter got killed.

Members not only described how the leaders cared for members, but how a supportive environment was created where members cared for one another as well. There was a deep sense of group cohesion as there was a sense of "we" in "The Family". The depth of this cohesion seemed to emerge from a connection that was forged out of difficult, painful, and fearful places. Strength was found in one another, but they also found a spiritual strength. The caring and love in the group was tangible and real.

Discussion

This study sought to examine the interrelationships among spirituality, transformation, and group-related themes in a community-based group that was culturally tailored to meet the needs of Bahamians. The model also incorporates key group therapy techniques, including supportive factors, group process, and role-playing to effect change (Abernethy et al., 2017).

The finding that connectedness to the group was the most pervasive theme supports the power of the group and the sense of community. Participants offered poignant examples of the power of the group process. Participants experienced the group as a supportive family, reflecting group cohesion, which is a key therapeutic factor in groups (Yalom & Leszcz, 2005). Group cohesion rests on the sense of connection among members and their connection to the leader. Group members described caring and concern for one another as well as deep appreciation for Dr. Allen's leadership. Interpersonal learning, another therapeutic factor (Yalom & Leszcz, 2005), was also a predominant theme and the fourth most referenced theme in participants' description of the group. Participants were not simply describing an emotionally and relationally powerful experience, but noted specific insights they gained that contributed to their learning and transformation. As depicted in the dendrograms, the themes related to sense of connection and learning from others were closely linked in analyses of both spirituality and group themes and spirituality and transformation themes (Figures 2 and 3). Group leadership plays a vital role in the efficacy of groups (Rutan, Stone, & Shay, 2014). Participants emphasised the power of Dr. Allen's leadership in the group. Members described his role in guiding the group and fostering emotional expression and highlighted his spiritual leadership in incorporating spiritual practices of prayer and singing. They not only identified common group leader characteristics but also emphasised a sense of spiritual connection as they experienced him as leader. This exemplifies a spiritually informed approach to group work in which the leader embodies a spiritual presence while demonstrating group expertise (Abernethy, 2012). This is consistent with Sandage and Shults' model of spiritual transformation (2007) where they highlight the importance of relational spirituality and the reciprocal influence of spirituality and interpersonal relationships. This embodiment is partially supported by the cluster analysis of all study themes as the sense of God's presence is most proximal to Dr. Allen's leadership (Figure 1).

Spiritual themes were also prominent in the interviews. Members described powerful moments when they were able to face perpetrators of violence against themselves and their loved ones with a heart of forgiveness. The forgiveness that they described was not a passive acceptance of a wrong committed against them. This type of forgiveness in a noxious environment might be associated with the more negative outcomes that McFarland et al. (2012) have found. This forgiveness was a bold, literally "in your face" forgiveness that reflected a deep recognition of the toxicity of maintaining a stance of vengeance. The work of these groups offers insight for one approach to reframing these traumatic stressful life experience using a spiritual perspective (Bray, 2010). Members noted experiencing hope as they sensed God's presence in a tangible way. In both dendrograms that depicted spirituality and either group or transformation themes, Hope and a Sense of God's presence were closely linked (Figures 2 and 3).

Transformational outcomes were also prominent, particularly Compassion for others and Transformation. Members experienced both compassion toward others and some degree of self-compassion. Vivid descriptions of change were shared as participants noted a gradual, sometimes elusive, process of transformation.

In terms of the interrelatedness of group, spirituality, and transformation-related themes, the themes clustered most closely within their categories, as might be expected. The major exception to this was Forgiveness. Forgiveness clustered in the categories associated with group themes in the group and spirituality dendrogram (Figure 2) and clustered with transformational themes in the spirituality and transformation dendrogram (Figure 3). Clearly, there are distinctions between the themes in these categories, but there is also overlap. Because many group members have been impacted by violence, a major goal of "The Family" is to encourage members to avoid engaging in retaliatory behaviour; thus moving toward forgiveness can have significant prosocial benefits. Yalom also identified three key mechanisms of change in group: imitation, identification, and internalisation (Yalom & Leszcz, 2005). Members come to "The Family" and imitate, identify, and ultimately internalise a hope-filled, forgiveness-oriented, non-retaliatory response. This is modelled in the group first, but eventually "The Family" becomes a model for a healthier way of being in the wider Bahamian community. This clustering of forgiveness more with group and transformational themes rather than spiritual themes was also supported in the thematic analysis in terms of a specific dimension of spirituality, God's presence. There were very few references to God in these responses. Even in a Christian sample although forgiveness may be understood in terms of God's action, human violation in the forms of murder and cycles of revenge may make God's forgiving posture less prominent in certain phases of transformation.

The most meaningful aspects of "The Family" are apparent throughout all of the responses, but particularly in the response to the meaningfulness questions, descriptions of support, God's presence, sense of hopefulness, forgiving others, and connection to the group. The power of this group to change lives is readily evident. Members experience violent crimes toward themselves and others and through their experience in "The Family", they witness others who have been on a similar journey. They realise that they are not alone and that they can obtain support. It is a support that is multifaceted: emotional, cognitive, relational, spiritual, tangible, and practical. They are able to share the depth of their pain and loss as well as their anger and rage. They are able to gain spiritual and psychological perspectives on their pain so that they do not need to engage in retaliation and vengeance. Some do not choose this path, but many do move on to forgiveness and a deeper commitment to help others in their community.

Limitations

Although this study depicts an innovative community-based intervention, this qualitative approach has several methodological challenges. The participants were recommended based on established criteria, but these participants neither fit a rigorous criterion of exemplars nor serve as representative of their groups. As noted above, only two groups were selected; thus the study did not include a broader sample of members in "The Family". This sample is not representative of "The Family" or the Bahamian population. This limits generalisability. The goal in purposive sampling was to be able to adequately address the questions of interest, but these responses come from an informed, but not representative group. Although Christians have strong representation in the Bahamas, the selection of Protestants rather than some representation of Catholics is a limitation of this study. The identified thematic categories are meaningfully derived, but there is conceptual overlap, particularly within the spirituality and transformation themes.

Conclusion

This integrated culturally tailored approach that draws on the cultural strength of spiritual resources, psychological group processing, and a collective communal context offers a powerful vehicle for change in the context of societal fragmentation. Significant insights were gained that helped identify specific characteristics in this group that contributed to transformation for these group members. The responses illumine that forgiveness that emerges and is sustained through this group process is one way that spiritual and social support work together to foster a positive relationship between forgiveness and health outcomes even in a more noxious environment (McFarland et al., 2012). These findings highlight the promise of an innovative, culturally responsive approach that may offer insight for addressing global challenges related to violence.

Disclosure statement

No potential conflict of interest was reported by the authors.

Funding

This work was supported by Templeton World Charity Foundation: [Grant Number TWCF 0073].

References

Abernethy, A. D., Allen, D. F., & Allen, M. (2017). Adapting group therapy to address real world problems: Insight from groups offered in the Bahamas. *International Journal of Group Psychotherapy*, 68(1), 17–34. doi:10.1080/00207284.2017.1335582

Abernethy, A. D. (2012). A spiritually informed approach to group psychotherapy. In J. L. Kleinberg (Ed.), *The Wiley-Blackwell handbook of group psychotherapy* (pp. 681–705). Chichester: John Wiley & Sons.

Allen, D. F., Allen-Carroll, M., Allen, V. S., Bethell, K. Y., & Manganello, J. A. (2015). Community resocialization via instillation of family values through a novel group therapy approach: A pilot study. *Journal of Psychotherapy Integration*, 25, 289–298. doi:10.1037/a0039563

Allen, D. F., Mayo, M., Carroll, M., Manganello, J., & Allen, V. (2014). Cultivating gratitude: Contemplative discovery pathway theory applied to group therapy in the Bahamas. *Journal of Trauma Treatment*, 3(3), Article ID 1000197. doi:10.4172/2167-1222.1000197.

Biggerstaff, D., & Thompson, A. R. (2008). Interpretative phenomenological analysis (IPA): A qualitative methodology of choice in healthcare research. *Qualitative Research in Psychology*, 5(3), 214–224. doi:10.1080/14780880802314304

Bray, P. (2010). A broader framework for exploring the influence of spiritual experience in the wake of stressful life events: Examining connections between posttraumatic growth and psycho-spiritual transformation. *Mental Health, Religion & Culture*, 13(3), 293–308. doi:10.1080/13674670903367199

Cole, B. S., Hopkins, C. M., Tisak, J., Steel, J. L., & Carr, B. I. (2008). Assessing spiritual growth and spiritual decline following a diagnosis of cancer: Reliability and validity of the Spiritual Transformation Scale. *Psycho-Oncology*, 17, 112–121. doi:10.1002/pon.1207 doi:10.1002/pon.1207

Grannum, G. D. (2017). An exploration of shame, spiritual practices, and compassion in a community based group (Unpublished doctoral dissertation). Fuller Theological Seminary, Pasadena, CA, USA.

Hwang, W. (2006). The psychotherapy adaptation and modification framework: Application to Asian Americans. *American Psychologist*, 61, 702–715. doi:10.1037/0003-066X.61.7.702

Jacques, J. R. (1998). Working with spiritual and religious themes in group. *International Group of Psychotherapy*, 48(1), 69–83. doi:10.1080/00207284.1998.11491522

Kurian, K. (2015). *The person of the worship leader: A qualitative study of communal worship* (Unpublished doctoral dissertation). Fuller Theological Seminary, Pasadena, CA, USA.

Lawler-Row, K. A., Hyatt-Edwards, L., Wuensch, K. L., & Karremans, J. C. (2011). Forgiveness and health: The role of attachment. *Personal Relationships*, 18(2), 170–183. doi:10.1111/j.1475-6811.2010.01327.x

McCullough, M. (2008). *Beyond revenge: The evolution of the forgiveness instinct*. San Francisco, CA:-Jossey-Bass.

McFarland, M. J., Smith, C. A., Toussaint, L., & Thomas, P. A. (2012). Forgiveness of others and health:

Do race and neighborhood matter? *The Journals of Gerontology: Series B: Psychological Sciences and Social Sciences*, 67(1), 66–75. doi:10.1093/geronb/gbr121

Nelson, J. M. (2009). *Psychology, religion, and spirituality* (pp. 475–506). New York, NY: Springer.

Pasick, R. J., D'Onofrio, C. N., & Otero-Sabogal, R. (1996). Similarities and differences across cultures: Questions to inform a third generation for health promotion research. Health Education Quarterly, 23, S142–S161. doi:10.1177/109019819602300S101

Pargament, K. I. (2002). The bitter and the sweet: An evaluation of the costs and benefit of religiousness. *Psychological Inquiry*, 13, 168–181. doi:10.1207/

S15327965PLI1303_02

Pargament, K. (2007). *Spiritually integrated psychotherapy: Understanding and addressing the sacred.* New York, NY: Guilford Press.

Pargament, K. I., Mahoney, A., Exline, J. J., Jones, J. W., & Shafranske, E. P. (2013). Envisioning an integrative paradigm for the psychology of religion and spirituality. In K. I. Pargament, J. J. Exline, & J. W. Jones (Eds.), *APA handbook of psychology, religion, and spirituality: Context, theory, and research* (Vol. 1, pp. 3–19). Washington, DC: American Psychological Association.

Paris, P. (1995). *The spirituality of African peoples.* Minneapolis, MN: Augsburg Fortress.

Robinson, O. C. (2013). Sampling in interview-based qualitative research: A theoretical and practical guide. *Qualitative Research in Psychology,* 11(1), 25–41. doi:10.1080/14780887.2013.801543

Rutan, J. S., Stone, W. N., & Shay, J. J. (2014). *Psychodynamic group psychotherapy* (5th ed). New York, NY: Guilford Press.

Sandage, S. J., & Shults, F. L. (2007). Relational spirituality and transformation: A relational integration model. *Journal of Psychology and Christianity,* 26(3), 261–269. Retrieved from https://www.questia.com/library/journal/1P3-1492333261/relational-spirituality-and-transformation-a-relational

Schultz, J. M., Altmaier, E., Ali, S., & Tallman, B. (2014). A study of posttraumatic spiritual transformation and forgiveness among victims of significant interpersonal offences. *Mental Health, Religion & Culture,* 17(2), 122–135. doi:10.1080/13674676.2012.755616

Smith, J. A., Flowers, P., & Larkin, M. (2009). *Interpretative phenomenological analysis: Theory, method and research.* Thousand Oaks, CA: SAGE Publications.

Smith, J. A., & Osborn, M. (2003). Interpretive phenomenological analysis. In J. A. Smith (Ed.), *Qualitative Psychology: A practical guide to research methods* (pp. 53–80). London: Sage.

Strelan, P., Acton, C., & Patrick, K. (2009). Disappointment with God and well-being: The mediating influence of relationship quality and dispositional forgiveness. *Counseling & Values,* 53(3), 202–213. doi:10.1002/j.2161-007X.2009.tb00126.x

Thompson, A. D. (2016). Toward a Caribbean psychology: Context, imperatives, and future directions. In J. L. Roopnarine, D. Chadee, J. L. Roopnarine, & D. Chadee (Eds.), *Caribbean psychology: Indigenous contributions to a global discipline* (pp. 15–44). Washington, DC: American Psychological Association. doi:10.1037/14753-002

Worthington Jr., E. L., & Sandage, S. J. (2016). *Forgiveness and spirituality in psychotherapy: A relational approach.* Washington, DC: American Psychological Association.

Yalom, I., & Leszcz, M. (2005). *The theory and practice of group psychotherapy* (5th ed.). New York, NY: Basic Books.

A Social Intervention for Court-Ordered Adolescents — The Family: People Helping People Project

David F. Allen, Keva Bethell, Denie Fountain and Marie Allen Carroll

Introduction

The Bahamas is an archipelagic nation situated between the southern tip of Florida and Cuba. The population of approximately 400,000 is 85 percent Afro-Bahamian and Haitian descent, with 15 percent made up of European, Asian, and Latin American. After democratically achieving Black majority rule, The Bahamas obtained its independence from Great Britain in 1973. The countrywide crack cocaine epidemic of the 1980s and its sequelae led to a serious familial and community disintegration manifested by burgeoning murder (Figure 14.1) and violent crime rates, domestic violence, child abuse, and poverty. Crack cocaine, one of the first drugs to feminize drug addiction, resulted in addicted mothers being absent from the home, leaving children to fend for themselves (Jekel, Allen, Podlewski, Clarke, Dean-Patterson, & Cartwright, 1986; Allen & Jekel, 1991). This led to the formation of violent youth gangs that terrorize the community. The average age of a murderer in the Bahamas is between 16 and 25 years and involves young men who have been traumatized by abuse and social deprivation.

In 2016, the authors approached the Court Social Workers to refer adolescents (aged 10-15 years) involved in minor violent crimes such as bullying, disorderly behavior, fighting, gang turf wars, and other destructive behaviors. Based on a carrot-stick approach, if the adolescent cooperates, they are released from their legal obligations. But if they refuse, they suffer the full consequences of the law. In this chapter, a pilot study of the court-referred adolescent program is presented.

Description of Program

Clients are referred to the program by social workers, probation officers, and guidance counselors in conjunction with the courts. The goal is to intervene in the lives of troubled adolescents to prevent them from entering a life of crime and violence. Once referred, an intake interview is scheduled for the adolescent and a parent/guardian in which the program is described and a thorough history is taken. Attendance is mandatory and the length of the program ranges from six months to two years, depending on the severity of their situation. Because many youth carried knives, screwdrivers, and other weapons which were used for protection, participants had to be screened prior to entering the program. Meeting twice a week, Mondays and Thursdays from 4:00-5:30pm, the adolescents would share their stories of trauma and shame in the presence of two facilitators. Their parents were mandated to attend a separate meeting on Wednesdays from 4:00-5:30pm. On average, 20 adolescents attended each session and 10 parents (mostly mothers) attended the patent group. This combination of the adolescents and their parents enabled a better understanding of their problems and domestic situation. The parent group assisted parents in understanding their adolescent's language, behavior, and anger patterns. Our program offered the parents a safe environment to share their concerns regarding their teens. Many parents were frustrated and felt distant from their child. But, after listening to other parents, they began to realize

Figure 14.1 Incidence of Murders in the Bahamas (1963-2018)
Source: Graph prepared by Keva Bethell, M.P.H

they were not alone in their challenges. Facilitators were able to teach parents the language of their child, the language of mind and heart. Once the mind connection began, the heart would follow. Parents came to realize the love and time they give or do not give their children can make or break them.

For most court-ordered adolescents, family life is non-existent or extremely chaotic. Many of the adolescents referred to the program have experienced some type of childhood abuse/trauma (either physical, sexual, or verbal) from a parent/guardian or other relative. While some of their grade point averages (G.P.A.) were unknown to the program facilitators, those that were known were very poor and ranged from 0.5—1.00. Because of the low educational achievement of most of the participants, a trained teacher was hired to come in once a week to teach basic literacy and math skills. Males and females were equally represented in the court-ordered group (1:1). Most of the adolescents attended regularly and felt very connected to the program. In fact, some of them would arrive one and a half hours early because they felt the program was a safe place. The adolescents displayed attention and behavioral issues but facilitators were adept at maintaining good dialogue and participation. The group process was made more difficult by the gang dynamics amongst some participants. After each meeting, the participants would often gather in their various gang groups to ensure their safe journey home.

Both therapists who facilitated the groups were Afro-Bahamian, committed Christians, and trained in psychotherapy. The male facilitator was a former gang leader who after being reformed obtained a college education. The facilitators, in many ways, were mother and father figures to these adolescents. The program is unique because "while leaders are clearly leaders and facilitators in the group, they are also community members exposed to similar trauma, violence, and community fragmentation" (Abernethy, Allen, & Allen-Catroll, 2017). According to one female facilitator:

> Our group sessions stand in the place of a family environment, where family members gather around the table to talk. With a listening ear, we are ready to absorb the pain, hurt, frustrations, and joy of the youth.
>
> What at-risk youth really need is a positive environment where they can recover and learn positive strategies to manage their anger and other emotions. Structure, discipline, and self-control are very important to these adolescents.

The idea was if facilitators could therapeutically impact traumatized adolescents/children (aged 10-15 years) involved in minor violent incidents, these youth could be deterred from committing more serious violent crimes in later years.

Method Used in Pilot Study

Over a period of one year (April 2016-May 2017), the facilitators submitted 81 praxes reports describing each session. These reports were analyzed for pertinent themes. To measure levels of trauma, post-traumatic stress disorder (PTSD), and depression of adolescents coming into the program, during the initial intake interview adolescents completed the Adverse Childhood Experience (ACE) questionnaire, the post-traumatic stress disorder (PTSD) questionnaire, and the Beck Depression Inventory (BDI).

Results of Pilot Study

Thematic Analysis

A thematic analysis of 81 group praxes submitted by the facilitators over the period of one year (April 2016—May 2017) was carried out (Figure 14.2). The leading theme discussed in the sessions was association with friends. The adolescents explained that

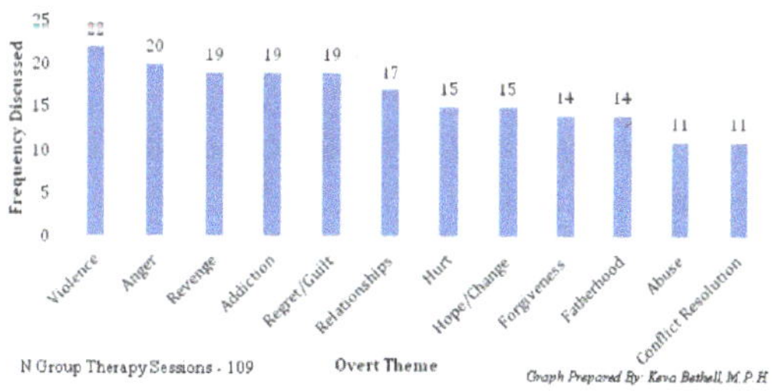

Figure 14.2 Overt Themes
Source: Graph prepared by Keva Bethell, M.P.H

friendship to them is about safety and not loyalty. For example, when asked how they felt about six teenage girls murdering one of their friends, they were not surprised. According to them, friendship may mean they are close today but if an altercation occurs, it could explode into violence. Sadly, some of the participants live under serious threats because of gang involvement. They have shown us pictures of hitmen dressed in hoodies sent to their phone. The gang often represents the masculine part of the single-parent family. In other words, the gang is a perverse rescuer in that it promises the participants relief but at the same time exposes them to greater danger and destruction (Brenneman, 2012).

Often, it takes a long time in the group before they share what is really troubling them. For example, one participant was in the group for a year before he shared that he witnessed a young man being murdered. Some of the adolescents showed a lack of empathy and remorse. After a severe stabbing at one of their schools, one of the young men was asked if he felt sorry for the victim. He said "Why should I? He's not one of my boys." The implication was that unless there is a direct association, there's no reciprocal empathy. When discussing education, many of the participants expressed no desire to continue their education. They did not believe they would live long enough to make it worthwhile.

ACE Questionnaire

A cohort of twenty-five (25) court-ordered adolescents was administered a 10-item questionnaire to measure their adverse childhood experiences (ACE) (Adverse Childhood Experience Questionnaire). Any score greater than three (3) is significant. The higher the score, the greater the impact of life experiences (Reavis, Looman, Franco, & Rojas, 2013). The results indicate that eight (8) of the participants (31 percent) scored four (4) or higher on the ACE questionnaire (Table 14.1). According to Dr Elinore McCance-Katz:

> young people who have experienced trauma are more likely to develop mental health conditions such as anxiety, depression, and substance use disorders. Young people exposed to trauma also have an increased probability of developing physical problems such as cardiovascular diseases later in life.
>
> (Greenberg, 2018)

Post-Traumatic Stress Disorder (PTSD)

A cohort of twenty-three (23) court-ordered adolescents (15 males and 8 females) were administered a questionnaire to measure post-traumatic stress disorder (PTSD) (Post-Traumatic Stress Disorder Self-Test}. The original questionnaire was altered slightly to make it more understandable for the adolescents. We used our clinical judgment to assess their level of traumatization and violence potential.

The results indicated that three (3) of the adolescents did not have PTSD; seven (7) had moderate PTSD; and thirteen (13) had severe PTSD. Test results indicated that 87 percent of the adolescents in the program had moderate or severe PTSD (Table 14.2). These results are significant because they support our hypothesis that many of our adolescents who are brought before the courts for minor infractions are in fact so traumatized that they

Table 14.1 Participant Scores on the Adverse Childhood Experiences (ACE) Questionnaire

ACE Test Score	Number of Participants
0	2
1	9
2	3
3	3
4	4
5	3
6	0
7	1
8	0
9	0
10	0

Table 14.2 Participant Scores on the Post-Traumatic Stress Disorder (PTSD) Questionnaire

Post-Traumatic Stress Disorder (PTSD) Score	Number of Participants
2	2
3	1
4	2
5	1
6	1
8	2
9	1
10	3
11	1
12	2
13	2
14	1
16	1
17	2
19	1

have a bona-fide diagnosis of post-traumatic stress disorder. This means that they have flashbacks, murderous rage, poor impulse control, and feel hopeless about their life and future (George & Berger, 2013; Walkup & Rubin, 2013). As a result, when they are enticed, either by an individual, gang, or personal desire, they may do the most destructive acts. These results are similar to what is being recorded by emergency centers dealing with violent injury in Chicago, Atlanta, and Detroit.

Beck Depression Inventory (BDI)

A cohort of twenty-three (23) court-ordered adolescents were administered the Beck Depression Inventory (BDI). The BDI showed that more than half (52 per cent) of the adolescents suffered from moderate to severe depression, involving deep-seated anger and rage. Seventeen (17) percent suffered from borderline clinical depression, 9 percent have a mild mood disturbance, and 22 percent have normal ups and downs (Table 14.3).

These scores indicated that the adolescents in the court-ordered group come with significant levels of post-traumatic stress and depression. Any treatment program must take these factors into consideration. Five individual case studies highlight these findings.

Table 14.3 Beck Depression Inventory (BDI) Test Results

Beck Depression Inventory (BDI) Score	Number of Participants
1-10	5
11-16	2
17-20	4
21-30	6
31-40	6
>40	0

Case Vignette #1

The adolescent with the highest PTSD (Post-Traumatic Stress Disorder Self-Test) score (19) was a female (aged 13 years) who showed strong destructive traits. She scored 38 on the BDI (Beck's Depression Inventory) indicating that she was severely depressed, with strong suicidal ideation. This participant claimed that she had given up on life and nothing mattered to her. On the other hand, her grade point average (G.P.A.) was 3.78, demonstrating that she had high intelligence and was doing well in school. She was cared for by her mother but had little attachment to her. She did not know her father and had no siblings. She was referred to the program by her mother (not the courts) due to her cutting behaviors. This phenomenon is not uncommon in adolescents who have deeply repressed anger with emotional numbness. The cutting and witnessing of blood is a masochistic defense which distracts youth from the pain of their depression and isolation (Peterson, Freedenthal, Sheldon, & Andersen, 2008).

Case Vignette #2

A male (aged 16 years) scored thirteen (13) on the PTSD questionnaire (Post-Traumatic Stress Disorder Self-Test), indicating severe PTSD. He was referred to the program by the courts for fighting. He scored 40 on his BDI (Beck's Depression Inventory), which indicated severe depression. Being of Haitian descent and now living as a minority in the Bahamas may have been a contributing factor to his depression. He believed that every young Bahamian male was out to get him. His parents were separated and he was especially angry at this father. He was overtly hostile and showed no signs of remorse or regret for his participation in fighting. Sadly, he claimed he lived in a constant state of fear of being stabbed or murdered. However, he would often say that he was willing to die if he was pushed to fight for his rights. During one of the therapeutic sessions, he was smiling while describing how he caused grievous harm to another person. This was a serious prognostic sign for further destructive, violent behavior. Despite his incongruent affect while describing violent behaviors he committed, this same young man was mannerly and respectful, though extremely angry.

Case Vignette #3

A female (aged 14 years) scored twelve (12) on the PTSD questionnaire (Post-Traumatic Stress Disorder Self-Test), indicating severe PTSD. She was referred to the program by the courts for fighting. She scored 23 on her BDI (Beck's Depression Inventory), which indicated moderate depression. She was extremely impulsive and could change her affect to become violent within seconds. She could remain aggressive, and if not encouraged to change, she could easily self-destruct. She was from a dysfunctional home and displayed a high level of anger. She was failing in school and her grade point average (G.P.A.) was 1.89. At the time, she was reading at a sixth-grade level, with little to no comprehension. Her attention span was also extremely short. In an instant, she could vacillate between actively participating in the session to sitting slumped on a chair as if falling asleep. She would often express anger towards her mother and stepfather for their lifestyle. She claimed both parents were alcoholics and that her stepfather was physically abusive.

Case Vignette #4

A male (aged 15 years) scored eleven (11} on the PTSD questionnaire (Post-Traumatic Stress Disorder Self-Test), indicating that he was severely traumatized. He also scored 32 on the BDI (Beck's Depression Inventory), which indicated a score in the severe depression range. He was referred to the program by the courts for fighting. At the time of his referral, he did not seem to have the capacity to understand the danger and vulnerability of his behavior. Although his grade point average (G.P.A.) was unknown, his reading ability was at a third-grade level. He had dropped out of school and was assigned to another institution for learning but refused to attend based on his Haitian nationality and gang affiliation. Being a minority, he was paranoid that Bahamian young males wanted to attack and hurt him because of his nationality. He had explosive anger and expressed no remorse or empathy for hurting others. In fact, he boasted of continuing this fight should they ever cross paths again.

Case Vignette #5

A male (aged 14 years) male scored nine (9) on the PTSD questionnaire (Post-Traumatic Stress Disorder Self-Test), indicating moderate/severe PTSD and 20 on the BDI (Beck's Depression Inventory), indicating borderline clinical depression. He presented as very angry and moderately depressed. He was referred to the program for fighting and causing harm. His two brothers had been murdered. He was a leader in the gang and had a cruel revenge streak. For example, he threatened to kill his mother because she wanted him to get a haircut. This young man was diagnosed with severe post-traumatic stress disorder. He was extremely impulsive with deep-seated murderous rage and could easily murder another person. In cases like these, the adolescent meets individually with the male facilitator — a reformed gang leader who has special expertise in dealing with young men in this predicament.

Outcomes of the Program

Since the inception of the program, there have been 49 adolescents who have fulfilled the requirements of the program and have been released from their legal obligations. Thirty-eight (38) of the adolescents or their parents/guardians were contacted via telephone and asked a series of questions (Table 14.4). Eighty-four (84) percent of those contacted indicated that since their release from the program, they had not had any trouble with the law. Almost 50 percent of them were able to secure employment. Only 37 percent of them were still enrolled in secondary school, some had left and others had graduated. Of particular note is that one participant had a Grade Point Average (G.P.A.) of 1.70 when he first started the program. Since successfully completing the program, he has graduated from secondary school. According to his stepmother, he graduated with a G.P.A. of 3.75. Seventy-six (76) percent of them said they no longer struggled with substance abuse. For those who still used, the drugs of choice included: marijuana, cocaine, and bidi. One parent indicated that her son was addicted to smoking cigarettes. Another parent disclosed that her son had to be admitted to the state mental hospital for severe cocaine abuse.

Table 14.4 Responses to Questions Asked during Follow-up Calls

	Yes	No	Not Sure
Trouble with the law?	5	32	1
Employed?	18	20	0
Attending School?	14	24	0
Substance Abuse?	9	29	0
Better decision making/anger management?	33	3	2
Better manages emotions?	33	4	1
Better choices in terms of friends?	29	7	2
Experienced any trauma?	29	6	3

Eighty-seven (87) percent of the adolescents said since their release from the program that they had better decision making, anger management skills, and were better able to manage their emotions. Seventy-six (76 percent said they now made better choices in terms of friends. Seventy-six (76) percent had not experienced any trauma since being released. However, one individual said there was a death in his family, another said he was almost ganged up by a group of men, and a third said there was a murder in his home. When asked about any noticeable changes, responses included: more goal-setting, attending church, less angry, all positive actions, more respectable, much better person, and helps out more. When asked for suggestions on how to improve the program, the majority of the participants indicated that the program was fine for them. Some suggested that we go to the schools to appeal to the students and another suggested that we get more parents involved.

According to Lewis there is a direct correlation between serious childhood abuse and murder in later teenage years (Lewis, 1992; Lewis 1998). Therefore, by simulating a positive family, The Family: People Helping People Project is an effective resocialization intervention based on empirical data. Research studies carried out on participants in The Family Project provided evidence that participants had a significant decrease in feelings of depression, suicidality, anger, and vengefulness. Involvement in illegal activity and abusive relationships also decreased. There were significant increases in intimacy with others, self-esteem, benevolence, quality of family relationships, gratitude, and forgiveness (Allen, Allen-Carroll, Bethel, & Manganello, 2015; Allen, Allen-Carroll, Bethell, & Manganello, 2017; Abernethy, Allen, & Allen-Caroll, 2017).

Universal Application

The hurt child, in any culture, is a smoking gun because a hurt child becomes a dangerous adult. According to the Contemplative Discovery Pathway Theory, children traumatized early in life are deprived of the three basic instinctual needs: safety (survival/security), connection (affection/esteem), and empowerment (power/control) (Keating, 2006). As a result, they develop impacted hurt leading to shame, with deep feelings of abandonment, rejection, and humiliation. Shame (Self Hatred Aimed at ME) is so painful to the human psyche that the brain, through a series of neuro-mechanisms, develops a defensive Shame False Self characterized by self-absorption, self-gratification, and control to protect the person from the negativity of shame (Allen, 2010; Allen et al., 2014). On the streets, the adolescents describe shame as being "dissed." When they win a gambling game or a turf war, they feel empowered. But when they are further shamed by experiencing abandonment, rejection, and humiliation, they experience murderous rage and enter the Evil Violence Tunnel. In this tunnel, they become destructive to themselves (masochistic/suicide) or others (sadistic/homicide) (Figure 14.3). This destructive behavior is triggered by provocation, loss, and intoxicating substances (e.g. strong alcohol such as brandy, cocaine, marijuana, and liquid ecstasy) (Allen, Bethell, & Allen-Carroll, 2016).

Like many adolescents in the United States and other cultures, those in the court-ordered program were born into difficult circumstances and have estranged or non-existent relationships with the parent/guardian. Most lack a father figure in their lives. Due to their traumatization, they have insecure, disorganized attachment to their parents or caretakers (Duke, Pettingell, McMortis, & Borowsky, 2010). Their decisions are mostly influenced by friends or gang members (Siegel, 2013).

Some of these adolescents have been sexually abused by a family member, leaving them extremely traumatized and shamed. Others have witnessed traumatic events such as the murder of a close friend or relative. Unfortunately, exposure to trauma, especially witnessing violence, is the norm for delinquent youth in juvenile detention (Abram et al., 2004). Some of the participants are grieving the loss of a parent or sibling and their lives are characterized by mood swings, distrust, and depression. The dream of being empowered has been shattered because they are failing in school and feel hopeless about the future. Their trauma leads to severe anger which they self-medicate by abusing substances, stealing, and fighting. Many of them have experienced the Evil Violence Tunnel and have been violent towards themselves (self-mutilation) or attempted to fatally wound others.

An article posted in The New York Times stated that childhood adversity can chemically change the way the brain works. The author warned that childhood trauma is one of the most important things that shape criminal behavior in adulthood. Her evidence-based research led to the conclusion that long before many inmates were perpetrators, they were victims. In reference to this, she advised that when interviewing inmates, we should shift the question from "What is wrong with you?" to "What happened to you?" (Burch, 2017).

Those working with teens in child welfare custody in the United States asserted that current psychiatric diagnoses of treatment for teens are limited, Medical charts may track multiple hospitalizations and medications but fail to trace traumatic pain. The authors of an article in Psychiatric News stated that complex PTSD will soon be added to the International Classification of Diseases and the symptoms will include: behavioral dysregulation, mood and anxiety issues, and attention and memory problems. As many teens who are traumatized are guarded and dismissive, the authors suggest that a tri-factor approach be implemented in assessing them: respect avoidance, respect resilience, and expect ambivalence. A respectful and validating approach can help to uncover the underlying issues, referred to as the "second story," according to the authors. Consequently, this "erauma-informed, developmentally appropriate approach can change the way the teen views himself or herself and the capacity to connect with others, change patterns of behavior and take control of the future" (Gerson & Heppell, 2019). In contrast to these findings, facilitators in The Family program work with the individual participants and not their psychiatric diagnoses.

The importance of offering this court-ordered program for juvenile offenders is to prevent them from entering the penal system, which can be more punitive than rehabilitative. Author Danielle Sered states that "imprisonment isn't just an inadequate tool; it's often enormously counterproductive — leaving survivors and their communities worse off." Prison deprives those incarcerated of the opportuni-

Figure 14.3 The Evil Violence Tunnel

ty to heal, be human, and break the cycle of violence (Sered, 2019). There have been circumstances in which both the perpetrator of the violent act and the victim have been referred to our program for therapy. As such, The Family: People Helping People Project can be compared to The Restorative Circle, a meeting in which offenders sit with their victims and a trained facilitator in an effort to support those in conflict.

According to an article in The New York Times by Michelle Alexander, a perpetrator is greatly impacted if they take full responsibility for what they have done and commit themselves to specific actions to repair themselves and others. The author stated that "a growing body of research strongly supports the anecdotal evidence that restorative justice programs increase the odds of safety, reduce recidivism, and alleviate trauma." In keeping with Dorothy Lewis' hypothesis that the perpetrators were once victims themselves, Alexander, citing Danielle Sered, concludes that:

> Violence is driven by shame, exposure to violence, isolation and instability to meet one's economic needs - all of which are core features of imprisonment ... Nearly everyone who committed violence has first survived it. Studies indicate that experiencing violence is the greater predictor of committing it.
> (Alexander, 2019),

Conclusion

According to the Diagnostic Criteria from DSM-5, adolescents with Oppositional Defiance Disorder (ODD) tend to be angry, easily annoyed, resentful, argumentative with authority figures, and spiteful (American Psychiatric Association, 2013). All the adolescents discussed seem to have different forms of ODD, as defined by the DSM-5. The major issue that stands out is the traumatized nature of their lives. If this early trauma is not addressed, it will lead to more destructive behavior such as murder in later teenaged years. We recognize that the program is a work in progress. One limitation of the pilot study thus far is that the adolescents are always under threat of serious violence or being killed. For instance, one of our participants only attended the program three times. When the facilitator called to follow up on him, his sister informed her that he had been murdered. There is evidence cited in our follow-up study that the program enhances resocialization and reduces violent behavior. For example, a young girl referred to the program for fighting had a special preference for attacking males because of her deep-seated anger toward her father. On the verge of being expelled from school, she was referred to the program for anger management and conflict resolution. Having a positive transference toward the female facilitator, the facilitator encouraged her to visualize her face in times when she felt violent. Returning to school, she was challenged to fight when a male student hit her. Picking up a chair to hit the student in the head, she envisioned the facilitator's face encouraging her not to fight. Putting the chair down, she walked away. The principal, who was watching unobtrusively from his office, was greatly impressed and asked the young girl what happened. She told him that remembering the facilitator's face and love for her prevented her from attacking the student. Very impressed, the principal reported this episode to the program administrator. As a result, he allowed the participant to repeat the grade to improve her grade point average in order to graduate. Presently she is a changed person, her G.P.A. is 2.90 and she is about to graduate from secondary school.

In conclusion, these early results are encouraging and motivate us to do more to develop the quality and quantity of the program. Major issues to still be addressed are the development of compassion fatigue or burnout of the facilitators, the recidivism rate of the participants, and the need for a longitudinal follow-up of many more participants to ascertain the program's effectiveness.

Acknowledgment

This work is funded by the Templeton World Charity Foundation.

References

Abernethy, A. D., Allen, D. F., & Allen-Carroll, M. (2017). Adapting group therapy to address real-world problems: Insights from groups offered in the Bahamas. International Journal of Group Psychotherapy, 68(2), 1-18.

Abram, K. M., Teplin, L. A., Charles, D. R., Longworth, S. L., McClelland, G. M., & Dulcan, M. K, (2004). Posttraumatic stress disorder and trauma in youth in juvenile detention. Archives of General Psychiatry, 61(4), 403-410.

Adverse Childhood Experience (ACE)Questionnaire (n.d.). Retrieved from: httpsi//iwww .ncjfcj-org/sites/default/files/Finding% 20Y our %20ACE%20 Score.pdf in June 2017.

Alexander, M. (2019, March 3). Reckoning with violence. The New York Times.

Allen, D. F. (2010). Shame: The human nemesis. Washington, DC: Eleuthera Publications.

Allen, D. F., & Jekel, J. F. (1991). Crack: The broken promise. London: MacMillan Academic and Professional Ltd.

Allen, D. F., Allen-Carroll, M. A., Bethell, K. Y., & Manganello, J. A. (2015). Community resocialization via instillation of family values through a novel group therapy approach: A pilot study. Journal of Psychotherapy Integration, 25 (4), 289-298.

Allen, D. F., Allen-Carroll, M., Bethell, K. Y., & Manganello, J. (2017). An instrument for assessment of longitudinal community resocialization through a group process intervention. Journal of Trauma and Treatment, 6(01).

Allen, D., Bethell, K., & Allen-Carroll, M. (2016). Anger and social fragmentation: The Evil Violence Tunnel. Journal of Psychotherapy Integration, 27(1), 79-92.

Allen, D. F., Mayo, M., Allen-Carroll, M., Manganello, J. A., Allen, V. S., & Singh, J. P. (2014). Cultivating gratitude: Contemplative discovery pathway theory applied to group therapy in the Bahamas. Journal of Trauma and Treatment, 3(3).

American Psychiatric Association (2013). Desk reference to the diagnostic criteria from DSM-5. Arlington, VA: American Psychiatric Association.

Beck's Depression Inventory. Retrieved from: https://www.bmc.org/sites/default/files/For_Medical_Professionals/Pediatric_Resources/Pediatrics__MA_Center_ for_Sudden_Infant_Death_Syndrome__SIDS_/Beck-Depression-Inventory-BDI. pdf in June 2017.

Brenneman, R. (2012). Homies and hermanoes: God and gangs in Central America. New York: Oxford University Press.

Burch, A. D. (2017, October 15). A gun to his head as a child. In prison as an adult. The New York Times. The Family: People Helping People Project 203

Duke, N. N., Pettingell, S. L., McMorris, B. J., & Borowsky, I. W. (2010). Adolescent violence perpetration: Associations with multiple types of adverse childhood experiences. Pediatrics, 125(4), 778-786.

George, D. T., & Berger, L. (2013). Untangling the mind: Why we behave the way we do. New York: HarperCollins Publishers.

Gerson, R., & Heppell, P. (2019, April 5). Beyond PTSD: The complexity of diagnosis and treatment for teens in child welfare custody. Psychiatric News, 54 (7), 14-15.

Greenberg, R. (2018). SAMHSA Child mental health event promotes trauma- informed approach. Psychiatric News, 53(12).

Jekel, J. F., Allen, D. F., Podlewski, H., Clarke, N., Dean-Patterson, $., Cartwright, P. (1986). Epidemic free-base cocaine abuse. Case study from the Bahamas. Lancet, 1(8479), 459-462.

Keating, T. (2006). Open mind open heart: The contemplative dimension of the Gospel. New York: Continuum International Publishing Group.

Lewis, D. (1992). From abuse to violence: Psychophysiological consequences of maltreatment. Journal of the American Academy of Child and Adolescent Psychiatry, 31(3), 383-391.

Lewis, D. O. (1998). Guilty by reason of insanity. New York: Random House.

Peterson, J., Freedenthal, S., Sheldon, C., & Andersen, R. (2008). Nonsuicidal self injury in adolescents. Psychiatry, 5(11), 20-26.

Post-Traumatic Stress Disorder Self-Test. Retrieved from: http://www-ptsd.ne.gov/pdfs/ptsd.pdf in June 2017.

Reavis, J. A., Looman, J., Franco, K. A., & Rojas, B. (2013). Adverse childhood experiences and adult criminality: How long must we live before we possess our own lives? The Permanente Journal, 17(2), 44-48.

Sered, D. (2019). Until we reckon: Violence, mass incarceration and a road to repair. New York: The New Press.

Siegel, D. J. (2013). Brainstorm: The power and purpose of the teenage brain. New York: Penguin Group.

Walkup, J. T., & Rubin, D. H. (2013). Social withdrawal and violence — Newtown Connecticut. The New England Journal of Medicine, 368(3), 399-401.

Community-Based Treatment of Suicide Through The Family: People Helping People Project

Corresponding author
David Allen, Allen Institute of Research & Training, Bahamas
Received: 16 July 2025
Accepted : 21 July 2025
Published: 06 August 2025

*

Katherine Farrington, Dr. David Allen, Keva Bethell
Allen Institute of Research & Training, Bahamas

Abstract
Suicide is a growing public health issue in The Bahamas. As more data emerges, it is becoming clear that suicide treatments are needed. Community-based treatments offer support, reduce isolation, and reduce stigmatisation. The current study examines whether The Family: People Helping People Project, a community-based support group, functions as an effective treatment for suicide. A qualitative observational design, where the researcher attends meetings and writes detailed field notes, was utilised. Data collection was conducted over eight weeks, involving approximately 100 participants, with demographic data withheld to maintain participant anonymity. Four central themes emerged: expression of suicidal struggles, social connection and belonging, coping, and sharing one's story. The study found that The Family group sessions provide a safe and supportive environment that encourages openness, reduces loneliness, offers practical coping skills, and facilitates healing through sharing one's story. Overall, the findings suggest that The Family is an effective and accessible community-based treatment for suicide.

Introduction

Suicide is a complex and deeply concerning public health issue. Historically, it has been seen as a moral failure or even a crime, especially in religious communities where suicide was believed to be a sin [1]. For example, during the Middle Ages, those who died by suicide were denied proper burials, and even attempting suicide was considered a crime in some parts of Europe [1]. Today, however, that view has shifted. Due to developments in science, psychology, and shifts in religious interpretation, suicide is now more commonly seen as the result of intense pain, mental illness, trauma, or being emotionally overwhelmed [1]. Thinkers like Emile Durkheim saw suicide as a social issue, influenced by things like isolation or instability [2]. Others like Freud believed suicide could come from turning anger inward [3]. More recent theories, like Thomas Joiner's interpersonal-psychological theory, argue that people die by suicide when they feel like a burden, feel isolated, and have the capacity to kill themselves [4]. There are also emotional and biological explanations. Childhood trauma, difficulty managing emotions like sadness or anger, and changes in brain chemicals all increase suicide

This article appeared in the *Japan Journal of Medical Science* risk. For example, research has shown low levels of serotonin and changes in the brain's stress response in people who have attempted suicide [1].

In The Bahamas, suicide is still heavily stigmatised and is often an unspoken issue. The most complete data available is from a 2014 study by Keva Bethell and Dr. David Allen, which reported 96 suicides between 2000 and 2013, with a male-to-female ratio of 7:1 [5]. In recent years, that number has remained steady, with six suicides reported in 2023, eight in 2024, and by March 2025, there have already been six [6].

Additionally, a nationwide mental health survey recently found nearly one in four Bahamian teens had considered suicide, one in five had attempted it, and more than a quarter reported ongoing feelings of hopelessness and sadness. Loneliness and self-harm have more than doubled since the late 1990s [7]. While the survey is based on self-reported data and therefore should be interpreted with care, it still highlights that suicide is a growing problem in The Bahamas, especially among young people.

Having determined the importance of suicide treatment in The Bahamas, the question becomes: What type of treatment is realistic and effective? Suicide disproportionately affects lower socio-economic communities, meaning high-cost interventions are often not feasible [8]. A strong alternative is community-based treatment of suicide.

Community-based treatments often focus on an upstream approach, meaning addressing root causes and preventing problems before they escalate. This strategy is focused on preventing suicide risk in the first place, identifying and supporting people at increased risk through treatment and crisis intervention, preventing reattempts, promoting long-term recovery, and supporting survivors of suicide loss [9]. Community-based treatments help reduce stigma and create a sense of belonging. They offer consistent support and help to reduce loneliness. By building problem-solving skills and helping individuals manage daily stress, these treatments lower the chances of someone feeling like suicide is their only option. Community-based treatments also give people a space to share their stories. According to the National Strategy for Suicide Prevention, effective prevention must include a wide range of voices and experiences, especially those informed by people who have lived through it themselves [9].

Within The Bahamas is a community-based treatment option called The Family: People Helping People Project. The Family encompasses all the aspects highlighted above through encouraging participants to share their stories and own their hurt. The Family reduces stigma, fosters belonging, promotes coping skills, and provides support [10,11]. Therefore, this study aims to understand if The Family serves as an effective community-based treatment for suicide in The Bahamas.

Methods

Design

The present study employed a qualitative observational design. By employing such an approach, our study aimed to understand whether The Family functions as an effective community-based treatment for suicide in The Bahamas by exploring how participants engage with and are impacted by the sessions. This research involved a series of in-person observations of The Family group sessions over eight weeks.

Participants

A total of approximately 100 participants were involved in the observed sessions over the study period. In terms of participant gender distribution, there was a mix of men and women, though exact numbers were not recorded to protect anonymity. Similarly, exact ages were not recorded to preserve confidentiality. At the time of the sessions, most members were from the capital, New Providence, Bahamas; however, a few were from outer islands such as Abaco, Bahamas.

Materials

The researcher used a pen and paper to make field notes after each session. Otherwise, no materials were used as the aim of the study was to observe The Family group sessions without interference by the researcher.

Procedure

The researcher would attend a Family group session

and be introduced as a student observer. All members were informed about the academic nature of The Family and its use in studies, and by attending, they consented to participate in these studies. Given the sensitive nature of the sessions, all details surrounding the individuals are confidential. The researcher then observes these sessions, paying attention to how The Family may or may not operate as a community-based treatment for suicide. The researcher does not take notes during the meeting as this could draw attention towards themselves and may interfere with the sessions. Instead, the researcher makes field notes after each meeting. The researcher attends 3 to 5 sessions a week for 8 weeks. Data is collected after every session.

Data Analysis

A deductive thematic analysis approach was taken to analyse the field notes. A deductive codebook was generated prior to the qualitative analysis based on the qualitative research aims and knowledge of sessions. Using this deductive codebook, the researcher initiated the coding process, systematically coding segments of the field notes to identify and capture recurring themes and patterns until the point of data saturation. Coding was conducted manually by the researcher without the use of qualitative analysis software. Four major themes and accompanying sub-themes began to emerge following comparisons of codes across notes; each was titled to reflect its meaning accurately.

Results

Over two months, observational data were collected from over 30 sessions of The Family.

Field notes focused on participant engagement, recurring themes, and personal disclosures related to mental health and suicidality. Four themes emerged: expression of suicidal struggles, social connection and belonging, coping, and sharing one's story.

Expression of Suicidal Struggles

Openness. Members of The Family do not shy away from difficult conversations, instead addressing them directly. Throughout the sessions, it was evident that individuals were open about their struggles, and this included suicidal struggles. Several members recalled times when they experienced suicidal ideation or attempts. Some stated they knew that they were trying to kill themselves, whereas others simply felt they were getting away from their pain. Many described experiencing overwhelming and unending suffering that they felt left them with no other choice. They were open enough to explain the attempts, going as far as to include the methods used, which included overdosing with pills, using a gun, or drinking bleach.

Environment. Members were able to open up about their suicidal struggles because of the environment that The Family group sessions provide. Members offer support to those who share both during the session and after. They offer similar stories, empathy, understanding, and no judgment. 'Holy moments' are held when one is sharing particularly painful experiences, where a moment of silence is held and respect and empathy are given to the individual.

Social Connection and Belonging

Community. The Family provides a sense of community to its members. Existing members are warm and inviting towards new members, for example, providing them with existing members' numbers to call so they can have support both during and after the sessions. Members also often stay after the sessions to converse and interact more with one another. These sessions are held five times a week, meaning members see each other often and grow close. The extreme level of honesty practised in these sessions means members know each other well and feel a sense of community among one another.

Reduced Loneliness. Many members have expressed experiencing extreme loneliness. For some, it is due to their work hours, which are so extreme that they do not have time for anything else; for others, it is because they are foreigners to the Bahamas, and for others, it is because of their poor mental health. Regardless of the reason, The Family sessions are proven to reduce loneliness [10]. The close connections formed, the regularity of the sessions, and the authentic stories shared all act to reduce loneliness.

Stigma Reduction. The Family discusses a multitude of topics, including shame, fear, abuse, suicide, and more. Discussing these taboo topics reduces the stigma associated with them. Individuals have expressed that when they shared their story, they quickly realised they were not alone, and this helped them change the way they perceived themselves and their experiences. This allows for stigma reduction.

Coping

Coping Strategies. The Family offers members coping strategies. When a member expresses an issue they are facing or shares an experience that happened to them, other members offer how they would cope. Several individuals suggest forgiveness both towards oneself and others. They also suggest surrendering the things one cannot control, trusting and relying on God, focusing on changing oneself rather than others, and continuing to attend sessions with The Family.

Empowerment. Through support and encouragement, The Family empowers its members to deal with the daily stressors they encounter. Members do this by reaching out to one another, providing advice, offering their strength, understanding, and shared experiences to help each other cope. Additionally, by working on themselves at these meetings, individuals express how they feel better equipped and empowered to handle these stressors on their own.

Sharing One's Story

Self-Healing. Through sharing their stories, members have said it allows them to begin the process of healing. Members state this allows them to reclaim their story, to address their shame, to understand their story better, to work through the hurt, forgive others and themselves, and start healing. Referring to Dr. Daniel Siegel's work, Dr. Curt Thompson explains: "An important part of how people change... is through the process of telling their stories to an empathic listener. When a person tells her story and is truly heard and understood, both she and the listener undergo actual changes in their brain circuitry. They feel a greater sense of emotional and relational connection, decreased anxiety and greater awareness of and compassion for others' suffering" [12].

Members share their stories repeatedly. Each time, they are asked questions as well as offered advice and support by participants in The Family. Members say it is this process that distances them away from the hurt, anger, and shame, and moves them towards acceptance and love.

Healing of Others. Sharing one's story is not only beneficial for the individual sharing but also for the others at the sessions. Members claim that hearing other people's stories allows them to apply the lessons learned to their own challenges. In doing so, growth is fostered.

Vignettes

1. A gentleman from a family island struggled with extreme loneliness. He became tired of drinking alcohol as a coping mechanism and attempted to drink bleach to end his life. He relocated to the capital, attends The Family Group, and is doing much better.

2. A man came to The Family Group and spoke of the extreme grief he experienced after his wife passed. He spoke of sitting alone on the beach and wanting to walk to another far away island. He began to walk to the water, but he heard a song from his childhood, and this stopped him. At the time, he did not see this as a suicide attempt, but later recognised it as such.

3. A woman came to The Family Group and spoke of a childhood full of unrelenting hardship. She spoke of attempting to take pills to end her life. She is now attending The Family Group and doing much better.

4. At a recent Family Group session a young man struggling with severe depression confessed that he had nearly taken his own life with a gun. Desperate for help, he reached out to the Program Director early in the morning, leading to a meeting where he was invited to the program that afternoon. There, he connected with one of The Family facilitators, who shared her own story of despair as a pregnant teenager. Her words deeply

resonated with him, as his mother had also given birth at age 14 years. Feeling an unexpected bond, he asked if he could call her "mother." The facilitator provided comfort, reminding him of God's love and the support around him. She continued to check on him daily, and through her care, he regained his will to live. As a symbol of love and prayer, she gifted him a special blue scarf that she knitted, reinforcing that he was not alone. Now, he has found purpose in helping others facing similar struggles, working to bring more people in crisis to The Family Program.

Discussion

The results of this study suggest that The Family is an effective model of community-based support for individuals experiencing suicidality in The Bahamas. Through open conversation, honesty, and support, members are able to work through their experiences, including grief, shame, anger, and suicidal ideation. These sessions create a space where people feel safe to share their pain, and that act of sharing allows for personal growth, healing, and a reduction in suicidal ideation. The Family Program is proven to be 98% effective in resocialising individuals who participate [13].

A large part of what is discussed in these sessions is grief. While some members grieve the death of loved ones, many grieve other forms of loss, such as the loss of innocence, safety, family, or identity. Grief often goes unspoken, but as Dr. David Allen expresses, "you cannot leave until you grieve." If a person tries to move forward without facing their grief, the pain will not leave. It lingers and begins to take new shapes, often showing up as anger, shame, or self-hatred. The Family gives members space to grieve openly, not just once, but over time. Two significant emotional responses to grief that came up throughout the sessions were anger and sadness. These emotions are not mutually exclusive; there is anger in sadness and sadness in anger. However, one emotion can dominate. For example, people who process their grief alone without the support of others can often direct their hurt inward, resulting in more anger than sadness. This anger, if not processed, can turn into the Evil Violence Destructive Tunnel [14]. When someone is deeply hurt, full of shame, and carrying unresolved anger, they may lash out. This could be homicide, where the pain is turned outward, or suicide, where the pain is turned inward. Both are a result of the same deep suffering. The Family helps to interrupt this process by offering connection, understanding, and support, which allows people to work through the grief.

Another recurring theme that plays a significant role in suicidal thoughts and behaviours is shame. Shame is Self-Hatred Aimed at ME, and it can present itself in many ways [15]. It is the gap between where one thinks they should be, who one thinks they should be, where others want them to be, and where they are. Shame says, "I am a mistake," as opposed to grief, which says "I made a mistake." Members often describe it as a darkness, or like a hole they cannot climb out of. Some have described it as a tiredness that seeps into their bones, or a pain that never ends. Shame causes people to believe they are broken, unworthy, or a burden to others. Some members shared that their suicide attempts were not necessarily about wanting to die, but about wanting the pain to stop and not seeing any other option. To survive shame, many people create defensiveness, such as the False Self. This is a version of themselves they show to the world, often as a form of protection. This False Self may be narcissistic, controlling, lack empathy, blame others, and lie [16]. However, underneath, it is often rooted in fear, shame, and the belief that the True Self is too broken to be accepted. If left unchallenged, this False Self can deepen disconnection and make suicidal thoughts even stronger. In The Family, people slowly begin to let go of the False Self. Through honest conversations, repeated storytelling, and being heard without judgment, members begin to accept parts of themselves they once rejected. This process requires vulnerability. As Bren'e' Brown expresses, "vulnerability is the centre of shame, scarcity, fear, anxiety, and uncertainty. But it is also the birthplace of belonging and love" [17]. When one can tell their story and face their shame through vulnerability, they can heal. Vulnerability allows people to move from shame to healing, and as shame decreases, the True Self emerges. The True Self is grateful, accepting, empathetic, accepts responsibility, and embraces the truth [16].

Conclusion

The results of this study show that The Family offers a space to grow and heal, to address one's hurt and begin their healing. The way The Family handles grief, shame, and pain mirrors what community-based treatment aims to do: provide consistent, safe, and accessible support. The Family does not offer quick fixes. Instead, it supports members as they learn to carry their pain, understand it, and grow through it. These findings also support what was outlined earlier, that community-based mental health treatment is both necessary and effective in contexts like The Bahamas, where traditional mental health services may be limited or inaccessible. The Family brings together the core components of the upstream approach previously mentioned; it addresses root causes and prevents problems before they escalate. It does this through creating a sense of belonging, offering support, reducing loneliness, providing ways of coping, and reducing stigma. These attributes make The Family an effective community-based treatment for suicide.

References

1. Tabbara, M. S. (2023). Clinical and conceptual foundations: Suicidality and the afterlife. In A. D. Abernethy (Ed.), Spiritual care in psychological suffering: How a research collaboration informs integrative practice (pp. 129–149). Lexington Books/ Rowman & Littlefield.
2. Durkheim, É. (1951). Suicide: A study in sociology (J. A. Spaulding & G. Simpson, Trans.). Free Press. (Original work published 1897)
3. Freud, S. (1917). Mourning and melancholia. In J. Strachey (Ed. & Trans.), The standard edition of the complete psychological works of Sigmund Freud. 14: 237-258. Hogarth Press. (Original work published 1917)
4. Joiner, T. E. (2005). Why people die by suicide. Harvard University Press.
5. Bethell, K., & Allen, D. (2014). Suicide in The Bahamas. Global Journal of Human Social Science: Sociology & Culture. 14: 21–30. https://globaljournals.org/GJHSS_Volume14/4-Suicide-in-the-Bahamas. pdf
6. Bowleg, E (2025, March 17). Officials concerned as suicides reach 2023's total. The Tribune. https://www.tribune242.com/news/2025/ mar/17/officials-concerned-as-suicides-reach-2023s-total/
7. Rolle, L. (2025, July 4). 1 in 5 teens has attempted suicide. The Tribune. https://www.tribune242.com/news/2025/jul/04/1-in-5-teens-has-attempted-suicide/
8. Omiyefa, S. (2025). Mental healthcare disparities in low-income U.S. populations: Barriers, policy challenges, and intervention strategies. International Journal of Research Publication and Reviews. 6: 2277–2290. https://connectwithcare.org/wp-content/uploads/2025/05/MentalHealthcareDisparitiesinLo w-IncomeU.S.Populations-BarriersPolicy-ChallengesandInterventionStrategies-1.pdf
9. National Academies of Sciences, Engineering, and Medicine. (2023). Reducing suicide: A public health imperative. In A. R. Insel & J. M. Gould (Eds.), Frameworks for suicide prevention (Publication No. NBK604170). National Library of Medicine. https://www.ncbi.nlm. nih.gov/books/NBK604170/
10. Allen, D. F., Carroll, M. A., Allen, V. S., Bethell, K. Y., & Manganello, J. A. (2015). Community resocialization via instillation of Family Values through a novel group Therapy Approach: A pilot study. Journal of Psychotherapy Integration, 25: 289–298. https://doi.org/10.1037/a0039563
11. Abernethy, A. D., Allen, D. F., & Allen-Carroll, M. (2017). Adapting group therapy to address real world problems: Insights from groups offered in the Bahamas. International Journal of Group Psychotherapy.https://doi.org/10.1080/00207284.2017.1335582
12. Thompson, C. (2010). Anatomy of the soul: Surprising connections between neuroscience and spiritual practices that can transform your life and relationships. Carol Stream, IL: Tyndale House.
13. Bethell, K., & Allen, D. (2022). Resocialization through the Family Project in the Bahamas: Using group therapy to heal adverse childhood experiences. In Child abuse and neglect. IntechOpen. https://doi.org/10.5772/intechopen.102515 14. Allen, D., Bethell, K., & Allen-Carroll, M. (2016). Anger and social fragmentation: The evil violence tunnel. Journal of Psychotherapy Integration, 27: 80–88. https://doi.org/10.1037/int0000022
15. Von Kahle, C., Allen, D., Bethell, K., Allen, M., & D'Alessandro, F. (2019). Shame and The Family Project: An interpersonal neurobiological per-

spective. NeuroQuantology. 17: 36-41. https://doi.org/10.14704/nq.2019.17.3.1987.

16. Allen, D. F. (2024). The Contemplative Discovery Pathway Theory: A Psychodynamic Therapy Model Addressing the Trauma of Shame. In Y. Shapiro (Ed.): Psychodynamic Psychotherapy A Global Perspective. New York: Nova Science Publishers, Inc.
17. Brown, B. (2019). The call to courage [Film]. Netflix. https://www.netflix.com/title/81010 Cite this article: Katherine Farrington, Dr. David Allen, Keva Bethell. (2025) Community-Based Treatment of Suicide Through The Family: People Helping People Project. Japan Journal of Medical Science 6 (2): 272-275.

www.ingramcontent.com/pod-product-compliance
Lightning Source LLC
LaVergne TN
LVHW081317110826
845149LV00006B/1532

9780997160963